Prophetic Precursors

Prophetic Precursors

Pointers Toward Muhammad or Christ?

TOM WILSON

WIPF & STOCK · Eugene, Oregon

PROPHETIC PRECURSORS
Pointers Toward Muhammad or Christ?

Copyright © 2020 Tom Wilson. All rights reserved. Except for brief quotations in critical publications or reviews, no part of this book may be reproduced in any manner without prior written permission from the publisher. Write: Permissions, Wipf and Stock Publishers, 199 W. 8th Ave., Suite 3, Eugene, OR 97401.

Wipf & Stock
An Imprint of Wipf and Stock Publishers
199 W. 8th Ave., Suite 3
Eugene, OR 97401

www.wipfandstock.com

PAPERBACK ISBN: 978-1-7252-6713-8
HARDCOVER ISBN: 978-1-7252-6714-5
EBOOK ISBN: 978-1-7252-6715-2

Manufactured in the U.S.A.   05/28/20

Biblical quotations taken from the Holy Bible, New Revised Standard Version®. NRSV®. All rights reserved worldwide.

With thanks to all my Christian and Muslim friends and colleagues who have helped me think more deeply about the biblical figures discussed in this book

Contents

Introduction: The Working Assumptions of This Book | 1
Creation, Adam and Eve | 8
Noah | 30
Abraham | 55
Joseph | 86
Moses | 110
David and Solomon | 137
Mary | 163
Jesus | 188
Postscript | 214

Bibliography | 215

Introduction
The Working Assumptions of This Book

THE PURPOSE OF THIS book is to enable Christians and Muslims to engage in detailed conversation about the Qur'an and the Bible. In recent years there has been a growing emphasis on the connection between these two sacred texts. But the nature of that connection has not always been clear, and Christians and Muslims have, at times, lacked the confidence and specialist knowledge needed to have anything other than superficial conversations. The introduction explains my own presuppositions in writing and outlines the structure of the chapters that follow.

My own thinking about the relationship between the Qur'an and the Bible is heavily indebted to Gabriel Said Reynolds. In his introduction to his commentary on the Bible and the Qur'an, Reynolds argues that the Qur'an is an independent literary work that presumes a working knowledge of the Bible.[1] By "working knowledge" Reynolds does not mean that the Qur'an engages with the written text of the Bible, which he acknowledges was not available in seventh-century Arabia. Rather, Reynolds argues that the Qur'an is engaged in conversation with biblical material, by which he means both narratives found in the biblical text and also subsequent extrabiblical speculations on and elaborations of those narratives. Reynolds has five key theses about the relationship between the Qur'an and the Bible. First, the Qur'an has a particular relationship with the Christian interpretive tradition, especially the Syriac Christian tradition. By this Reynolds means that where there are differences between Christian and Jewish understandings, the Qur'an tends to engage more with the former than the latter. Second, the Qur'an is a polemical or an apologetic text. It is not simply recounting biblical narratives,

---

1. Reynolds, *Qur'an and Bible*, 2–3.

but engaging with them for a particular purpose. Third, that purpose is most succinctly explained as the theological and prophetic focus on Muhammad as the Seal of the Prophets, the Final Messenger of God. Fourth, the Arabic language of the Qur'an is crucial to interpreting the text. Fifth, the relationship between the Qur'an and the Bible is complex and multifaceted.[2]

It will be obvious to even a casual reader that this book has been strongly influenced by Reynolds's five theses. But that does not mean I have accepted them uncritically or in their entirety. I have at least four caveats. First, the metaphor of the Bible and Qur'an in "conversation" is not entirely accurate. Conversation implies a back-and-forth process of speaking and listening. But the Bible does not speak to, listen to, or engage with the Qur'an in any overt way. It would be more precise to say the Qur'an reacts or responds to oral accounts of biblical narratives, understanding "biblical" to mean both the text of the Bible itself and also subsequent retellings, interpretations and speculations related to that text.

Second, it is important to distinguish between correlation and causation. It is possible, for example, to show that while Noah in the Genesis is a silent Prophet, early Christian interpreters (including 2 Peter) turn him into a preacher. This does not mean the Christian understanding caused the Qur'an's account of Noah as a preacher of righteousness. Rather it is an interesting point of correlation that is worth exploring further. In the past scholars produced reductionist accounts of the Qur'an as being merely derived from Christian scripture and preaching. I am not arguing for this view. The Qur'an interprets the stories of the Prophets in order to bring Muhammad into greater prominence as the Final Messenger, much as Christian interpreters find types of Christ in the Old Testament.

Third, while I recognize the importance of original languages for understanding a text, I do not read classical Arabic (or Syriac), and have very limited Hebrew, and so am reliant on translations.

Fourth, the Qur'an and the Bible are very different texts. The Bible is more properly described as a collection of texts, with multiple authors, written over a considerable historical period, in three languages. The Qur'an claims a single author, was revealed over a short period, in a single language. As Reynolds explains, at its heart the Bible is "an account of God's relationship with the patriarchs, Israel, and finally (in the New

---

2. Reynolds, *Qur'an and Bible*, 12–15.

Testament), with those who follow Jesus."³ The Qur'an, by contrast, is divine direct speech, God's warnings to people of the past and to people of Muhammad's day. It is thus, as Reynolds proposes, more like a Christian sermon than the Christian scriptures.

I am not proposing to engage with the debate about the composition of either text. To do so would distract too much from the main purpose of this book, which is to juxtapose the extant text of the Bible and the Qur'an, to discuss the similarities and differences that are found there, and so develop dialogue between Christians and Muslims. I will treat each text on its own terms, trying to engage with the interpretive strategies of each community as far as I am able to.

Echoes of Christian Narratives within the Qur'an

The basic thesis of this book is therefore that there are echoes of Christian narratives within the Qur'an. Reynolds points out that for most of Muhammad's life he was interacting with pagan culture and beliefs, but there is relatively little evidence of this in the pages of the Qur'an, which in fact engages far more with biblical ideas. Moreover, the text of the Qur'an actually engages primarily with Christian ideas and interpretation. Reynolds illustrates this claim with reference to the story of the temptation of Adam and Eve in the garden of Eden. Christian, but not Jewish, tradition identified the serpent with Satan. The Qur'an, Reynolds proposes, "seems to accept the Christian interpretation," not mentioning the serpent, but simply stating Satan was in the garden.⁴ Reynolds argues that the Qur'an is aware of "oral traditions about biblical characters but not of the Bible itself." Those Prophets whom the Qur'an focuses on were the subjects of popular stories, and the Qur'an makes no distinction between canonical biblical text and stories in Jewish and Christian legends.⁵ Thus, the Qur'an presumes its audience knows who some of the characters are. For example, Potiphar is referred to as *al-'aziz, the mighty one*, which is a fitting description of the commander of the king's guard. But he is nowhere named within the text itself.⁶

---

3. Reynolds, *Emergence of Islam*, 102.
4. Reynolds, *Emergence of Islam*, 121–22.
5. Reynolds, *Emergence of Islam*, 126.
6. Reynolds, *Emergence of Islam*, 128.

Sinai argues you must combine comparison with biblical literature with study of the Qur'an as a literary work in its own right. He explains that the historical-critical approach to the text can help us see what the text actually says, rather than succumbing to confirmation bias, whereby we presume the text confirms what we already believe. Moreover, rigorous historical-critical analysis can disclose hitherto unnoticed literary features that mean we develop a greater appreciation of the text itself.[7] In addition to Sinai's two points, we can add that reading the Bible and Qur'an side by side, gives Christians a greater appreciation of what the Bible says (and does not say), as well as greater clarity as to what Christians believe.

While Sinai recognizes that the Qur'an presumes knowledge of biblical figures and cites reference to Pharaoh as an example (Q 85:17–18), he also cautions against overestimating the Christian presence in the Arabian interior in Muhammad's day. It is possible that there were orthodox and/or heterodox branches of Christianity present, but there is no certainty as to whether this is the case. He conjectures there may have been syncretism, a fusion of Jewish, Christian and pagan beliefs and practices, and that the Qur'an reacts against an amalgamation of beliefs rather than discrete schools of thought.[8] This means that while the Qur'an is familiar with the Bible and biblical lore, this does not mean familiarity with the biblical text. Rather, the Qur'an contains allusions, paraphrases and echoes of biblical phrases and stories. The main familiarity comes through oral transmission of the text. But we cannot access this oral tradition directly, nor is there any extant Arabic Christian or Jewish literature from the period that we can engage with. We must therefore rely on other languages and more distant parallels.[9] This is the task of this book.

What This Book Does—and Does Not—Do

Any exercise in comparing and contrasting the Qur'an and the Bible must limit itself; otherwise the task of writing would be never-ending and any output unreadable. The purpose of this book is to start conversation, not offer definitive solutions or advance novel academic theories. Most of the scholarship is attributed to specialists who contributions are

---

7. Sinai, *Qur'an*, 2–4.
8. Sinai, *Qur'an*, 62–65.
9. Sinai, *Qur'an*, 138–41.

Introduction

acknowledged throughout the text. Any mistakes or misunderstandings are, of course, my own. While the precise format differs from chapter to chapter, the basic structure remains the same. I retell the story of a biblical figure, engaging both with intrabiblical and also extrabiblical interpretations of that story. Relevant texts from a variety of ancient literature are introduced, in order to shed light on how that figure's story was interpreted and retold from both a Christian and at times a Jewish perspective. The retelling found in the Qur'an is also discussed, together with a small selection of Islamic interpretations and elaborations. At times, I engage with detailed debate about Qur'anic interpretation, for example, on the identity of the son whom Abraham offers in sacrifice, or exactly what the Qur'an teaches about the death of Jesus.

The conclusion to each chapter discusses what the Christian understanding of this figure teaches about Jesus and what the Islamic understanding teaches about Muhammad. This final section is written as a stimulus for discussion, a way for Christians and Muslims to discover where they agree and disagree, in a spirit of friendship and mutual learning. This book is therefore primarily a way into conversation, rather than the last word on whom the Prophets pointed toward.

Where to Begin?

Before diving into comparisons of key figures, it is worth beginning the exchange by looking at how the Bible and the Qur'an begin. Both texts begin with God, but there the similarity ends. Genesis, the book of beginnings, starts at the start, explaining that the God whose actions and will this book describes is the sovereign Creator, far greater and more powerful than things others might choose to worship: the sun, moon and so forth. The climax of this creation story is the account of how human beings were made. While the Qur'an does discuss this creation story a number of times, it is not mentioned in *surah al-Fatihah, the Opening*. Rather this first *surah* is a prayer, offering praise to God as Lord of all creation, Master of the Day of Judgment, whom the faithful seek to serve and obey. The opening sentences of the two books therefore set very different tones.

The Bible begins:

> In the beginning when God created the heavens and the earth, the earth was a formless void and darkness covered the face of

> the deep, while a wind from God [or while the spirit of God] swept over the face of the waters. (Genesis 1:1–2, NRSV)

By contrast, the Qur'an commences:

> In the Name of God, the Merciful, the Compassionate. Praise (be) to God, Lord of the worlds, the Merciful, the Compassionate, Master of the Day of Judgment. You we serve and You we seek for help. God guide us to the straight path; the path of those whom You have blessed, not (the path) of those on whom (Your) anger falls, nor of those who go astray. (*Al-Fatihah* 1:1–7, Droge)

Beginnings are important, because they orientate the reader, setting the tone of what will follow. The opening sentences often demonstrate the main priorities of the text in question. If this is true of the Qur'an, then the main purpose of the text is to set out appropriate conduct for worship of God, explaining who speaks on behalf of God, what their message is and how this message is to be followed. By contrast, the Bible begins with an account of God as Creator, who makes the world and humanity in order to enter into relationship with them, a subtle, but important, difference. As an aside, Reynolds argues that *surah al-Fatihah* has "some similarities" to the Lord's Prayer, as a prayer of commitment and orientation of the self toward God.[10]

Matthew's Gospel records Jesus teaching the Lord's Prayer as follows:

> When you are praying, do not heap up empty phrases as the Gentiles do; for they think that they will be heard because of their many words. Do not be like them, for your Father knows what you need before you ask him. Pray then in this way:
>
> Our Father in heaven, hallowed be your name.
> Your kingdom come.
> Your will be done, on earth as it is in heaven.
> Give us this day our daily bread.
> And forgive us our debts, as we also have forgiven our debtors.
> And do not bring us to the time of trial, but rescue us from the evil one.
>
> For if you forgive others their trespasses, your heavenly Father will also forgive you; but if you do not forgive others, neither will your Father forgive your trespasses. (Matthew 6:7–15)

Before you begin contrasting the figures of faith in the chapters that follow, a useful warm-up exercise is to begin by contrasting the Lord's

---

10. Reynolds, *Qur'an and the Bible*, 29.

Prayer with *al-Fatihah*. There are many similar themes, about submission to God and longing for his rule, but also clear differences, such as whether forgiveness is mentioned, the place of human action and the guidance God is expected to give.

This book is written to begin conversations, to open up possibilities for exploration, not to close them down. May this encourage you to develop friendships between Christians and Muslims.[11]

---

11. You can read more of my understanding of interfaith in Wilson, *What Kind of Friendship?* and Wilson, *Hospitality, Service, Proclamation.*

Creation, Adam and Eve

Overview of the Chapter

THIS CHAPTER IS DIVIDED into four main sections. Section 1 discusses the biblical account of the creation of people and their rebellion against God. Section 2 sets out the Qur'an's understanding of these two same points. Section 3 then focuses on Adam in Christian and Muslim thought before section 4 draws the threads together, pointing out the similarities and differences between the accounts found in the Qur'an and the Bible, and making suggestions for productive discussion of these issues.

Both the Qur'an and the Bible presume that God created the world. In addition to the two accounts found in Genesis, there are also scattered references to God as Creator throughout the Hebrew scriptures. To give an example, Psalm 19 is a meditation on God as Creator and giver of the Torah; the two are aspects of the same move of divine self-disclosure as God reveals himself as Creator with particular expectations of his creation. Similarly, the Prophet Isaiah regularly presumes that God is Creator; see for example Isaiah 40:28; 42:5; 45:18.

The Qur'an is also interested in the fact of divine creation. For example, it states:

> Surely your Lord is God, who created the heavens and the earth in six days. Then he mounted the throne. The night covers the day, which it pursues urgently, and the sun, and the moon, and the stars are subjected, (all) by His command. Is it not (a fact) that to Him (belongs) the creation and the command [that is, God creates and then controls the universe from his throne]? Blessed be God, Lord of the worlds! (*al-A'raf* 7:54; see also *Fussilat* 41:9–10)

Thus the Qur'an presumes a six-day creation, as set out in Genesis 1 and 2, although *Fussilat* 41:12 states that God finished the *seven heavens in two days*. Moreover, there is a significant omission from the biblical account: there is no Sabbath command. This is arguably because the notion of the divine resting is seen as diminishing God. Why would God need to have a rest? Does that not imply that he is somehow weak and fallible? The implications for humanity are interesting, as the Sabbath command is one that the Bible argues applies to people on the basis of creation in the divine image. The lack of a Sabbath command also influences the structure of worship. For Muslims, Friday may be the day of congregational prayer, but it is not a day of Sabbath as observed by Jews, and to an extent transferred by Christians to Sunday. Rest is not a divinely mandated activity.

Finally, as an aside, I note that in Islam, as in Christianity, there is debate as to how to understand the story of six-day creation. For some in both faiths, this is literal and scientific fact, while for others it is a metaphorical tale of divine origins. In the third century, the great church teacher Origen, for example, stated very clearly that he understood Genesis 1–3 as a cosmic myth, not a historical account. This debate has been running for centuries and I am not proposing to enter into it here. Instead I simply note that while Christians and Muslims would agree that their sacred texts teach a doctrine of divine creation, they hold a range of views as to how that came about. The focus of this chapter is on the biblical and Qur'anic understandings of Adam in particular, and it is on him that our discussion centers.

The Creation of People and Their Rebellion against God (Genesis 1–3)

This section discusses three points. First, the creation of people in Genesis 1:26–27; second, the creation of Eve in Genesis 2:18–25; third, the temptation and fall of humanity.

The Creation of People in Genesis 1

In Genesis 1, the creation of people is the pinnacle of the account of creation.

> Then God said, "Let us make Adam in our image, according to our likeness. Let them have dominion over the fish of the sea,

over the birds of the air, over the cattle, over all the earth and over every crawling thing that crawls on the earth." And God created Adam in his image; in the image of God he created him; male and female he created them. (Genesis 1:26–27, adapted NRSV)

Christians down the centuries have discussed these verses in great detail. I have included a few ancient and modern commentaries on these verses, primarily for the purpose of provoking discussion. Gregory of Nyssa in *On the Origin of Man* states that while heaven was made without deliberation, God debates (*let us . . .*) at the creation of human beings, because *God deliberated about the best way to bring to life a creation worthy of honor.*[1]

For other ancient Christian commentators, these verses indicate that the Father and the Son cooperate in creation, and people are made in the image of the image of God, that is, in the image of Jesus, who is himself the image of God. Thus Marius Victorinus in *Against Arius* states:

> Moses says what was said by God: "Let us make man according to our image and likeness." God says that. He says "let us make" to a co-operator, necessarily to Christ. And he says "according to our image." Therefore man is not the image of God, but he is "according to the image." For Jesus alone is the image of God, but man is "according to that image," that is, image of the image. But he says "according to our image." Therefore both Father and Son are one image.[2]

For many commentators, the use of the plural in 1:26–27 indicates the Trinity. Thus for example Irenaeus explains:

> In previous times man, it is true, was said to have been made according to the image of God, but he was not revealed as such. For the Word according to whose image man was made was still invisible. Therefore also man easily lost the likeness. For on the one hand he truly showed the image by becoming what his image was. On the other hand he firmly established the likeness by the co-assimilation of man to the invisible Father through the visible Word.[3]

Finally, Gregory of Nyssa explains that humans are made in the image of God in order to display God's goodness to the world:

---

1. Louth, *Genesis 1–11*, 28.
2. Louth, *Genesis 1–11*, 29.
3. Louth, *Genesis 1–11*, 31.

> God creates man for no other reason than that God is good; and having this as his reason for entering upon the creation of our nature, he would not exhibit the power of this goodness in an imperfect form, giving our nature some one of the things at his disposal and grudging it a share in another: but the perfect form of goodness is here to be seen by his both bringing man into being from nothing and fully supplying him with all good gifts. But since the list of individual good gifts is a long one, it is out of the question to apprehend it numerically. The language of Scripture therefore expresses it concisely by a comprehensive phrase, in saying that man was made "in the image of God," for this is the same as to say that he made human nature participant in all good; for if the Deity is the fullness of good, and this is his image, then the image finds its resemblance to the archetype in being filled with all good.[4]

Turning to modern interpreters, in his discussion of scholarly interpretation of the plural *us* in Genesis 1:26, Hamilton outlines six possible interpretations. First, *us* indicates other gods, a hangover from a pagan prestory. Second, it refers to the heavenly court, the angelic host. Third, God is speaking to something recently created, that is, the earth. Thus, humanity originates from both God and ground. Fourth, it is a plural of majesty. Fifth, it is a plural of deliberation, God speaking to himself. Sixth, it is a "plural of fullness" that has hints of Trinitarian thinking. That is not to say the author had a Trinitarian understanding, but rather that he recognized a degree of plurality within the unity of God. He is most persuaded by this final alternative.[5]

The second area of discussion is over the meaning of *image* and *likeness*. Wenham explains that the idea that image indicates physical resemblance has gained little traction amongst interpreters, largely because they recognize that Genesis sees God as without physical form. Some see the two terms as distinct, indicating mental and spiritual qualities, although exactly how they are to be distinguished is questionable. The idea that *image* means human beings are God's representatives on earth has merit, not least because both Egyptian and Assyrian texts describe the king as the image of God. It is therefore likely that Genesis democratizes the idea, making all people bear this function. Finally, being made in the image of God may indicate human capacity to relate to the divine, but

---

4. Louth, *Genesis 1–11*, 34.
5. Hamilton, *Genesis 1–17*, 133–34.

the precise way this works needs spelling out; presumably it involves an amalgamation of the ideas noted above. Given the shift between Adam in the singular and plural humanity as male and female, the discussion cannot be about an individual but about all people.[6] Regarding image, Hamilton agrees with Wenham's proposal that Genesis 1 takes the concept known in Mesopotamian and Egyptian society, namely, that a king was "the image of God," and applies that to all humanity. Thus the text "democratizes the royalistic and exclusivistic concepts of the nations that surround Israel." The term *likeness*, he argues, may be present to tone down the concrete specificity implied by *image*, or conversely, may strengthen the relationship between God and humanity, indicating that by understanding humanity we can understand something about God.[7]

The Creation of Eve

Genesis 2 contains a second account of the creation of humanity. In this account the Lord God forms Adam from the dust of the ground (*adamah* in Hebrew), and breathes the breath of life into him, making him a living creature (Genesis 2:7). God plants a garden in Eden, filling it with plants and rivers. He places Adam in the garden and commands him, *You may freely eat of every tree of the garden; but of the tree of the knowledge of good and evil you shall not eat, for in the day that you eat of it you shall die* (Genesis 2:16–17). God then says it is not good for man to be alone, so resolves to make him a helper. God then makes animals and birds, bringing them to Adam to name, which he duly does. But no suitable helper for Adam is found amongst them. So God sends Adam into a deep sleep, removes a rib from the man and makes a woman. Adam then says, *This at last is bone of my bones and flesh of my flesh; this one shall be called Woman* [Heb. *ishah*] *for out of Man* [Heb. *ish*] *this one was taken* (Genesis 2:23). The text concludes that for this reason a man leaves his parents, and cleaves to his wife, the two becoming one flesh. Adam and Eve are naked, but unashamed (Genesis 2:24–25).

The early Christian commentators on this text are very much men of their era. Thus, for example, while Tertullian explains that woman is a blessing, he does so in entirely male-centered terms:

---

6. Wenham, *Genesis 1–15*, 29–34.
7. Hamilton, *Genesis 1–17*, 134–36.

> [In goodness God] provided also a help meet for [the man] that there might not be anything in his lot that was not good. For God said that it is not good for man to be alone. He knew full well what a blessing the gender of Mary would be to him and also to the church.[8]

Ephrem the Syrian, by contrast, has a more egalitarian understanding:

> After Adam's rib had been taken out in the twinkling of an eye, God closed up the flesh in its place in the blink of an eyelash. The bare bone took on the full appearance and all the beauty of a woman. God then brought her to Adam, who was both one and two. He was one in that he was Adam, and he was two because he had been created male and female.[9]

Third, Augustine is typical in reading the creation account typologically as referring to Christ. He argues that woman is one with man as Christ is one with the church, and so

> Adam's sleep was a mystical foreshadowing of Christ's death, and moreover, both men and women are divine creations. If she was made from the man, this was to show her oneness with him; and if she was made in the way that she was, this was to prefigure the oneness of Christ and the church.[10]

Augustine finds equal spiritual significance in the account of marriage:

> From the law we heard: "Therefore a man leaves his father and his mother and cleaves to his wife, and they will become one flesh." This is a great and sublime prophecy. Who actually leaves his father and mother when he takes a wife? This is the meaning of the words: man in his original condition loved and worshipped God, his father, and the Holy Spirit, his mother. He did not have any other love. In order to take a wife, man leaves his mother and father, those whom I mentioned above. His mind is thereby diverted by this world. His soul and mind are driven away from God and drawn into this world that he adores and loves "as a man loves the wife of his youth."[11]

---

8. Louth, *Genesis 1–11*, 64.
9. Louth, *Genesis 1–11*, 69.
10. Louth, *Genesis 1–11*, 70.
11. Louth, *Genesis 1–11*, 71–72

Hamilton points out that Genesis 2:15 indicates that work enters the garden before sin does, and so physical labor is not a consequence of sin. He adds that "Eden certainly is not a paradise in which man passes his time in idyllic and uninterrupted bliss with absolutely no demands on his daily schedule."[12] Discussing the naming of the animals in 2:19, Hamilton proposes this is the first fulfillment of God's directive to humanity in 1:26, 28 because conferring a name indicates authority.

Turning to the creation of Eve, Hamilton argues that "none of Israel's neighbors had a tradition involving a separate account of the creation of the female. In biblical thought the woman is not subsumed under her male counterpart." He proposes this second account of the creation of people complements the first in Genesis 1. The equality between men and women is emphasized by Hamilton's suggestion that the word conventionally translated as *rib* in Genesis 2:21 is better translated as *side*, which means the "passage states that woman was created from an undesignated part of man's body rather than from one of his organs or from a portion of bony tissue." Thus the woman is not subordinate to, but equal to the man; both are made in the image of God.[13] Thus the reference to *bone of my bones* (Genesis 2:23) indicates common, reciprocal loyalty between Adam and Eve. Finally, on "leaving and cleaving" for marriage, Hamilton understands the emphasis to be on loyalty; that is to say, the man severs loyalty to his parents and becomes loyal to his wife.[14]

The Temptation and Fall of Humanity

Perhaps the most striking aspect of the story found in Genesis 3 is what might be termed the chain of blame. The chapter begins with a description of the serpent as the craftiest of all creatures. He questions the woman as to exactly what God has said to them; she replies with a more stringent command that than recorded in Genesis 2. According to Eve, God told them that they may not even touch the tree or they will die. The serpent disputes this claim, telling the woman that if she eats of the tree, her eyes will be opened; she will be like God, knowing good and evil. *So when the woman saw that the tree was good for food, and that it was a delight to the eyes, and that the tree was to be desired to make one wise, she took of its*

12. Hamilton, *Genesis 1–17*, 171.
13. Hamilton, *Genesis 1–17*, 177–78.
14. Hamilton, *Genesis 1–17*, 179–81.

fruit and ate; and she also gave some to her husband, who was with her, and he ate (Genesis 3:6). Their eyes are then opened; they realize they are naked and make clothes for themselves from fig leaves.

They then hear God walking in the garden, and hide from him. God calls out to Adam, asking him where he is. Adam replies that he heard God in the garden, and was afraid because he was naked, so hid himself. God asks how Adam has come by this knowledge, and Adam replies, *The woman whom you gave to be with me, she gave me the fruit from the tree, and I ate* (Genesis 3:12). When God then questions the woman, she blames the serpent, saying he tricked her. God then issues a series of curses, first to the serpent, who will crawl on his belly, eating dust all his life, and there is enmity between the serpent's offspring and the woman's. The woman is also cursed: *I will greatly increase your pangs in childbearing; in pain you shall bring forth children, yet your desire shall be for your husband, and he shall rule over you* (Genesis 3:16).

The man is also cursed:

> Because you have listened to the voice of your wife, and have eaten of the tree about which I commanded you, "You shall not eat of it," cursed is the ground because of you; in toil you shall eat of it all the days of your life; thorns and thistles it shall bring forth for you; and you shall eat the plants of the field. By the sweat of your face you shall eat bread until you return to the ground, for out of it you were taken; you are dust, and to dust you shall return. (Genesis 3:17–18)

God then makes clothes for Adam and Eve, but nevertheless expels them from the garden, placing a guardian angel to prevent a human attempt to return to the tree that they were forbidden to touch.

John of Damascus explains that the serpent was a close associate of Adam and was used by the devil to spread his deceit. But for Augustine, *the serpent signifies the devil*. Ephrem the Syrian argues for human culpability, stating: *the words of the tempter would not have caused those two to be tempted to sin if their avarice had not been so helpful to the tempter.*[15] Irenaeus finds a typological salvific relationship between Eve and Mary:

> As Eve was seduced by the word of a [fallen] angel to flee from God, having rebelled against his word, so Mary by the word of an angel received the glad tidings that she would bear God by obeying his word. The former was seduced to disobey God

---

15. Louth, *Genesis 1–11*, 75–77.

[and so fell], but the latter was persuaded to obey God, so that the Virgin Mary might become the advocate of the virgin Eve. As the human race was subjected to death through the act of a virgin, so it was saved by a virgin, and thus the disobedience of one virgin was precisely balanced by the obedience of another.[16]

Irenaeus also sees significant symbolism in Christ's defeat of the devil, as the one who took human form through birth from a virgin (Mary) defeats the one who first deceived another virgin (Eve):

> Christ completely renewed all things, both taking up the battle against our enemy and crushing him who at the beginning had led us captive in Adam, trampling on his head . . . The enemy would not have been justly conquered unless it had been a man made of woman who conquered him. For it was by woman that he had power over man from the beginning, setting himself up in opposition to man. Because of this the Lord also declares himself to be the Son of Man, so renewing in himself that primal man from whom the formation of man by woman began, that as our race went down to death by a man who overcame, and as death won the palm of victory over us by a man, so we might by a man receive the palm of victory over death.[17]

In Hamilton's discussion of Genesis 3, he describes the exchange between the serpent and Eve as a mixture of "misquotation, denial and slander," which is "reinforced even by the ambiguity of the passage in Hebrew." Hamilton is clear that both Adam and Eve are tempted by the fantasy of deification, which he describes as difficult to repress. There is a difference between their sins: Eve is guided by her own mind and judgment, committing "a sin of initiative," while Adam is more passive, neither challenging nor raising questions, neither approving nor rebuking, committing "a sin of acquiescence." Hamilton is cautious about reading too much into Genesis 3:15, but recognizes that it does promise that a future human will strike out against the serpent's seed, even if the specific promise of Christ cannot necessarily be read from this verse. He concludes that the overall thrust of these verses is that sin and disobedience have consequences, but also that they do not go unchallenged.[18]

---

16. Louth, *Genesis 1–11*, 78–79.
17. Louth, *Genesis 1–11*, 90–91.
18. Hamilton, *Genesis 1–17*, 189–201.

The Creation of People and Their Rebellion against God as Told in the Qur'an

The purpose of this chapter is to enable readers to contrast biblical and Qur'anic material. But these are two different texts, written for two different purposes, in two different languages. Comparison will therefore not be straightforward. The discussion that follows touches on the same three points as section 2, namely, the creation of Adam, the creation of Eve and human rebellion against God. But the Qur'anic account has its own unique features, notably, rebellion of Iblis, which must also be discussed.

The Accounts of Creation of Adam and Eve

There are four accounts of the creation of Adam in the Qur'an (*al-Baqarah* 2:28–39; *al-A'raf* 7:10–25; *al-Hijr* 15:19–48; *Ta' Ha'* 20:115–22). The Qur'an states that God's hands formed Adam (*Sad* 38:75) before he breathed the spirit of life into him (*al-Hijr* 15:29; *Sad* 38:72). Qur'anic commentators have discussed these anthropomorphisms extensively, and the consensus view is that they are not to be taken literally. There is also agreement that this one being is the father of all humanity. Thus, there is a *hadith (saying)* of the Prophet that *God created Adam from a handful of dirt which was taken from the entire earth, thus the children of Adam correspond to the earth in being red, black, white, and other colors, plain, rugged, pleasant or ugly.*[19] God is described as discussing the being he will create with the angels. The angels are skeptical as to the benefit of this being. But God still makes him, informing Adam of the names of all created things. Adam thus possesses knowledge, and power, which the angels do not, and so they are ordered to prostrate themselves before him. They all comply, except for Iblis/Satan, a topic to which I will return.

The Qur'an does not state that Eve was created from Adam's rib, but that they were both created from one soul, and that through them *spread countless men and women far and wide* (*al-Nisa* 4:1; see also *al-A'raf* 7:189). While the story of creation from a single rib is not in the Qur'an, commentators on the text do mention it; thus Ibn Abbas narrates that God took Adam's shortest rib from his left side while he was sleeping, and from it created Eve. When she was presented to Adam, he asked her first who she was, to which she replied *a woman*, and second, what she

---

19. Wheeler, *Prophets in the Qu'ran*, 17–18.

was created for, to which she replied, *so you could seek comfort in me.* The angels then asked Adam her name, and he said *Hawwa* (Eve). When asked why, he explained, *because she was created from something living.* Notice also that Eve is only named in the extra-Qur'anic tradition; the text itself does not give her a name.

Adam and Eve are used within Islam to present a paradigm of marriage. The Qur'an is clear that both celibacy and monasticism are human inventions, specifically Christian creations, which in fact the Christians are not even able to maintain properly (*al-Hadid* 57:27). For Muslims, Adam and Eve teach us that "man and woman cannot live without each other, otherwise they become unsettled, and worse."[20] Jesus also uses Adam and Eve to set out a paradigm for marriage, although this is a specific response to questions about divorce, and in contrast with the Muslim understanding, Jesus includes teaching that remaining single and celibate may also be a calling from God (Matthew 19:1–12).

The Prostration of the Angels

My second area of discussion is the prostration of the angels before Adam. References to the prostration of the angels appear in seven different *surahs* (*al-Baqarah* 2:34; *al-A'raf* 7:11–12; *al-Hijr* 15:28–33; *al-Isra* 17:61–62; *al-Kahf* 18:50; 20:115–16; 38:71–78). To cite one example:

> Certainly We created you, (and) fashioned you. Then We said to the angels, "Prostrate yourselves before Adam," and they prostrated themselves, except Iblis. He was not one of those who prostrated themselves. He said, "What kept you from prostrating yourself when I commanded you?" He said, "I am better than him. You created me from fire, but You created him from clay." (*al-A'raf* 7:11-12)

Nasr gives three possible explanations for the prostration of the angels. First, some interpreters understand it to be merely symbolic in nature, while second others argue that the angels were bowing to God, and taking Adam as their *qiblah*, or direction of prayer. Third, prostration may indicate recognition of the spiritual greatness of another.[21] Iblis refuses to prostrate himself because he believes that he, a being made of fire, is superior to humanity, who are made of clay. Yet the message of the

---

20. Haleem, *Understanding the Qur'an*, 136.
21. Nasr, *Study Qur'an*, 409.

Qur'an is the reverse, implying that clay is more beneficial and better than fire. The *Stories of the Prophets* suggests this is because in clay there are qualities of serenity, gentleness, perseverance and growth, while fire has qualities of frivolity, impatience, haste and burning. Similarly, Ibn Kathir explains that Satan's claim that the fire is more honored than mud was also false, because mud has the qualities of wisdom, forbearance, patience and assurance; mud is where plants grow, flourish, increase and provide good. To the contrary, fire has the qualities of burning, recklessness and hastiness. Moreover, Adam has knowledge that the angels do not possess; he is given the names of creation. This knowledge also implies power over creation, a point reinforced by Adam's role as *khalifa*, a point to which I will return (*al-Baqarah* 2:30). The prostration of the angels also teaches about the nature of the devil's fall from heaven. There is tension between the devil and humanity. God banishes the devil from heaven (*al-A'raf* 7:13) but the devil requests and receives a reprieve of some sort up until the Day of Resurrection (*al-A'raf* 7:14–15). While in heaven, the devil is called Iblis, but once he has fallen, he is called *shaytan*. Iblis is a rebel against God, while *shaytan* is the tempter of humanity.

Adam as Khalifa

Third, Reynolds discusses some of the problems with traditional Islamic exegesis concerning how to translate the title *khalifa*, which is given to Adam. The Qur'an states, (*Remember*) *when your Lord said to the angels, "Surely I am placing on the earth a khalifa"* (*al-Baqarah* 2:30). The word is normally rendered *representative* or *vicegerent* or *viceroy* or even *deputy*. But this representative function can be understood as implying that man has some type of divine quality, when Islam teaches that God is utterly distinct from his creation. Thus a better translation would be *successor*. This role is explained as human beings as successor to the *jinn*, who rebelled and were so impious that God decided to create humanity to be their successor.[22]

Reynolds adds that the idea of *khalifa* as *representative* is also problematic for the story of the prostration of the angels, as if he is God's representative, then it sounds very much like the angels are worshipping Adam. Qur'anic exegetes tell stories to deal with this issue: first, there is a suggestion that the command to prostrate was designed to flush out the

22. See also Reynolds, *Qur'an and the Bible*, 35–36.

devil's pride, exposing him as a rebel against God; second, the distinction is drawn between prostration in worship of God, and prostration to give honor to a person, as with the prostration before Joseph in *Yusuf* 12:100.[23]

All of this points toward a very different understanding of the status and role of human beings when contrasted with the biblical notion of humanity made in the image of God. The differences are subtle, but important. In the Qur'an, Adam is told the names of the animals, so the knowledge comes from God. By contrast, in Genesis Adam names the animals himself, indicating that he produces the knowledge; a reflection of his being made in God's image. Second, as we will see below, the account of what happens in the garden places the emphasis in different places: in Genesis the blame lies primarily with people, while in the Qur'an Satan is more culpable. The response also differs. Fundamentally, the difference in emphasis is that the Genesis accounts focus on the proximity of humanity and the divine, while the Qur'an focuses on the distance between them.

In his discussion that contrasts Genesis 1:26 with *al-Baqarah* 2:30, Lodahl points out that the biblical notion of creation in the divine image refers to function not physical resemblance, a point made clear in Psalm 8. This, Lodahl suggests, means the difference between the Qur'an and the Bible may not be as great as it first appears, as the Qur'an does also assign humanity a function of service and representation of God. But, Lodahl adds, the understanding of humanity is different, a point exemplified by the naming of the animals. Lodahl argues that human beings use language "to bring order to our experience of the world."[24] Thus, by naming the creatures, Adam rules over them, assigning them meaning and function. In the Qur'an, by contrast, it is God who rules, as it is only he who knows the names of the creatures. Indeed, in Islam the *Qadariyya* were condemned for their belief that people had the power to innovate and create, for only God creates. Thus, in the Qur'an Adam does imitate God, but he must learn from God, remaining submitted to him.

Human Rebellion

One Qur'anic text that tells of the time Adam and Eve spend in the garden is *al-A'raf* 7:10–25. The first section (7:10–18) concerns the story of creating Adam and the prostration of the angels, discussed above. God then

---

23. Reynolds, *Qur'an and Its Biblical Subtext*, 40–46.
24. Lodahl, *Claiming Abraham*, 85.

places Adam and Eve in the garden, forbidding them to eat the fruit of a particular tree. But *then Satan whispered to them both, to reveal to them both what was hidden from them of their shameful parts. He said, "Your Lord has only forbidden you both from this tree to keep you both from becoming two angels, or from becoming two of the immortals"* (7:20). Adam and Eve are deceived, and they eat from the tree; they realize they are naked and are ashamed, fashioning clothes for themselves from leaves.

Again, the commentators expand on this. To give three examples, Wahb b. Munabbih states, *The tree's branches were intertwined and it bore fruit which the angels ate to live forever, and it was this fruit that God prohibited to Adam and Eve,* while Abu al-Aliyah explains *Adam and Eve ate of the tree. It was a tree which made whoever ate from it defecate but faeces were not allowed in Paradise, so God drove Adam and Eve out of Paradise.*[25] Unal summarizes the Qur'an's teaching about human disobedience in four points. First, angels do not have the capacity to do evil, but Satan has no capacity to do good. Human beings can do both good and evil, because they have a dual nature belonging to both the physical and the metaphysical realm. Second, this dual nature, combined with our free will, means our inner world is an area of struggle between good and evil. Third, what distinguishes people from Satan is that Adam and Eve felt remorse for their actions, but Satan, who is arrogant and vain, excludes himself from God's mercy with his continued defiance to the divine command. Fourth, Adam and Eve's repentance teaches us that we must have an accurate understanding of our own helplessness before God, our dependence on his mercy and our need for forgiveness for wrongdoing.[26] As a result of their disobedience, Adam and Eve are expelled from the garden, but because they repent, they receive God's forgiveness, and the matter ends there.

A central feature of the Qur'anic account of the garden is that no distinction is made between Adam and Eve, a point emphasized by the fact that there are twenty-eight occurrences of grammatically dual forms in *al-A'raf* 7:19–22 (the dual is an Arabic grammatical form that indicates the actions of two people). This is a key difference from Genesis 3. There is no passing of blame from one to another; rather Adam is rebuked for forgetting the covenant he has made with God with no mention of a chain of temptation from Satan to Eve to Adam (*Ta Ha* 20:115). In one

---

25. Wheeler, *Prophets in the Qur'an*, 23.
26. Unal, *Qur'an*, 313–14.

tradition recorded in *Stories of the Prophets*, Adam spends forty years lamenting his failure until God finally accepted his repentance.

In the Qur'an, both Adam and Eve are expelled from the garden, but there is no discussion of the hereditary consequences of this rebellion such as that found in Genesis 3. The closest link to the generational consequences of rebellion is found in the repeated affirmation that when they leave the garden, they will do so with *some of you an enemy to others* (*al-A'raf* 7:24; *Ta Ha* 20:123). In contrast to the repeated use of the dual in the discussion of Adam and Eve's sin, the grammar now shifts to the second-person plural, suggesting that *you* here is humanity in general. All humanity suffers but at the same time individual culpability for personal sin is made plain:

> Sons of Adam! Do not let Satan tempt you, as he drove your parents out of the Garden, stripping both of them of their clothing in order to show both of them their shameful parts. Surely he sees you—he and his ilk—from where you do not see them. Surely We have made the satans allies of those who do not believe. (*al-A'raf* 7:27)

As this *ayat* makes clear, human beings continually face temptation and so are encouraged to seek refuge in the mercy of God. The consequences of the subtle difference in emphasis of the stories are far-reaching. Islam does not have a doctrine akin to the Christian understanding of original sin (or inherited corruption as some might term it). This is why there is no doctrine of baptism in Islam either. For those Christians who believe in infant baptism, part of the purpose of the rite is cleansing from the stain of original sin. Even for those who do not hold with infant baptism, within teaching on adult baptism there is still a core understanding that we were all born in rebellion against God. It is only by turning to Christ that this rebellion can be dealt with. By contrast, Islam teaches the notion of original innocence, in the sense that children are not held to be personally liable for their actions until they reach the age of maturity. Traditionally within Islam this is understood as puberty. Thus, prepubescent adolescents are not obligated to pray, fast, give and so forth, but are expected to learn to do so, in order that once they attain the age of personal moral responsibility they are already practicing their faith.

For some commentators, this mercy is on the basis of God's love for the Prophet Muhammad. Thus Umar b. al Khattab narrates the story in some detail:

The Prophet Muhammad said: "When Adam committed his sin he said: "O Lord, I ask you by the right of Muhammad, will you forgive me?" God said, "How do you know about Muhammad, I have not yet created him?" Adam said: "Lord, because when you created me with your hand and breathed into me from your spirit, I raised my head and saw what was written on the foundation of your throne: There is no god but God and Muhammad is the Apostle of God. I knew that you would not place his name there unless he is the most beloved of creation to you." God said, "You are right, Adam. He is the most beloved of creation to me. When you ask me in the right of his name, I will forgive you. If only for Muhammad did I create you."[27]

The implications of the slight differences in emphasis of the stories of the garden are significant. Christians and Muslims can use their different stories of the first temptations as a way of discussing their different conceptions of temptation, sin, personal responsibility, the existence and activity of the devil and much more. In a world that increasingly ignores these ideas, the power of these ancient stories to ignite debate and discussion remains as strong as it ever did.

Adam in Jewish, Christian and Muslim Thought

This section contrasts the Adam Christology of the New Testament with the Qur'an's understanding of Adam's role. But first, I introduce some Jewish and Christian material that develops biblical material in a manner not dissimilar to the interpretation found in the Qur'an.

Jewish and Early Christian Views of Adam

Although the idea of angelic prostration before Adam is not found in Genesis, we should note that Jewish traditional exegesis also contains some of these ideas. For example, commentators understand Psalm 8:4 (*what are human beings that you are mindful of them, or the son of Adam that you care for him?*) to be the angels' response to God's declaration, *let us make man in our image* (Genesis 1:26).

Thus, in the Babylonian Talmud we read:

---

27. Wheeler, *Prophets in the Qur'an*, 30.

> When the Holy One, blessed be He, wished to create man, He [first] created a company of ministering angels and said to them: Is it your desire that we make man in our image? They answered: Sovereign of the Universe, what will be his deeds?—Such and such will be his deeds, He replied. Thereupon they exclaimed: Sovereign of the Universe, What is man that thou art mindful of him, and the son of man that thou thinkest of him? Thereupon He stretched out His little finger among them and consumed them with fire. The same thing happened with a second company. The third company said to Him: Sovereign of the Universe, what did it avail the former [angels] that they spoke to Thee [as they did]? The whole world is Thine, and whatsoever that Thou wishest to do therin, do it (*Sanhedrin* 38b).[28]

The implication of this is that the Qur'an is drawing on contemporaneous Jewish debate, shaping the interpretation for its own purposes. In his discussion of *al-A'raf* 7:11–12, Reynolds proposes that Christian speculation about what happened in the garden of Eden lies behind the Qur'anic account. He cites the Syriac Christian text *Cave of Treasures* as evidence to support his claim. In this text, the angels prostrate themselves before Adam, except for Satan, who refuses to do so:

> Moreover the angels and celestial powers heard the voice of God saying to Adam, "See, I have made you king, priest and prophet, Lord, leader and director of all those made and created. To you alone have I given these and I give you authority over everything I have created." When the angels and archangels, the thrones and dominions, the cherubims and seraphims, that is when all the celestial powers heard this voice, all of the orders bent their knees and prostrated before him . . . When the leader of the lesser order saw the greatness given to Adam, he became jealous of him and did not want to prostrate before him with the angels. He said to his hosts, "Do not worship him and do not praise him with the angels. It is proper that you should worship me, since I am fire and spirit, not that I worship something that is made of dirt" (*Cave of Treasures*, 2:22–25; 3:1–2).[29]

The point to note is that although this material is not biblical, it nevertheless shows how Christians and Jews developed the story found in Genesis in a fashion that is not dissimilar to the interpretation found in the Qur'an.

28. Translated by Schlater and Freedman, *Sanhedrin*.
29. Cited in Reynolds, *Qur'an and the Bible*, 252.

Adam in the New Testament

In the New Testament, the Apostle Paul describes Adam as a type of Christ in 1 Corinthians 15:21–22, 45–49 and Romans 5:12–21. Fee argues that for Paul, Christ "stands at the beginning of the new humanity in a way analogous to, but not identical with, the way Adam stood at the beginning of the old order, both temporally and causally."[30] Paul's point is that our common lot as humans (sinfulness, death) comes from our being *in Adam*, that is, being born into Adam's race and therefore tainted by the sin and death that came from him. In the same way, those who are *in Christ*, that is, those who have entered the new humanity through God's grace, will enter into the shared life of the risen Christ. Paul's use of the analogy in 1 Corinthians 15:44–49 presumes the usage earlier in the chapter, and advances the argument that just as there is a natural body, so too there is a spiritual body. His reference to the *last Adam* in 15:45 is a reference to the eschatological reality of Christ's resurrection and the reference to the *second man* in 15:47 indicates the spiritual body of Christ.[31]

Thiselton adds that for Paul, Adam is "both an individual and a corporate entity." That is, he is what his name signifies, humanity. Thus, human beings, bound up in the "solidarities, vulnerabilities and consequences" of Adam, are offered assurance of salvation if they are bound up in the "solidarities, atoning work and resurrection victory and promise" of Jesus Christ. Thiselton notes that Paul stresses the common humanity of both Adam and Christ, whilst also emphasizing the qualitative difference between the two, as Paul's argument focuses on contrast and reversal.[32] As Hamilton explains Paul drew on this analogy in order to correct three misunderstandings of the resurrection. First, there is a resurrection, made possible by Christ; second, this resurrection is physical; and third, it is spiritual, immortal and permanent.[33]

Paul also uses Adam-Christ typology in Romans 5:12–21. Kruse outlines the structure of Paul's argument. First, Paul introduces his comparison between Adam and Christ (Romans 5:12), before digressing to explain how sin entered the world before the law was given to define sin (Romans 5:13–14). Then he highlights the difference between Adam's actions and Christ's actions (Romans 5:15–17). Then Paul states his full

---

30. Fee, *1 Corinthians*, 751.
31. Fee, *1 Corinthians*, 751–91.
32. Thiselton, *1 Corinthians*, 1225–28.
33. Hamilton, *Genesis 1–17*, 218.

comparison between the two figures, emphasizing the dire consequences for humanity of Adam's actions in contrast with the potential blessings offered through Christ (Romans 5:18–21).[34]

Paul's point here is that Adam is a (negative) type of Christ. As Moo notes, he adopts a corporate perspective, teaching that all people stand in relationship to one of two men. Either we belong to Adam, and so are under sentence of death because of Adam's disobedience, or else we belong to Christ, and so are assured of eternal life because of Christ's obedience.[35] For some Christians this is explained in a theological term "federal headship," which means that Adam's actions have implications for all his (natural) descendants and Christ's actions for all his (spiritual) descendants. Adam's decision to eat of the fruit of the tree was an act of rebellion against the express will of God, and this tendency to rebel has been passed down the generations, so that every human being has an innate propensity to sin, to reject the reign of God. Adam's one act of trespass against the commands of God resulted in condemnation for all people for all time. Until, that is, Christ came. Paul argues in Romans 5 that Jesus' one act of obedience to his Father's will was more than sufficient to deal with Adam's one act of rebellion against the Father's will. In an exegetical move that contrasts a (relatively) minor act with a (relatively) major act, Paul argues that Adam's single act of rebellion had dire consequences for everyone, but Jesus' single act of obedience overcomes and overpowers the disobedience of many, so that all who have faith in Jesus are now free of guilt and condemnation. Grace now reigns for those who accept its rule.

Adam in the Qur'an

The discussion thus far has made it clear that the Qur'an and the Bible understand Adam somewhat differently. In Genesis, God establishes a covenant with Adam, authorizing dominion and promising blessing. Haleem proposes that the Qur'an uses the story of Adam to make eight distinct moral points.[36] First, to prove the power of God in comparison with human beings, by stating that men were made from dust and their spouses from men themselves (*ar-Rum* 30:20–21; see also *Hud* 11:61;

---

34. Kruse, *Romans*, 240.
35. Moo, *Romans*, 315.
36. Haleem, *Understanding the Qur'an*, 136–38.

al-An'am 6:2; al-Hijr 15:26; al-Mu'minun 23:12; as-Sajdah 32:7; Fatir 35:11; as-Saffat 37:11). This point is also found in the Genesis account. Second, the creation of Adam from dust indicates that God can raise the dead from that same dust; humans thus return to the earth only to be raised again from the earth at a time of God's choosing, presumably to face judgment (Ta Ha 20:55). While this does not occur in Genesis, arguably this thought lies behind Paul's discussion of life after death found in 1 Corinthians 15. Third, although Adam is made of dust, he has the spirit of God breathed into him, was taught the names of all things and the angels bow down before him (which Haleem says is implied in *Fatir* 35:28; *al-Mujadilah* 58:11). There is an interesting contrast here with the account in Genesis. As noted above, in the Qur'an it is God who teaches the names, while in Genesis God brings the animals before Adam *to see what he would call them; and whatever the man called each living creature, that was its name* (Genesis 2:19).

Fourth, Adam was created without a father, as was Jesus. This similarity is used in the Qur'an to argue in favor of the virgin birth whilst refuting claims to Jesus' divinity. Fifth, the fact that all humanity was created from one man and one woman means humanity is one family; hence, people should behave justly to the poor and the weak and cannot claim superiority on the basis of tribe, race or class. One of the more commonly cited *ayat* in an interfaith context is:

> People! Surely We have created you from a male and a female, and made you different peoples and tribes, so that you may recognize one another. Surely the most honorable among you in the sight of God is the one among you who guards (himself) most. Surely God is knowing, aware. (*al-Hujurat* 49:13)

There are echoes of the themes of the first eleven chapters of Genesis in this verse: the notion of diverse humanity made for relationship with one another and with God. The narrative of Babel is perhaps the closet equivalent to this *ayat*, although the ending of that story is very different. In Genesis 11:8 God scatters the people across their differences because when they were united they attempted to become like God.

Sixth, there is a strong connection between humanity and the earth. Although there is not a direct statement that parallels the command given in Genesis—*Be fruitful and multiply, and fill the earth and subdue it; and have dominion over the fish of the sea and over the birds of the air and over every living thing that moves upon the earth* (Genesis 1:28)—nevertheless, there is a Qur'anic expectation of both mastery over and also responsibility for creation. Seventh, Satan's refusal to recognize Adam's superiority is a warning to people that Satan is the accuser who will tempt and mislead people. The reality of ongoing temptation is made clear in *al-A'raf* 7:27, quoted above, which spoke of accusers (*Satans*) allied with the unbelievers to trap the unwary faithful. Eighth, as noted above, God teaches Adam and Eve how to repent after they sin; there is no sense of guilt being passed down the generations. Haleem suggests that the story is repeated throughout the Qur'an in order to remind people of its morals and lessons and ensure they are properly embedded in their lives.

Kaltner and Mirza discuss the way that *Stories of the Prophets* adds dramatic detail to the sparse information provided by the Qur'an. The narrators explain that the angels and *jinn* were initially skeptical about the creation of Adam, and imagine what happened after he was created. In one story cited above, when Adam opens his eyes, he saw written on the throne of God the Muslim declaration of faith (*There is no God but God, and Muhammad is his messenger*). In another, Adam wants to be with his wife, but the angels prevent him from doing so until he has paid her dowry. When Adam questions the angels as to what the dowry is, the angels reply that it is *to pray for Muhammad, peace and blessings be upon him, three times*. When Adam questions who Muhammad is, he is informed that this man is *the last of the prophets from among your sons. If it were not for Muhammad, you would not have been created*. Thus, the tradition teaches that the primary purpose of creation is the coming of Muhammad.[37]

Conclusions and Pointers for Further Discussion

The purpose of this chapter has been to compare and contrast Christian and Muslim understandings of creation and Adam and Eve. It does not claim to be a definitive exposition of either Islamic or Christian doctrine, but rather a way into conversation. By way of conclusion I will recap five possible areas of discussion that have emerged so far. First, the question of Sabbath rest. The Sabbath is central to Judaism, but also an important concept within Christianity. Christians place different levels of emphasis on the importance of one day in seven when no work is done, and many Christians are wary of a legalistic enforcement of total abstinence from work. At the same time Christians also adopt the concept of Sabbath rest

---

37. Kaltner and Mirza, *Bible and the Qur'an*, 18–19.

and apply it to faith in Christ, an understanding that is particularly explored in Hebrews 4. By contrast Islam does not emphasize the Sabbath in any way. What are we to make of this difference?

Second, what are the similarities and differences between the Christian understanding of humanity made in the image of God and the Islamic concept of Adam as *khalifa*? Are they two ways of saying essentially the same thing, or are there important differences between them? Adam's role in naming the animals in Genesis, in contrast with his receiving the names from God in the Qur'an, is one interesting way into this discussion.

Third, how do we understand the teaching on human sinfulness? Christianity centers on a concept of corporate responsibility, that somehow when Adam and Eve sinned, all human beings were culpable. This teaching is encapsulated in phrases such as "inherited corruption" or "original sin." By contrast, in the Qur'anic telling of the story of human rebellion, Adam is responsible only for his own actions; they do not affect his descendants in the same way as Genesis teaches that they do. Adam is seen as making a personal mistake, which is rectified, rather than as committing a mortal sin that affects the whole of humanity.

A fourth, related area of discussion is whether Adam points toward Christ or Muhammad. The Apostle Paul develops an "Adam Christology" as one way of understanding and explaining the work of Jesus Christ in bringing salvation, while within Islamic tradition Adam is understood as pointing toward Muhammad. Are these complementary or mutually exclusive understandings?

Finally, how is Eve understood within Islamic and Christian tradition? The quotations from the early church fathers above indicate a fascinating comparison between Eve and Mary. Yet the Qur'an does not even name Eve. How important a figure is she, and what can we learn from the stories of her life?

Noah

THE CHAPTER FIRST PRESENTS the biblical material, beginning with the account in Genesis, before discussing other references to Noah in the New Testament. The second section sets out the Qur'anic presentation. The third section then contrasts the presentation of the Christian and Islamic perspectives on Noah, and his relationship with both Christ and Muhammad.

The Christian Understanding of Noah

Noah in Genesis 6–9

Genesis 6 begins with a tale of the slide toward wickedness, as the *sons of God* (or *of the gods*) decide that because human women are beautiful, they want to marry them (Genesis 6:2). The identity of these beings is the cause of much speculation. Wenham suggests three options: godlike beings like angels, demons or spirits; superior humans such as kings; or godly men, meaning the descendants of Seth, rather than the godless descendants of Cain. He notes that the first, angelic option has the strongest pedigree and also the most modern support among Christian commentators. The idea that these beings were kings gained traction in later Jewish interpretation, partly on metaphysical grounds (how do angels have sexual intercourse?) and partly to shift speculation from angelic to other routes.[1]

Hamilton's discussion of the options for identifying the *sons of God* also examines three views. He rejects the suggestion that they are angels because, although the expression has that meaning elsewhere in the Old

---

1. Wenham, *Genesis 1–15*, 139–40.

Testament, contextually it is problematic. There are three reasons for this. First, in the New Testament Jesus teaches angels do not marry (Matthew 22:29–30; Mark 12:24–25; Luke 20:34–36), and second, these beings sin. Why would humans be punished for the sins of angels? Third, elsewhere in the Old and New Testaments, angels do not take physical form.

There are two other interpretations that Hamilton suggests have more merit. First, the *sons of God* are dynastic rulers, an early aristocracy. The daughters of men constitute a harem and thus the sin is of polygamy. This allows the text to contain primarily historical data, with no mythological elements. But the disadvantage is that there is no attestation of groups of kings being called *sons of God*. A final interpretation is that the *sons of God* are godly Sethites and the daughters of humanity are ungodly Cainites (or the other way around, with the sons of God the ungodly Cainites and daughters of men as Sethites). If this interpretation is followed, then the sin is of yoking believer and unbeliever, that is, intermarriage that dilutes the divinely chosen line.[2]

Whichever option is preferred, the point is that God mourns the failure of humanity to live as he wants them to; human life span is shortened, and then God decides to wipe humanity from the face of the earth. Noah alone finds favor in God's eyes (Genesis 6:8). God speaks to Noah, explaining that he will destroy the earth because of the wickedness of people. Hamilton explains that divine punishment is not arbitrary or amoral, but the direct consequence of disobedience. "God is moved to anger by man's deliberate violations of the code by which God wills his world to live."[3] Lodahl comments that the divine grief of Genesis 6:5–8 is, for the Qur'an, "not worthy of Allah" and so all reference to it is omitted.[4] In Genesis Noah is therefore to make himself an ark. He is given detailed instructions as to the dimensions of the craft, and how many of which animals he is to take with him. God establishes his covenant with Noah, and promises that Noah, his wife, his sons and their wives will all be saved (Genesis 6:18). Noah does exactly as he is commanded.

The Lord then warns Noah again that the flood is coming, commanding him to take seven pairs of the clean animals and one pair of unclean animals into the ark, before the rain comes, for forty days and forty nights (Genesis 7:1–5). Noah does as he is told, embarking the animals.

2. Hamilton, *Genesis 1–17*, 262–64.
3. Hamilton, *Genesis 1–17*, 273.
4. Lodahl, *Claiming Abraham*, 115.

Noah is six hundred years old when *the fountains of the great deep burst forth, and the windows of the heavens were opened* (Genesis 7:11). Noah and his family enter the ark and the waters continued to rise for forty days and forty nights. The whole of the earth is flooded, such that *all the high mountains under the whole heaven were covered*, to a depth of nearly seven meters (Genesis 7:19–20). Every living creature dies—humans, animals, birds—leaving only Noah and those with him in the ark.

The situation seems desperate, *but God remembered Noah and all the wild animals and the domestic animals that were with him in the ark* (Genesis 8:1), and sends wind to drive back the waters, which slowly recede over the next one hundred and fifty days, until the ark comes to rest on the mountains of Ararat (Genesis 8:4). The waters continue to go down, and eventually Noah opens a window in the ark, and sends out a raven, which just flies back and forth (Genesis 8:7). He then sends out a dove, which flies around and comes back to Noah. He takes it back into the ark, waits seven days, and then sends it out again. It returns that evening with *a freshly plucked olive leaf* in its beak. Noah sends the dove out for a third time, and it does not return (Genesis 8:8–12).

On the first day of the first month of Noah's six hundred and first year, the waters had dried up, and so Noah removed the covering of the ark. But it is not until the twenty-seventh day of the second month that the earth had completely dried and God told Noah to come out of the ark, together with his family and all the living creatures that have been shut up with him (Genesis 8:13–19). Noah built an altar, took some of the clean animals and offered a sacrifice to God. The aroma of this sacrifice is pleasing to God, who resolves to never again curse the entirety of humanity, even though *the inclination of the human heart is evil from youth* (Genesis 8:21). God likewise resolves to not wipe out all living creatures. The promise is made that *as long as the earth endures, seedtime and harvest, cold and heat, summer and winter, day and night, shall not cease* (Genesis 8:22).

God then blessed Noah and his sons, telling them to be fruitful and increase, to fill the earth. He promises that *the fear and dread of you* will fall on all creatures—birds, fish and animals—and that they can eat all these living beings, but must not eat meat with its lifeblood still in it. A particular demand of accountability is made in relation to human beings, who are made in God's image (Genesis 9:1–7). God then established a covenant with Noah, his descendants, and all living creatures that never again will a flood destroy all life. The sign of this covenant is the rainbow

(Genesis 9:8–17). In his discussion of the covenant made between God and humanity in Genesis 9, Hamilton notes deterioration from Genesis 1. In that first covenant human beings were vegetarian; they had no authority to exploit animals for food. But in Genesis 9 the relationship with the animal world changes and now humans will eat meat. Prohibitions against drinking blood and murder remain, even when an animal is responsible. The flip side of this is that God includes animals within the covenant he establishes. The sign of this covenant is the rainbow, which becomes a symbol of peace and well-being.[5]

In the final episode Noah plants a vineyard, makes wine, drinks some of it, becomes drunk and lies naked in his tent. His son Ham sees his father's nakedness and informs his two brothers. They walk into the tent backwards, holding a cloth to cover their father. When Noah awakes and learns of what has happened, he curses Ham and his descendant Canaan, saying his descendants will be slaves to his brothers. Noah then blesses Shem and Japheth, asking God to extend their territory and ensure Canaan serves his brothers (Genesis 9:20–27). Noah then lives a further 350 years before dying at the age of 950 (Genesis 9:28–29). Regarding Noah's drunkenness, Hamilton notes that Genesis neither approves nor condemns Noah's actions. He notes that later texts allow for—even commend—moderate consumption of alcohol, while forbidding excess. Equally, we do not know why Noah was naked. The crime committed by Ham appears to be that he saw his father's nakedness and did nothing about it, while Shem and Japheth act commendably. The reason why Canaan is cursed, not Ham, is also unclear. Perhaps it is simply an indication that sin impacts down the generations.[6]

The covenant that God makes with Noah is described in Jewish thought as forming the seven Noahide Laws, which are seen as having universal scope and application. The laws are: first, do not profane the unity of God in any way; second, do not curse your Creator; third, do not murder; fourth, do not eat the limb of a living animal; fifth, do not steal; sixth, harness and channel the human libido, recognizing the family unit as foundational for society; and seventh, establish courts of law and ensure justice in the world. The details of this covenant are drawn out from the experience of Noah and the commands that God gives him and are regarded by Jewish rabbis as being applicable to all human beings for all

---

5. Hamilton, *Genesis 1–17*, 313–18.
6. Hamilton, *Genesis 1–17*, 321–25.

time. The implications of this are that Noah's covenant is for all creation; Noah's generation is, implicitly at least, a type of every generation, even if there are no explicit links made with subsequent ages.

Other Old Testament References to Noah

This section discusses reference to Noah in Isaiah and Ezekiel. The first Old Testament presentation of Noah is found in Isaiah 54:9, which reads:

> This is like the days of Noah to me:
>> Just as I swore that the waters of Noah
>> would never again go over the earth,
> so I have sworn that I will not be angry with you
>> and will not rebuke you.

Motyer titles Isaiah 54:1–17 as an "Invitation to sing: security, peace and righteousness," noting motifs of family (54:1–5), marriage (54:6–10) and city (54:11–17). The reference to Noah and the flood is thus in the context of a reconstituted marriage; the point is that an act of judgment has taken place (the flood, the exile) and now that justice has been satisfied, peace comes and reconciliation can take place.[7] Oswalt entitles 54:1–10 "A wife restored," remarking that the emphasis in this section is on the wonder of God's love for his people, a hymn of praise because Israel, who has been described as a childless, rejected wife, is now going to be restored to her husband, who promises his everlasting love and the blessing of children to fill the earth. This is shown by the fact that Noah was rescued from the flood and that God's anger was only operative for a limited time. God then promises to never send a flood again. Oswalt argues that Isaiah's point is that this same God of promises is active in the postexilic era, enabling the people to return to the land.[8] Childs concurs that the point is "a renewed promise of an everlasting covenant."[9]

The second usage is in Ezekiel, where Noah is listed together with Daniel and Job as paragons of righteousness (Ezekiel 14:14, 20). The point made in the passage is that even these exemplary characters are only able to save themselves by their righteousness. That is to say, everyone is personally culpable for their own sinfulness and benefits personally from their own righteousness. That much is uncontroversial; the point

---

7. Motyer, *Isaiah*, 444–49.
8. Oswalt, *Isaiah*, 411–22.
9. Childs, *Isaiah*, 429.

that Ezekiel also makes is that the presence of a righteous man, such as Noah, was not enough to save that whole generation. This contradicts the "presumption that the presence of sufficient righteousness would save a land under the just judgment of God."[10]

Jenson argues that Job and Noah are chosen as examples of righteous Gentiles, albeit an alcoholic in Noah's case, chosen because they promulgate the divine law to Gentile lands. Jenson adds that the Daniel mentioned here is not the Old Testament Prophet, but a contemporaneous ruler, famed for his righteousness and wisdom. The three figures are selected to indicate that their personal righteousness is only personally effective; that is to say, even these paragons of virtue can save only themselves for the impending judgment of God. The primary point is thus of personal culpability before the divine.[11] Allen concurs, arguing that Ezekiel is attacking a counterclaim of the exiles, "appealing to a solidarity of virtue that could outweigh the liability of punishment." Noah and Job may have been righteous men, and the ruler Daniel may have been a good judge, "judging widows and trying the cases of orphans," but even so this would not create a shield to protect others from divine wrath.[12]

Block describes Noah and Job as "two pious men who survived unspeakable disasters because of their righteousness," adding that Ezekiel's point is that if Noah had been alive in Ezekiel's day and Noah had been the only righteous person, this would have been insufficient to save even Noah's sons. Block is unconvinced that the Daniel of Ezekiel 14 is the pagan ruler that Jenson and Allen identify, proposing rather that he is the Old Testament Prophet, a paragon of virtue demonstrated by his refusal to compromise to Nebuchadnezzar's demands.[13] For the purposes of our discussion, it does not really matter who Daniel is, only that he, like Noah, is a paragon of virtue that Ezekiel uses to teach personal responsibility before God.

These two examples show that in the Old Testament Noah was understood primarily as an example of a righteous man. He has little agency, and his backstory is of little interest to the prophetic discourse. There is greater interest in Noah in the extrabiblical material, which is discussed below.

10. DuGuid, *Ezekiel*, 194.
11. Jenson, *Ezekiel*, 120–22.
12. Allen, *Ezekiel 1–19*, 218.
13. Block, *Ezekiel 1–24*, 449.

Christian References to Noah in the New Testament

In the New Testament, there are six presentations of Noah. The first is in Luke's genealogy, where Noah is listed (Luke 3:35) amongst the generations that go back from Joseph to Adam and so ultimately to God. There is no particular focus on him as an individual; he is simply another link in the chain. The next two references occur in the Synoptic Gospels, in Matthew 24:37–39 and Luke 17:26–27. In Luke's account, Jesus says:

> Just as it was in the days of Noah, so too it will be in the days of the Son of Man. They were eating and drinking, and marrying and being given in marriage, until the day Noah entered the ark, and the flood came and destroyed all of them.

In both cases, the point drawn from the Noah story is the sudden nature of judgment. As Wilson explains, the two uses of Noah in Luke and Matthew are from different contexts; in Luke it is in the discussion with a Pharisee about the coming of the kingdom of God, while in Matthew it is part of the discourse of the destruction of the temple and the end times. This leads Wilson to conclude that Jesus used the topos of Noah on multiple occasions to emphasize that judgment could happen at any moment.[14]

In his discussion of Matthew 24:37–39, Nolland explains that the focus is on the ordinary rhythms of life. "The entry of Noah into the ark does not change the behavior of the people; it frees God to bring the intended judgment."[15] He further suggests that the phrase *they did not know until* is Matthew's insertion into the Genesis account. Nolland proposes that the opportunity for repentance was long past by the time God declares his intention to flood the earth in Genesis 6:7. Thus judgment is not something the people have been warned about, but comes as a surprise. This contrasts with Jewish use of the story to emphasize the certainty of judgment. Keener concurs, arguing that "like the flood, the Son of Man's coming (Dan 7:13–14) would arrive as sudden and unexpected judgment, without explicit warning."[16] France agrees, explaining that the time of the second coming is unknown, but it is unmistaken, sudden and universal. "In all these ways the sudden and universal onset of the Flood as described in Gen 7:6–24 provides a powerful analogy; people were

---

14. Wilson, *Noah, the Ark and the Flood*, 3.
15. Nolland, *Matthew*, 993.
16. Keener, *Matthew*, 591.

caught unawares, no one could evade it, and only those who had made advance preparations escaped."[17]

Turning to Luke 17:26–27, Nolland notes there is a tradition in Jewish and Christian literature of appealing to the flood as a sign of the certainty of God's judgment on sinners. The point is that in the midst of human complacency, judgment will still fall; that is, there is an emphasis on uncertainty of timing held in tension with human unwillingness to recognize the reality of the possibility of judgment.[18] Green suggests the discussion of Noah sits in the middle of a chiasm:[19]

A Disciples will ask, "Where?" (17:22–24)
  B Jesus: repudiation and suffering (17:25)
    C Readiness in anticipation of calamitous judgment (17:26–30)
  B' Disciples: abandonment of life (17:31–35)
A' Disciples ask, "Where?" (17:37)

Thus, God's judgment "breaks inescapably, surprisingly, abruptly into the mundane of life."[20] As in Matthew, there is no real focus on the wickedness of Noah's people, but on everyday activities of eating, drinking, marrying and giving in marriage. For the Gospels, then, Noah is a paradigm of the certainty of sudden judgment, a warning that we are to be prepared for the judgment we know will come while we are about our daily business.

Wilson argues that the letter to the Hebrews uses Noah as an example of faith motivating action:

> By faith Noah, warned by God about events as yet unseen, respected the warning and built an ark to save his household; by this he condemned the world and became an heir to the righteousness that is in accordance with faith. (Hebrews 11:7)

Noah is held up as a paradigm of the type of faith mentioned in Hebrews 11:1; that is, he was warned of things to come, which he had not yet seen, and acted to save both himself and his family. The word used to describe Noah's motivation (*eulabeomai*) occurs only here in the New Testament; Wilson suggests it is best translated as *with reverent obedience*. According to Hebrews, Noah's actions have two spiritual outcomes.

---

17. France, *Matthew*, 940.
18. Nolland, *Luke 9:21—18:34*, 860.
19. Green, *Luke*, 631.
20. Green, *Luke*, 632.

First, his actions condemned the world, something that Wilson notes is not explicitly stated in Genesis. Second, Noah *became an heir to the righteousness that is in accordance with faith.* The fact that he is the only one specifically listed in this regard in Hebrews 11 implies, Wilson argues, that the author of Hebrews is particularly impressed by the quality of the faith that Noah displays in building the ark. Noah is probably cited as an example to the audience of Hebrews both to create a typological correspondence with the work of Christ and also as one who exhorts his hearers to heed the warning from heaven of the judgment that is to come.[21] DeSilva agrees, arguing that Noah presents an analogy with the audience of Hebrews: both live just before the dawning of the coming judgment. Thus they are invited to imitate Noah, believing that God will judge the disobedient and reward the loyal, condemning the world by their ongoing loyalty and obedience, their faithful worship of God. DeSilva notes two significant points made from Noah's example. The first is that his trust in God was the means by which the world was condemned, which may pick up on some of the Jewish traditions discussed below. The second is Noah's righteousness, which comes by faith, where faith is understood as persevering, trusting in God's promises and warnings, and shaping life accordingly.[22]

Noah is also used as an example in both 1 Peter and 2 Peter. In 1 Peter 3:19–21, Noah is used as an example of divine patience. God waited while Noah built the ark before he exercised judgment through the flood. The waters of that deluge are viewed by Peter as corresponding spiritually with the water of baptism.[23] Michaels describes 1 Peter 3:21–22 as a "kind of Christian midrash" on the story of Noah, based on Jesus' saying that *as it was in the days of Noah, so too it will be in the days of the Son of Man* (Luke 17:26; Matthew 24:37). The main point is the sudden judgment: in Noah's day, people ate, drank etc. until the flood; so people will be eating, drinking etc., until the sudden coming of the Son of Man. First Peter develops the comparison through reference to salvation by the waters of the flood being analogous with baptism.[24]

Michaels argues that in 1 Peter the focus is on mercy and salvation, in contrast with 2 Peter, where attention is given to a delicate balance

---

21. Wilson, *Noah, the Ark and the Flood*, 5–6.
22. DeSilva, *Hebrews*, 391–92.
23. Wilson, *Noah, the Ark and the Flood*, 7.
24. Michaels, *1 Peter*, 200.

between mercy and judgment.[25] He adds that in 1 Peter 3:20–22, "the two analogies that attract Peter's attention are, first, God's patience or longsuffering; and second, salvation through water."[26] The implicit reference to patience is probably based on the interval between the sin of the angels (Genesis 6:1–4) and the arrival of the floodwaters (Genesis 7:11), an interval traditionally understood to have lasted 120 years (Genesis 6:3). God appears to be doing nothing, but in actual fact he is giving the ungodly time to repent. The main metaphor is of salvation through water, the flood as analogy for baptism, salvation from physical death as analogy for salvation from spiritual death.

Hamilton understands the analogy somewhat differently. He explains that many commentators suggest 1 Peter develops the flood story, arguing that Noah and his family are saved *through* water, as opposed to the Genesis text that argues they are saved *from* water. This is because for 1 Peter water symbolizes baptism; thus, the argument moves from antitype back to type. His counterproposal is that the two can be reconciled if the phrase in 1 Peter is not understood instrumentally (by means of water) but locally (so Noah was saved by going through water and into the ark). Thus, it is not the flood that is a type of baptism, but that passing through death to salvation is the type that 1 Peter discusses.[27]

The precise details of Peter's analogy need not detain us too long. The main point, of Noah as a type of Christ, is evident. Ben Witherington summarizes the argument as follows:

> Here we have a story about the proclamation of judgment on the principalities and powers, and the triumph beyond death of Christ in glory. Its relevance to the Jewish Christian audience is quite apparent. Peter is telling them that they are following the same trajectory as Christ, and indeed of Noah even earlier. Though others may be reviling, slandering and abusing them during their earthly life, nevertheless despite their current suffering, they will one day triumph over their foes whose "doom is sure."[28]

He adds that the analogy in 3:20 is to provide reassurance: just as God saved his people in Noah's day, even though there were only a few of them, so he will save his people in Peter's day, even though there are only

---

25. Michaels, *1 Peter*, 200–201.
26. Michaels, *1 Peter*, 212.
27. Hamilton, *Genesis 1–17*, 328.
28. Witherington, *Letters and Homilies for Hellenized Christians*, 189.

a few of them. The analogy of the flood and baptism suggest something to the effect that the waters of Noah's day are a prefiguring of the greater judgment and salvation on offer through Christ, which is symbolized by baptism. Witherington adds that Noah was a common hero figure amongst the people of Asia Minor, where Peter's audience resides; thus, Peter has picked a figure from popular imagination, a logical choice to use to encourage the struggling and frightened believers.[29]

Turning to 2 Peter, there are two uses of Noah: 2:4–5 and 3:6. Witherington explains that 2 Peter 2:4 indicates that Genesis 6:1–4 is understood as referring to angels, not men. These angels sinned and were consigned to Tartarus (see also *1 Enoch* 20:2). Tartarus was the very lowest region of Hades, reserved for disobedient gods and rebellious humans; it acted as more of a holding tank than a final destination. Second Peter 2:5 presumes the flood is universal, not local. The point is that there is plenty of historical precedent for God acting in judgment, but also in redemption. None of these are the final judgment; that is yet to come.[30] Wilson explains that in 2 Peter 2:5, Noah is described as a preacher of righteousness, an expansion on the Genesis text, which is also attested in Jewish literature, some of which is discussed below. In 2 Peter 3:6, the flood of Noah's day is used to frame the discussion of judgment, which in Noah's day was by water but in the future will be by fire when Jesus returns.[31] Bauckham concurs with the description of Noah, describing him as "a type of faithful Christians who will be preserved from the present world to inherit the new world after the judgment."[32]

Thus, within the New Testament Noah is used to indicate the reality of both sudden judgment and also divine salvation, based primarily on God's grace not human merit. In a sense he is both a type of Christ and also a type of Christian, but in either case is an example to be admired and imitated. The focus remains primarily on Noah's positive actions, his response of faith to the revelation God gave him, with little or no attention paid to Noah's generation, who all perish.

---

29. Witherington, *Letters and Homilies for Hellenized Christians*, 190.
30. Witherington, *Letters and Homilies for Hellenized Christians*, 351–52.
31. Wilson, *Noah, the Ark and the Flood*, 8–9.
32. Bauckham, *Jude, 2 Peter*, 250.

Bridging Contexts: Extrabiblical References to Noah

This section first examines the church fathers' views of Genesis 6–9 before turning to other extrabiblical references. Ephrem the Syrian regards the limited lifespan of 120 years that is now allotted to humanity in Genesis 6:1–4 as sufficient to ensure they are able to repent. *Grace granted one hundred and twenty years for repentance to a generation that, according to justice, was not worthy of repentance.*[33]

Augustine sees clear symbolism in the instructions for making the ark in Genesis 6:11–16: undoubtedly the ark is a symbol of the city of God on its pilgrimage in history. It is a figure of the church, which was saved by the wood on which there hung the *mediator between God and men, himself man, Jesus Christ* (1 Timothy 2:5). Augustine goes on to explain how the physical measurements of the ark point to Christ.[34] Moving on to Noah's preparations to enter the ark (Genesis 7:6–9), Augustine also sees pointers toward Christ. Thus he says, *Christ was also represented in Noah, and the world, in that ark. For why were all living creatures shut up in that ark except to signify all the nations?* Elsewhere he adds: *Was not Noah a holy man, who alone in the whole human race together with his whole house deserved to be delivered from the flood? And is not the church prefigured by Noah and his sons? They escape the flood, with wood (which symbolizes the cross) carrying them.*[35]

Turning to Genesis 9:18–29, the church fathers explain away the episode of Noah's drunkenness. Thus, Ephrem the Syrian explains: *Noah's drunkenness was not from an excess of wine but because it had been a long time since he had drunk any wine.* Chrysostom proposes that wine itself is not evil, but the problem is drinking to excess. Finally, for some, Noah's drunkenness prefigures the passion of Christ. Thus Jerome states: *After the deluge Noah drank and became drunk in his own house, and his thighs were uncovered and he was exposed in his nakedness. The elder brother came along and laughed; the younger, however, covered him up. All this is said in type of the Savior, for on the cross he had drunk of the passion: "Father, if it is possible, let this cup pass away from me." He drank and was inebriated, and his thighs were laid bare—the dishonor of the cross. The*

---

33. Louth, *Genesis 1–11*, 125.
34. Louth, *Genesis 1–11*, 131.
35. Louth, *Genesis 1–11*, 136.

older brothers, the Jews, came along and laughed; the younger, the Gentiles, covered up his ignominy.[36]

For the church fathers, Noah is understood as a type of Christ; as such he is presented as a righteous figure whose blemishes are glossed over. The primary concern is to ensure God's saving work is presented in as compelling a manner as possible.

Noah also features in a number of apocryphal texts, including Ben Sira (dated to the second century BCE) and the Wisdom of Solomon (dated to the mid first century BCE). Noah is not necessarily named, as these two quotations from the Wisdom of Solomon illustrate:

> When the earth was flooded because of him, wisdom again saved it, steering the righteous man by a paltry piece of wood. (Wisdom of Solomon 10:4)

> For even in the beginning, when arrogant giants were perishing, the hope of the world took refuge on a raft, and guided by your hand left to the world the seed of a new generation. For blessed is the wood by which righteousness comes. (Wisdom of Solomon 14:6–7)

Noah is here seen as an example of righteousness, a hero of the past whose obedience to God meant that humanity was preserved. The point is also made more explicitly:

> Noah was found perfect and righteous; in the time of wrath he kept the race alive; therefore a remnant was left on the earth when the flood came. (Ben Sira 44:17)

These texts presume a knowledge of Genesis 6–9, and arguably also of legends that grew up from that text. Speculation about the angels and their role in the flood was a key part of this mythology. *First Enoch* 6–16 tells of the fall of angels: their decision to form a pact, to go down on earth together, to wed human women and have sexual intercourse with them. The children borne of these unions are giants; the fallen angels teach them all manner of evil practices and bring upon themselves the judgment of God. Thus, in *1 Enoch* 10 God sends a messenger to Noah to warn him of the deluge that will come on the earth, that will drown all the wicked, leaving only the righteous.

> And you cleanse the earth from all injustice, and from all defilement, and from all oppression, and from all sin, and from

---

36. Louth, *Genesis 1–11*, 156–58.

all iniquity which is being done on earth; remove them from the earth. And all the children of the people will become righteous, and all nations shall worship and bless me; and they will all prostrate themselves to me. And the earth shall be cleansed from all pollution, and from all sin, and from all plagues, and from all suffering; and it shall not happen again that I shall send these upon the earth from generation to generation and forever (*1 Enoch* 10:20–22).[37]

Enoch then intercedes for the fallen angels, but his prayer is not answered. Instead he is given a tour of heaven, seeing visions of the splendor of God. *First Enoch* returns to Noah a number of times. In 54:7–10 the story of the flood is recounted briefly; 65:1—67:13 give a much longer account, including a dialogue between Noah and Enoch in which the latter explains that judgment has been handed down from God, and Noah also hears from God about the punishments he has prepared for all rulers and angels who have denied him. In 89:1–9 Enoch has another vision of the flood, with elements not found in the Genesis account; and in 106:13–18 judgment and the salvation of Noah and his family are recalled.

In the *Sibylline Oracles*, Noah is told to prepare for the flood:

Noah alone among all was most upright and true, a most worthy man, concerned for noble deeds. To him God himself spoke as follows from heaven: "Noah, embolden yourself, and proclaim repentance to all the peoples, so that all may be saved." (1:125–29).[38]

Noah is then instructed to build the ark, and in what follows he preaches repentance (*Sibylline Oracles* 1:147–98). Noah explains that the evil deeds of the people have not escaped divine notice, but will be punished. The only proper response is repentance, standing in awe of the God who made everything, entreating him for life and mercy in the face of his wrath. The people, however, are not interested: *When they heard him they sneered at him, each one, calling him demented, a man gone mad* (*Sibylline Oracles* 1:171–72). Noah resumes his preaching, becoming more vehement and vitriolic in his condemnation of their deeds. He himself will lament, mourning the destruction of the earth from the safety of the ark that God will preserve. After Noah had finished preaching, God tells him to board the ark, with his sons and wife and daughters-in-law, together

---

37. Translation from Charlesworth, *Old Testament Pseudepigrapha*.
38. Translation from Charlesworth, *Old Testament Pseudepigrapha*.

with the animals whom God chooses (*Sibylline Oracles* 1:199–216). God then sends the flood on the earth, and the ark alone is saved. The sight of the flood terrifies Noah, as he wonders if they will ever be able to escape. But he sends out a dove, which returns the first time with nothing, then the second time with an olive twig. Noah then sends out a *black-winged bird* that does not return, and eventually the ark makes land (*Sibylline Oracles* 1:217–60). The ark arrives on Ararat, and Noah and his family go forth. This generation repopulates the earth; there is no mention of Noah's drunkenness as found in Genesis 9.

Reynolds cites two examples in which Noah is introduced as a preacher of righteousness. First, Ephrem and Jacob of Serugh, as well as other Syriac Christian fathers, taught that Noah's preaching continued for one hundred years. Ephrem adds that during this time the people mocked Noah:

> Although Noah was an example to that generation by his righteousness and had, in his uprightness, announced to them the flood during that one hundred years, they still did not repent. So Noah said to them, "Some of all flesh will come to be saved with me in the ark." But they mocked him, "How will all the beasts and birds that are scattered throughout every corner of the earth come from all those regions?"[39]

Second, the Babylonian Talmud, *Sanhedrin* 108a, gives details of Noah's sermon:

> The righteous Noah rebuked them, urging, "Repent; for if not, the Holy One, blessed be He, will bring a deluge upon you and cause your bodies to float upon the water like gourds, as it is written, He is light [that is, floats] upon the waters. Moreover, ye shall be taken as a curse for all future generations."[40]

The extrabiblical material can be therefore classified into two types: first, those that use Noah as a *paragon* of righteousness in the face of divine judgment; and second, those that advance that idea further, making Noah a *preacher* of righteousness, an understanding that is developed in some detail within the Qur'an. These texts add a further layer of complexity to the discussion. We cannot necessarily argue that these extrabiblical texts are the origin of the Qur'an's story of Noah, but we can notice

---

39. Ephrem, *Commentary on Genesis* 6:9, cited in Reynolds, *Qur'an and the Bible*, 348.

40. Cited in Reynolds, *Qur'an and the Bible*, 858.

correlation between the different accounts. This also forces Christians to ask what exactly the Bible teaches about Noah, and what is a consequence of later elaboration and speculation.

The Qur'anic Presentation

There are twenty-nine *surahs* that feature Noah; to discuss them all in detail would be exhausting and overly repetitive. I have chosen to focus primarily on two instances: the portion in *Hud* (11) and *Nuh* (71, Noah), with references to other accounts where these are appropriate (*al-A'raf* 7:59–64; *Yunus* 10:71–74; *al-Mu'minun* 23:23–30; *ash-Shu'ara'* 26:105–22; *al-Qamar* 54:9–17). The story of Noah has a different emphasis in the Qur'an from that of the biblical account. Tottoli describes the Qur'an's version as "the story of punishment *par excellence*," suggesting that it is for this reason it occurs frequently in the Qur'an.[41]

Surah Hud (11)

This *surah* is made up of stories of different messengers, one of whom is Noah, whose story is told in verses 25–49. Noah is described as *a clear warner* (*Hud* 11:25), who warns the people of the demand of monotheism and the reality of the coming judgment. His audience responds by branding him a liar and a gullible human being. He counters that he is in fact a clear sign of God, who has received mercy from God. Interestingly, that mercy is described as being *obscured* from them, indicating that God's mercy is not forced upon anyone. Noah engages in a dispute with his people, proclaiming that he has not asked for money from anyone, nor does he have any allies amongst his people, whom he describes as ignorant and unwilling to assist in driving away the rebels against God.

Noah is then commanded to build the ship, which he duly does, to the mockery and scorn of those who pass by. Eventually the time comes for the judgment of God to be enacted, described as the time when *the oven boiled* (*Hud* 11:40, taken as a reference to Jewish tradition that the waters of the flood were boiling). Noah is told to *load into it two of every kind, a pair, and your family—except the one against whom the word has (already) gone forth—and whoever has believed* (*Hud* 11:40). The *Enlightening Commentary* explains:

41. Tottoli, *Biblical Prophets*, 23.

This verse, on the one hand, refers to the wife of Noah and his son 'Kan'an', who, deviating from the path of belief and being in collaboration with the sinners, had broken off their relationship with Noah and were not entitled to embark on the Ark. On the other hand, it refers to the limited success that Noah (as) had had in persuading people to follow his way of life during his long years of continuous struggle that had resulted in getting only a small number of believers.[42]

The member of Noah's family who does not believe is revealed in the subsequent three verses to be Noah's son. Noah is commanded to begin sailing the ship, which he duly does, proclaiming the mercy of God as he does so. Evidently Noah's son is not on board, as Noah calls to him, while the boat runs through waves as big as mountains, urging him to sail with them and not be with the unbelievers. Noah's son, however, is unconvinced, seeking refuge in the mountains. This is to no avail, and he drowns (*Hud* 11:42–43). Reynolds suggests that in this passage the Qur'an is primarily responding to Ezekiel 14, not Genesis. The Qur'an takes Ezekiel's hypothetical son and makes him a real son, who drowns.[43]

There is no record in *surah Hud* of the duration of the flood, as the next sentence is the divine command, *Earth! Swallow your water! And sky! Stop!* The waters duly subside, and the ship comes to rest on *al-Judi* (*Hud* 11:44). Droge comments that this is traditionally identified as a mountain in Mesopotamia, near Mosul, but adds that it may have been the name of a mountain in Arabia, with echoes of the biblical account, where the ark comes to rest on the mountains of Ararat (Genesis 8:4).

There follows a dialogue between Noah and God about the fate of Noah's son. Noah says, *My Lord, surely my son is one of my family, and surely Your promise is the truth, and You are the most just of judges* (*Hud* 11:45). This appears to be Noah interceding, albeit slightly obliquely, for divine mercy to be shown to his son who has perished in the flood.

The divine response is unequivocal: *Surely he is not one of your family. Surely it is an unrighteous deed. So do not ask me about what you have no knowledge of. Surely I admonish you not to be one of the ignorant* (*Hud* 11:46). That is to say, God is clear that this unbelieving son is not a member of Noah's family, and Noah's intercession on his behalf is an act that has no merit, indeed is wrong. Notice that Noah is not condemned

---

42. https://www.al-islam.org/enlightening-commentary-light-holy-quran-vol-7/section-4-fate-those-who-disbelieved-noah#surah-hud-verse-40.

43. Reynolds, *Qur'an and the Bible*, 349.

as sinful, but rather warned for being ignorant. This is a reprimand for a faithful servant rather than condemnation of an unbeliever. Thus the *Enlightening Commentary* explains:

> Allah tells Noah that he was not of his kind, on the contrary, he was an evil doer; a man of misdemeanor, whose family relationship was of no value and kinship of no avail owing to the fact that he was cut off from Noah's school of thought, as such Noah should not make any requests about which he had no knowledge and therefore he should not be among the ignorant.[44]

This interpretation is supported by Noah's response: he asks for forgiveness, recognizing that he has asked about things of which he has no real knowledge, and that he needs divine mercy if he is to survive. This is duly given to him, as God says, *Noah! Go down with peace from Us, and blessings on you and on the communities of those who are with you* (*Hud* 11:48). It is not entirely clear if Noah is being instructed to disembark from the boat or to descend from the mountain, but either way, the main point is that he does so as a recipient of divine mercy. The episode closes with a reminder that Noah has received a divine message, which others have either not received or have ignored. There is a warning to the faithful to guard themselves lest they share the fate of the unrighteous.

Surah Nuh (71)

The *surah* begins with a reminder that Noah was sent as a warner to his people that a painful punishment would come upon them (*Nuh* 71:1). The message is that judgment will come, it is inescapable and the only refuge is found in dependence upon the mercy of God. Noah speaks with God and explains that he has been tireless in warning the people, speaking both in public and also in private. In reference to *Nuh* 71:5, Ibn Abbas explains that when Noah despaired of them, after calling them to faith for 950 years, and they refused to believe or heed his advice, he said, "*My Lord, surely I have called my people night and day*," but this had no impact on them.[45]

The offer Noah makes is of repentance followed by blessing; that is, if the people ask for forgiveness, then they will receive it and also he will

---

44. https://www.al-islam.org/enlightening-commentary-light-holy-quran-vol-7/section-4-fate-those-who-disbelieved-noah#surah-hud-verse-40.

45. Guezzou, *Tanwir al-Miqbas*, 697.

increase you with wealth and sons, and make gardens for you and make rivers for you (*Nuh* 71:12). The rationale for believing this is that God is the divine Creator; if he made everything, then it is easy for him to bless the people whom he has made.

Noah's message falls on deaf ears; he laments to God that the people have disobeyed him (*Nuh* 71:21) and have determined to not forsake *Wadd nor Suwa nor Yaghuth and Ya'uq and Nasr* (*Nuh* 71:23). They are presumably local gods, named only here in the Qur'an, although scholars debate whether they were worshipped in Noah's day or in Muhammad's. There is no account, then, of the building of the ship, nor the details of the flood. The *surah* simply ends with this summary:

> They were drowned on account of their sins, and forced to enter a fire, and they found they had no helpers other than God. Noah said, "My Lord, do not leave any of the disbelievers as an inhabitant on the earth. Surely You—if You leave them, they will lead Your servants astray, and will give birth only to depraved disbelievers(s). My Lord, forgive me and my parents, and whoever enters my house believing, and the believing men and women, and increase the evildoers only in destruction!" (*Nuh* 71:25–28)

Ibn Abbas suggests that the reference to *my house* is also taken as indicating both *my mosque* and also *my ship*, as in the ark that Noah travelled in, arguing that this is a plea from Noah that Allah increase the disbelieving idolaters in loss and destruction, "like the destruction of those people whose Prophet received the revelation but refused to believe in him."[46]

There are numerous ways in which this and other Qur'anic accounts differ from that found in Genesis. Two notable omissions are the discussion of the dimensions and construction of the ship and what happens after the flood. Two notable additions are that Noah is a speaking prophet, although, as noted above, later Jewish tradition does have him speak. On a number of different occasions the Qur'an records an account of the disputation between Noah and the people, as the people mock Noah for building an ark (see *Hud* 11:25–49; *Al-Anbiya'* 21:76–77; *Al-Mu'minun* 23:23–30; *Ash-Shu'ara* 26:105–22; as well as *Nuh* 71). In the Qur'anic version of the story, Noah, eventually wearied of pointless disputation, calls on Allah to save himself and his family and to punish

---

46. Guezzou, *Tanwir al-Miqbas*, 711.

a corrupt generation (*as-Saffat* 37:75–76; *Al-Anbiya'* 21:76; *Ash-Shu'ara* 26:117–18). According to the *hadith*, Muhammad is reputed to have said that Noah even warned his generation of the coming antichrist, but to no avail.

The second notable addition is the fact that Noah's son dies. This is not the only family member to perish. Later in the Qur'an we find the warning:

> God has struck a parable for those who disbelieve: the wife of Noah and the wife of Lot. They were under two of Our righteous servants, but they both betrayed them. Neither of them was of any use at all to either of them against God, when it was said, "Enter the fire, both of you, with the ones who enter!" (*at-Tahrim* 66:10)

Nasr points out that this is the only reference to Noah's wife betraying him, although there are other references to Lot's wife.[47] The point is that neither Noah nor Lot, two paradigms of righteousness, were able to be of any assistance to their wives in the face of divine judgment; the believer faces the judgment and mercy of God alone (a theme also found in the biblical book of Ezekiel). Reynolds cites *Tafsir al-Jalalayn*, which explains that *Noah's wife, called Wahila, used to say to his people that he was a madman*. Reynolds adds that 2 Peter 2 also presents Noah and Lot in parallel, intimating this may be antecedent to the Qur'anic presentation. Finally, Reynolds cites the fourth-century church father Epiphanius as an example of a Christian who promulgated negative teaching about Noah's wife. The *Panarion of Epiphanius* 90–91 explains that the Gnostics taught that Noah's wife (whom they named Nuria) was not allowed to join Noah in the ark after she burnt it down three times.[48]

Kaltner and Mirza suggest that the son of Noah who perishes represents those unbelievers who cling to false gods. There is also the point that even a prophet's own family can make wrong choices; salvation is therefore not guaranteed on the basis of lineage or biological connections, for as Noah and God speak of the fate of this son, it becomes clear that family is formed on the basis of belief, not of biology, as shown in *Hud* 11:45–46.[49] Ibn Abbas expands on the number who were saved, arguing it was eighty people: Noah, his wife, his three sons Shem, Ham and

---

47. Nasr, *Study Qur'an*, 1391.
48. Reynolds, *Qur'an and the Bible*, 840–41.
49. Kalter and Mirza, *Bible and the Qur'an*, 137.

Japheth and their wives, Jurhum and seventy three sons of Seth who also believed.⁵⁰

Kaltner and Mirza also point out that although God punishes, chapter eleven stresses divine mercy, with Noah speaking of this quality four times (*Hud* 11:28, 41, 43, 47). Moreover, Muhammad is addressed directly (*Hud* 11:35, 49), with clear links being drawn between Muhammad's experience and Noah's experience. Therefore, this story, as with many others in the Qur'an, "functions as an interpretive lens for Muhammad, his audience and later readers that attempts to legitimate his prophetic career."⁵¹

The *Stories of the Prophets* expands on the story of Noah, adding in extra details. For example, *al-Tarafi* explains how Noah planted trees for twenty years, and did not preach to the people during this time. As he cut down trees and began to build the ark, the people began to mock him, commenting that the Prophet had become a carpenter. The size of the ark, the numbers of animals and their location within the ark, the sending out of the raven and then the dove are all discussed, supplying information found in Genesis but not in the Qur'an. The *Stories of the Prophets* also debates whether Noah's wife, who is mentioned in the Qur'an as one of the unbelievers, entered the ark. Most commentators presume she perished, because Noah prays that God will destroy all unbelievers. Finally, some commentators suggest that God took the ark on a tour of various religious sites. According to these stories, as they passed Jerusalem a voice cried, *Oh Noah, this is Jerusalem where the prophets of your children will live*. Then, it is explained, the waves took the boat to Mecca, where it circled the Ka'ba seven times, copying the way in which Muslims perform the ritual during the Islamic pilgrimage.⁵²

Contrasting the biblical and Qur'anic Accounts

Both Islam and Christianity use Noah in a similar fashion: the basic story is recalled and moral lessons are drawn from that story, primarily to emphasize the salvation of the righteous and the reality of judgment. However, the presentations and understanding are by no means identical, and the understandings of Noah differ. Lodahl suggests that while in Genesis

---

50. Cited in Wheeler, 2002a, 59.
51. Kalter and Mirza, *Bible and the Qur'an*, 138.
52. Kalter and Mirza, *Bible and the Qur'an*, 139.

Noah is a new Adam, the new head and progenitor of the human race, in the Qur'an he is simply another of the Prophets.[53] This is an important distinction. In Genesis, the promise and command that God gives Noah echoes that given to Adam; the covenant with Noah is for all people in all times, and arguably also echoes the instruction given to Adam. But for the Qur'an, Noah is simply another in a long line of Prophets whose message is largely ignored by a people who are not interested in receiving revelation. In what follows I will first discuss five points of contrast before drawing conclusions about whether Noah is a precursor to Muhammad or to Christ.

One striking point for reflection is the Noahide Covenant. While this precise formulation does not have much currency in Christian or Islamic thought, the notion of Noah as a paradigm and his relationship with God setting a standard by which others are judged does have currency within both faith traditions. There is scope for more detailed reflection on what precisely this covenant has to teach Christians and Muslims about what God expects of us.

Second, a crucial difference concerns who is saved. The New Testament in particular makes a great deal of the fact that eight people are saved (Noah, his wife, his three sons and their three wives). Although some have tried to argue for typological significance in this number (the eighth day being somehow equivalent to Easter Sunday, for example), the arguments are not persuasive. More likely, the focus is on the salvation of a whole family, which stands in marked contrast with the Qur'anic emphasis that family membership does not necessarily equate with salvation. That is not a point that the Bible disputes. Jesus himself is recorded as explaining that his family are those who do the will of God (Mark 3:31–35 and parallels), and of acting independently of his family, ignoring his brothers' advice on when to appear in public and what to say (John 7:1–10). The difference here is therefore not so much in the theological point being made as the means by which it is made. The New Testament does not often use the fate of unbelieving family members as a way of persuading others to demonstrate greater faith, although the incident with Ananias and Sapphira in Acts 5 is a notable exception.

Third, the lack of details about the flood in the Qur'anic accounts suggests that the story is presumed to be known; arguably later commentators supply the missing information because they are no longer

---

53. Lodalh, *Claiming Abraham*, 122.

confident that readers of the Qur'an will have any knowledge of biblical texts. This poses an interesting question for discussion: much as Christians cannot really understand the New Testament without reading the Old, might it be argued that Muslims cannot really understand the Qur'an without reading both Old and New Testaments? Moreover, would people of all Abrahamic faiths not also benefit from at least a passing familiarity with some of the other literature associated with their traditions? The material in *1 Enoch*, for example, is relevant for understanding the New Testament's and the Qur'an's presentations of the story of Noah.

Furthermore, Genesis 9 includes the episode where Noah gets drunk, lies naked in his tent and is seen by Ham, but not Shem and Japheth. The function of the story is to introduce the genealogy of Ham, father of the Canaanites, bitter enemies of Israel; it is important to note that while later commentators interpret this incident negatively, the text itself offers no judgment.[54] Its omission from the Qur'an may therefore simply be because that rivalry is of no relevance. But there is arguably also a second, and probably more significant, reason for the omission, and that concerns attitudes toward the Prophets. In biblical accounts, Prophets are often fallible people, whose very faults become the means by which God works in and through them. The Qur'an tends to present Prophets more as paradigms of righteous conduct, shining exemplars whose weaknesses did not hinder their being used by God, as seen by the fact that Noah is merely gently chastised for daring to pray for his son. The story of Noah, used by the Qur'an as a type of Muhammad, therefore provides an interesting way into a discussion of how Prophets are viewed in Islam and Christianity.

Fourth, the fact that Noah is silent in Genesis but vocal in the Qur'an must be considered in the light of extrabiblical material. *First Clement* presumes Noah was a preacher of righteousness, as do the *Sibylline Oracles* and other Jewish texts. In *1 Clement* we read:

> Let us review all the generations in turn, and learn that from generation to generation the Master has given an opportunity for repentance to those who desire to turn to him. Noah preached repentance, and those who obeyed were saved. (7:5–6)

Thus, Noah is portrayed as a preacher of righteousness, as in 2 Peter. *First Clement* refers to Noah again in chapter 9, explaining that *Noah, being found faithful, proclaimed a second birth to the world by his ministry,*

---

54. Lodahl, *Claiming Abraham*, 123.

and through him the Master saved the living creatures that entered into the ark in harmony (9:4).

This picks up echoes of the Genesis account that are not used in the other Christian texts cited above. Furthermore, Josephus also makes a similar point:

> For many angels of God coupled with women, and begat sons that proved unjust, and despisers of all that was good, on account of the confidence they had in their own strength; for the tradition is, that these men did what resembled the acts of those whom the Grecians call giants. But Noah was very uneasy at what they did; and being displeased at their conduct, persuaded them to change their dispositions and their acts for the better. But, seeing they did not yield to him, but were slaves to their wicked pleasures, he was afraid they would kill him, together with his wife and children, and those they had married; so he departed out of that land. (*Antiquities* 1.73–74)

The silence of Noah, and indeed of God, in the Bible in relation to judgment must therefore be held in tension with these traditions that presume a divine message was communicated. The conversation should perhaps be primarily about when, why and how God speaks of judgment, who he uses and whether they are heard.

Fifth, the Qur'an presumes the flood is of much more limited impact than the Bible, although some more critical scholars presume that the biblical account is actually really referring only to a more local event. There is theological significance in this difference. The notion of a universal flood makes sense of the universal promise of continuity and care for creation that God makes in Genesis 9. The rainbow thus means much more to Christians than it does to Muslims. The significance of this difference is the nature of covenant relationship between God and his people. Christians have appropriated Jewish conceptions of covenant and redefined them in the light of Jesus. Islam has not done the same in the light of Muhammad. A fifth possible area of discussion is therefore the notion of covenant. Who does God make covenants with, on what terms, and what happens if and when those covenants are broken?

Glaser and Kay argue that the flood account shows God wrestling with the challenge of human sinfulness. This is significant because, they explain, it is only in the most intimate relationships that we reveal the struggles of our hearts, and so in Genesis 6–9 we are invited as readers into the very heart of God. Returning to the theme of sacrifice, Glaser and Kay add that Cain and Abel respond to God with sacrifice, as does Noah as soon as he emerges from the ark. Indeed, after the flood God establishes a covenant with his people. They add that

> for the God who is love from eternity, the tension between his justice and salvation is found right in his own heart. Sin breaks the relationship between him and people, and, in love, he longs to restore us to that place of intimacy.[55]

In Genesis, the flood story is thus a tragic love story, of God being spurned by the people whom he loves and restoring the world to reset the relationship of love anew. By contrast, the passages in the Qur'an that feature Noah are all Meccan; that is, they are revealed in the context of Muhammad's struggle against opposition. Thus, Noah becomes a type that Muhammad also conforms to. That is to say,

> The qur'anic Noah's opposition is also similar to that experienced by Muhammad. The Qur'an offers details such as plots, accusations of madness or forgery and continued idolatry, all of which parallel what happened to Muhammad in Mecca. And, like Muhammad, the qur'anic Noah grieves over his people's disbelief. He prays for them, exhorts them, and pleads with God when he is rejected.[56]

Although the Christian and Muslim understandings of Noah are basically similar, there are subtle differences. The most crucial difference is whom they point toward. For the New Testament, Noah warns us of the sudden nature of judgment, but also of the importance of perseverance, which results in saving faith. Judgment is held in tension with mercy, a point displayed most supremely in the life of Christ. By contrast, the Qur'an focuses primarily on the messenger who is not heard, echoing Muhammad's own experience of one whose preaching fell on many deaf ears. To put this differently, for Muslims, Noah is primarily understood as a precursor to Muhammad, whose experience is mirrored in Muhammad's own. But for Christians, Noah is both a precursor for Christ, but also a paradigmatic believer in the salvation that is offered through Christ alone.

---

55. Glaser and Kay, *Thinking Biblically about Islam*, 42.
56. Glaser and Kay, *Thinking Biblically about Islam*, 64.

Abraham

Jews, Christians and Muslims all look to Abraham as a father figure, foundational to their faith. Yet what we believe about Abraham (*Ibrahim* in Arabic), the stories we tell of his life and faith, differ from faith to faith, never mind within each faith. The variety of understandings of Abraham within the Abrahamic faiths is a vast subject, and any attempt to write about it could very quickly become a lengthy book, if not series of books. My specific intention in this chapter is to introduce some primers for discussion between Christians and Muslims as to their different understandings of this pivotal figure. The first section gives a brief overview of the story of Abraham as told in Genesis. The shape of the next five sections comes from a lecture heard at a conference on the influence of the Bible on the Qur'an, held at the British Academy in October 2018. The speaker on Abraham was Nicolai Sinai, who divided references to Abraham in the Qur'an into five groups, which he admits are subjective, but provide a helpful framework for analysis. These five are, first, the so-called disputation cluster, that is, texts that record Abraham's confrontation of idolatry. This is not in Genesis, but is found in postbiblical traditions. Second, the so-called annunciation cluster, when angels tell Abraham he will have a son. There is an account in Genesis 18, as well as postbiblical references. There are significant differences between Genesis and the Qur'an, which will be explored below. Third, the "sacrifice cluster" is different in who is offered, as well as the awareness and willingness of the son to be sacrificed. There is a debate within Islamic exegetical tradition as to whether it was Isaac or Ishmael who was offered, and I will outline this debate below. Fourth, there are passages unique to the Qur'an, the so-called sanctuary cluster, that is, texts that establish the covenant and the Meccan sanctuary. There is no pre-Qur'anic attestation of the episode, although the underlying concepts do exist. Sinai's fifth category is miscellaneous references. The two points I will focus on are the reference to Abraham as a friend of God and as a *hanif*. Having discussed these five categories, the seventh area of focus will be Christian retelling of the story of Abraham, with particular focus on the Pauline usage in Galatians and Romans. Finally, in the eight section, the rival Christian and Muslim claims for Abraham are assessed.

The Story of Abraham as Told in Genesis

The story of Abraham begins with the genealogy in Genesis 11, which traces Terah's family line, and includes Terah's son Abram. The account of his life is found in Genesis chapters 12–25. Limitations of space preclude a detailed exegesis of the whole story, but I will outline the basic shape. God calls Abram to leave the land of his family and go and settle in Canaan, the land that God directs him to. When he is first called, Abram receives this promise:

> I will make of you a great nation, and I will bless you, and make your name great, so that you will be a blessing. I will bless those who bless you, and the one who curses you I will curse; and in you all the families of the earth shall be blessed. (Genesis 12:2–3)

Discussing the call of Abram in Genesis 12, Hamilton points out that his faith is "in operation prior to his commitment to be Yahweh's servant."[1] The covenant and promise of blessings come afterwards, as Abram agrees to be both recipient and conduit of God's favor. On the strength of divine reassurance, Abram travels first to Canaan, but then when there is a famine he goes down to Egypt. Fearful that his beautiful wife, Sarai, will be so attractive to the Egyptians that they kill him to get her, Abram instructs Sarai to say she is his sister. She does so, but when Pharaoh takes her into his palace, God afflicts Pharaoh and his family with serious diseases. Pharaoh, on learning that Abram is in fact Sarah's wife, sends him on his way. Abram then returns to the Negev, where he and his nephew Lot separate, because their livestock have become too numerous to share the same pastures. Lot goes to the plains where the towns of Sodom and Gomorrah lie, while Abram settles near Mamre at Hebron, and builds an altar to the Lord.

---

1. Hamilton, *Genesis 1–17*, 371.

In Genesis 14, Lot, and all the people of Sodom, are subsequently captured, and Abram takes 318 trained men, and goes and rescues him and those with him. As Abram returns, Melchizedek, who is described as king of Salem and priest of God Most High (Genesis 14:18), comes out to greet Abram and blesses him, saying: *Blessed be Abram by God Most High, maker of heaven and earth; and blessed be God Most High, who has delivered your enemies into your hand!* (Genesis 14:19–20).

Abram responds by giving Melchizedek a tenth of the plunder, returning the rest to the king of Sodom and the people. God then makes a covenant with Abram, tell him that his offspring will be numberless, like the stars in the heavens. Abram believed the Lord, who *reckoned it to him as righteousness* (Genesis 15:6). The covenant is sealed in a sacrifice where Abram cuts a heifer, a goat and a ram in half, also sacrificing a pigeon and a dove. Abram guards the sacrifice till dusk, when a blazing torch passes through the halves of the animal carcasses, sealing the promise.

In Genesis 16, Sarai, recognizing she is barren, offers Hagar, her Egyptian servant, to Abram for him to have children with. Abram sleeps with her, and she becomes pregnant. In her pregnancy she *looked with contempt on her mistress* (Genesis 16:4), so Hagar is sent into the desert. She is found there by an angel, who tells her to return and submit to her mistress, which she duly does, having been promised that she will give birth to a son, *Ishmael*, a name that is a wordplay on the Hebrew *God hears*. Ishmael is born when Abram is eighty-six.

In his discussion of the story of Hagar and Ishmael in Genesis 16, Hamilton points out that no reason is given for Sarai being barren. Moreover, she never refers to her maidservant by name, only by her function. Hamilton sets out parallels in other ancient texts whereby a wife who cannot conceive a child herself can provide her husband with a female slave to bear a son on the wife's behalf. He suggests that such an action was obligatory for a woman in Sarai's position, as a male heir was essential for the continuity of the family line. The problem comes when everyone fails to act appropriately. Hamilton argues that Sarai shows false blame, Hagar pride and Abram false neutrality. Abram and Sarai have acted on their own initiative to fulfill God's promises, but do not accept the consequences of their actions.[2]

Arguably Hagar comes out in the best light. Didymus the Blind argues Hagar must be a woman *not to be despised* because an angel spoke with her.

---

2. Hamilton, *Genesis 1–17*, 441–58.

Moreover, he takes the fact that Sarai chose to her sleep with Abraham as indicating Hagar was *a person of [religious] zeal*.[3] Although Hagar flees to save herself and her son, when she meets the angel of God, whom Hamilton correctly notes should probably be identified with God himself, she is obedient to the divine instruction to return to her mistress. Hagar is "a lady of faith and obedience."[4] This faith is rewarded with blessing; she is told she is bearing a son who will become a great nation. Moreover, his name, *Ishmael*, means *Yahweh has been attentive to your humiliation*.[5] Hagar's response is a further demonstration of her faith, as she rejoices, not in the fact of bearing a son, but in receiving divine revelation (Genesis 16:13). Hagar thus stands as an example of obedient faith even in difficult circumstances. Her son is also a recipient of divine grace. Hamilton points out that although Ishmael does not receive the covenant promises (Genesis 17:20–21), he does receive the covenant sign of circumcision, marking him as a recipient of divine grace (Genesis 17:23–27).

Thirteen years later, when Abram is ninety-nine, the Lord appears to him and renews his covenant with him. Abram's name is changed to Abraham; Abram is argued to mean something like *exalted father*, while Abraham means *father of many*. Sarai's name is changed to Sarah. Abraham is given the covenant of circumcision; from this moment every male child is to be circumcised at eight days old. Abraham is reassured that God's promise will be fulfilled through Sarah, through a son to be called Isaac. In chapter 18, the promise comes closer to fulfillment.

> The LORD appeared to Abraham by the oaks of Mamre, as he sat at the entrance to his tent in the heat of the day. He looked up and saw three men standing near him. When he saw them, he ran from the tent entrance to meet them, and bowed down to the ground. (Genesis 18:1–2)

Abraham persuades the three visitors to stay and eat with him. When they have eaten, they ask where his wife Sarah is. He tells them, and then reply that they will return in a year, to see the son whom Sarah will have given birth to. She laughs at this idea, and the Lord questions Abraham as to why she laughed. She denies it, but the Lord repeats the comment. Sarah's laughter is held by commentators to be the etymology of Isaac's name, as it is a wordplay on the Hebrew for *he laughs*.

---

3. Sheridan, *Genesis 12–50*, 46.
4. Hamilton, *Genesis 1–17*, 452.
5. Hamilton, *Genesis 1–17*, 453.

In his discussion of the annunciation story in Genesis 18, Hamilton focuses initially on the shift between the singular and the plural in reference to Abraham's visitors. He points out this also occurs in Genesis 19, when the angels visit Lot, and in Judges 6:7–24, when Gideon talks with an angel of God. Hamilton is clear that any Trinitarian reading of the text is more eisegetical than exegetical, that is, read into the text rather than read out of it. But he does allow for the possibility of a fluidity of understanding the divine as both single and plural.[6] Regarding the fact that the visitors eat, Hamilton suggests this is a "concession by God to Abraham's ignorance of the one who stands in front of him incognito."[7] Hamilton points out that Isaac's name, which is conferred on him by Abraham in Genesis 21:3, was chosen for him by God before he was even born (Genesis 17:19). This fact is significant, reinforcing the notion that Isaac is the chosen heir. As noted above, the name Isaac means *he laughs*, although it is unclear whether it is God, Abraham or Isaac (or Sarah) who is laughing.[8]

Genesis 18 continues with a discussion between Abraham and the Lord, as Abraham pleads for the city of Sodom, asking that it might be spared from judgment if fifty, forty, thirty, twenty, ten or even five righteous people can be found there. But this does not happen; judgment falls on Sodom and Gomorrah; only Lot and his daughters escape. In Genesis 20, Abraham moves into the territory of Abimelech, and again pretends that Sarah is his sister, not his wife. But God reveals the truth to Abimelech in a dream, and Abimelech sends Abraham on his way.

The second record of conflict between Sarah and Hagar is found in Genesis 21:8–21.[9] Genesis 21:9 records that Ishmael was *playing*; the text is unclear what this actually means. Later translations, such as the Septuagint, add *with Isaac*, and many interpreters presume this means Ishmael was somehow abusing or hurting Isaac. This is the interpretation Paul offers in Galatians 4:29, where he states that Ishmael persecuted Isaac. Ephrem the Syrian suggests that *Sarah also saw how much Ishmael shared the characteristics of his mother, for just as Sarah was despised in the eyes of Hagar, so too did Ishmael mock her son*. Ambrose proposes that Sarah, aware of her own and Abraham's advanced age *was afraid that in the event of their sudden passing Ishmael would, on the score of his being*

---

6. Hamilton, *Genesis 18–50*, 6–8.
7. Hamilton, *Genesis 18–50*, 9.
8. Hamilton, *Genesis 18–50*, 73–74.
9. Hamilton, *Genesis 18–50*, 75–86.

born of an association with the patriarch, endeavor to thrust himself into his father's inheritance and become a sharer of it with Isaac.[10]

Hamilton discusses possible interpretations of Genesis 21:9, proposing that perhaps *playing* be understood in the sense of displaying sporting prowess. Thus Ishmael tries to draw the attention that should be Isaac's at the feast celebrating Isaac's weaning. This clear rivalry is too much for Sarah, who decides she must be rid of Ishmael, whom she feels threatens her own son's inheritance (Genesis 21:10). Her jealousy is coincidentally in-line with God's sovereign purposes. God has decreed that his blessing to Abraham will come via Isaac, and so a "family squabble becomes the occasion by which the sovereign purposes and programs of God are forwarded."[11] By this time Ishmael is a teenager. Abraham entrusts him to the care of his mother Hagar, placing provisions on her back as they set out into the desert. The provisions only last for a while, and so Hagar leaves her son in the shade of a desert shrub, either to protect him from the sun or so he can die as peacefully and painlessly as possible. The only thing Hagar can do now is pray, which she does. Her prayer is answered direct from heaven. She is reassured that God will make her son into a great nation; God also opens her eyes to see a well. Ishmael learns to live in the wilderness, becoming a skilled hunter, the only way to survive in such harsh conditions. Chrysostom takes this as a sign of the Lord's loving kindness, and takes God's provision of a spring of water as a reminder that *whenever God wishes, even if we are utterly alone, even if we are in desperate trouble, even if we have no hope of survival, we need no other assistance, since God's grace is all we require.*[12]

Meanwhile, Abraham and Abimelech make a treaty with each other. Then God tests Abraham, asking him to offer his son Isaac as a sacrifice. Abraham complies, and it is only when Isaac is bound on the altar and Abraham has his knife raised to kill him that God speaks, telling him to substitute a ram for the sacrifice and praising his faith. The promise of blessing is repeated; Abraham will become a great nation and through him all nations will be blessed, because he has obeyed God.

In his opening remarks about Genesis 22, Hamilton points out that the chapter is contextually related to the previous one. Having lost Ishmael to the desert, is Abraham now to lose Isaac to the altar? What

---

10. Sheridan, *Genesis 12–50*, 94–95.
11. Hamilton, *Genesis 18–50*, 81.
12. Sheridan, *Genesis 12–50*, 98.

exactly is the difference—if anything—between Abraham sending Hagar and Ishmael into the desert at Sarah's command and his placing Isaac on an altar at God's command?[13] Jewish tradition (*Genesis Rabbah* 56:8) suggests Isaac is 37 by now. The rabbis reached this age by presuming that Sarah, having given birth at age 90, subsequently died, at age 127, of the shock of discovering Abraham's willingness to sacrifice his son. This potentially gives Isaac a far greater role in the story. Christians have not speculated on Isaac's age, focusing more on the obedience of Abraham and the faithfulness of God. Thus, Hamilton argues that the real test for Abraham is not his willingness to sacrifice his beloved son, but whether he will sacrifice "the one person who can perpetuate the promises of God" especially the promise of descendants who will become a great nation.[14] Hamilton goes on to discuss the appropriateness of God demanding Abraham sacrifice his son, arguing the narrative must be read as a whole, rather than focusing exclusively on the command of Genesis 22:2. In that way the reader sees the graciousness and mercy of God and is reminded that it is only by that grace and mercy that people can survive and thrive.

Isaac is clearly aware of what is happening; his question to Abraham about where the sacrifice will come from (Genesis 22:9) makes that plain. Abraham's answer, that God will provide, can be taken as indicating the patriarch's faith that Isaac will be raised by God. Abraham's willing obedience is sufficient for God to halt the sacrifice and provide an alternative, just as Abraham had said he would. The covenant promises of blessing are then reiterated as father and son return home.

The New Testament authors make much of this text, especially Paul, and their views are discussed below. For the moment I simply note that Clement of Alexandria is typical in his description of Isaac as a type of Christ, who carried the wood for his sacrifice as Jesus carried his cross. Clement also says, *Isaac rejoiced for a mystical reason, to prefigure the joy with which the Lord has filled us, in saving us from destruction through his blood*. Ephrem the Syrian spoke of Abraham's victory:

> In two things then was Abraham victorious: that he killed his son although he did not kill him and that he believed that after Isaac died he would be raised up again and would go back down with

---

13. Hamilton, *Genesis 18–50*, 97–123.
14. Hamilton, *Genesis 18–50*, 104.

him. For Abraham was firmly convinced that he who said to him, "through Isaac shall your descendants be named," was not lying.[15]

In Genesis 23 we hear of the death of Sarah, and in chapter 24 of the quest to find a suitable wife for Isaac. Then in chapter 25 Abraham dies.

The Disputation Cluster

The most commonly cited tradition about Abraham that is found in the Qur'an but not in the Bible is his attempt to persuade his people away from polytheism toward monotheism. In these stories, Abraham's father is the main opponent, and Abraham destroys idols (*al-An'am* 6:74–83; *Maryam* 19:41–50; *al-Anbiya'* 21:51–57; *ash-Shu'ara'* 26:69–86; *al-'Ankabut* 29:16–27; *as-Saffat* 37:83–98; *az-Zukhruf* 43:26–27; *al-Mumtahanah* 60:4). This experience is shared by Muhammad, and is also found in nonbiblical Jewish sources. The longest conversation between Abraham and his father is found in *Maryam* 19:41–50. The narrative is poignant, showing Abraham's desperate attempts to persuade his father to a new path and his father's blunt rejection of change.[16] In his discussion of *surah Maryam*, Unal argues that "Faith, emigration, and striving in God's cause are the three pillars of a single, sacred truth."[17] He explains that every new message from God has been resisted by some of those it was given to. The original recipient of the message must strive to master his own spiritual growth, the *jihad al-akbar*, or *greater struggle*. He then rises to radiate the light of belief throughout the world, which results in spiritual and physical migration as the message is spread.

Reynolds explains that according to the Qur'an, Abraham became a monotheist after first worshipping the stars, the moon and the sun (*al-An'am* 6:76–79). As each set in the west, he realized they were unworthy of worship and resolved to only worship the Creator. As the *Enlightening Commentary* puts it: "A thing that has rising and setting is objective to some regularity, not in a position of subjugating them. A thing that has movement is 'creatable' and a creatable thing cannot be God."[18] The Qur'an also teaches that Abraham opposed idolatry, rebuking his father,

---

15. Sheridan, *Genesis 12–50*, 105.
16. Kaltner and Mirza, *Bible and the Qur'an*, 12.
17. Unal, *Qur'an*, 595.
18. https://www.al-islam.org/enlightening-commentary-light-holy-quran-vol-5/section-8-submission-allah-abrahams-arguments#surah-al-anam-verse-76.

then his people. He destroyed the idols and the people, who in turn sought to kill him (*as-Saffat* 37:82–97). "Thus the Abraham in the Qur'an is a self-taught monotheist and opponent to the idolaters."[19]

Bakhos recounts an Islamic birth legend in some detail:

> According to al-Tha'labi, when Abraham's mother begins to feel labour pains, she goes into a cave and gives birth to Abraham. She supplies him with all the necessary provisions, seals him in the cave, and departs for home. When she later returns to the cave, she finds him sucking his thumb, and indeed whenever she returns to the cave she finds him doing so. When she examines his fingers, she notices that from one finger he sucks water, from another he sucks milk, from another honey, and from yet another clarified butter.[20]

Reynolds recounts the story of Abraham's origins as told by *Tafsir Muqatil*. Abraham is reputed to have been born in Kuta, a city ruled by the pagan tyrant Nimrod. Nimrod's priests warn him that a child is to be born who will destroy both Nimrod's rule and also the gods that Nimrod and the people worship. To stave off this threat, Nimrod orders the separation of men and women, except during a woman's period, in order to ensure no children can be born. But a man named Azar disobeys, and his wife conceives Abraham. When Abraham is born, his mother digs a burrow and hides the baby there, covering it with a stone to protect the baby from wild animals, returning regularly in secret to nurse Abraham. The baby grows phenomenally, increasing in size in a single day at a rate that takes most babies a month, and growing in a month to a size that most babies attain in a year. As he grows, Abraham first contemplates worshipping Venus (or Jupiter), but when Venus sets, he turns to the moon, but when it sets, the sun. Then when the sun sets, Abraham concludes that only the Creator is to be worshipped, and resolves to do so, going into the city and discovering that the people worship idols.

Reynolds adds that there are other versions, one of which has Azar in the role of astrologer to Nimrod. The stars play a central part in this narrative, both predicting Abraham's birth and also guiding him to worship of the true Creator. In a third version, Azar is not an astrologer but an idol maker. In this account, Nimrod orders all pregnant women to be imprisoned, and kills their babies on birth. God keeps Abraham's mother's

---

19. Reynolds, *Qur'an and Its Biblical Subtext*, 71.
20. Bakhos, *Family of Abraham*, 97.

pregnancy concealed. She escapes to a cave, and gives birth while hidden there. Abraham is concealed in the cave; his mother informs Azar that his son has died. Abraham grows up in the cave, and there contemplates worshipping the stars, as he knows no better. Reynolds recounts discussion amongst commentators as to what Abraham's people worshipped. The suggestion from Zamakhshari is that they worshipped the sun, moon and stars. According to Zamakhshari's retelling, Abraham himself never actually joined in this worship, merely pretending to do so in order to gain an audience with the people, whom he rebuked for their false belief. Ibn Kathir concurs, suggesting that Abraham gradually escalated his rejection of idolatry in a planned tactic to rebuke his people.[21]

Wessels adds to this, describing Nimrod as the first tyrant on earth; Jewish and Muslim tradition both hold he engaged in confrontation with Abraham. Nimrod is the archetype of an idolater and a tyrant. Wessels recounts a story in which Nimrod throws Abraham in the fire, but an angel intervenes to cool the fire. Nimrod becomes an archetype of the cruel biblical kings Pharaoh and Nebuchadnezzar. Nimrod is held to have built the tower of Babel because he wanted to see Abraham's God. Abraham has to leave Nimrod's land and his dominion in order to practice monotheism in peace.[22] Wheeler recounts similar traditions; in Ibn Ishaq's retelling, as the wood is lit to burn Abraham, *the heavens and the earth and all that was created in it except the humans and the Jinn screamed to God in a single voice*, begging for permission to intervene to save Abraham, as he is the only human on earth who worships God. But God replies that they can only act if Abraham calls for aid. If Abraham does not call out, then God himself will act. Abraham is indeed silent, and so God speaks: *Fire, be cold and peaceful for Abraham.*[23]

Reynolds discusses the biblical subtext to the disputation cluster. The first text he refers to is the Jewish text *Jubilees*, which describes Abraham's conversion from paganism to monotheism. Abraham confronts his father Terah, proving that worship of idols is foolish. Terah agrees but warns his son to be quiet, for the idolaters may want to kill him. The key episode is in *Jubilees* 12:16–17. Philo also knows of this legend. He describes the idolatry of the Chaldeans, amongst whom he includes Abraham, before describing how Abraham's eyes were opened to the truth of

---

21. Reynolds, *Qur'an and Its Biblical Subtext*, 71–75.
22. Wessels, *Torah, the Gospel and the Qur'an*, 66–67.
23. Wheeler, *Prophets in the Qur'an*, 91–92.

monotheism through his studying of the stars (*De Abrahamo* 70). Josephus tells a similar story, suggesting that Abraham infers the existence of God by studying nature (*Jewish Antiquities* 1.154). In the *Apocalypse of Abraham* 7–8 (dated to the second century CE), Abraham confronts his father Terah, who is guilty of paganism. Abraham tells his father, *I shall seek before you the God who created all the gods supposed by us (to exist)* (*Apocalypse of Abraham* 7:10). Terah's guilt means God destroys him and his house; as Abraham leaves his father's house, *the sound of a great thunder came and burned him and his house and everything in his house, down to the ground* (*Apocalypse of Abraham* 8:6).

Reynolds suggests that the two Old Testament verses that shape these interpretations are Genesis 15:5 and Deuteronomy 4:19. In Genesis 15:5, God is explaining his promise to give Abram descendants. He takes Abram outside and tells him, *look toward the heavens and count the stars, if you are able to count them*, promising that this will be the number of his descendants. The implication of this verse, Reynolds argues, is that human beings must rely on God to understand creation, implying that nothing created is worthy of worship, but only the one who created it. The second verse comes in a recap of the Israelites' experience of deliverance from Egypt and encounter with God at Mount Sinai. Moses orders them to not make any idols, including this injunction: *And when you look up to the heavens and see the sun, the moon, and the stars, all the host of heaven, do not be led astray, and bow down to them and serve them, things that the LORD your God has allotted to all the peoples everywhere under heaven* (Deuteronomy 4:19). This warning against idolatry and worship of celestial bodies is the same as that which Abraham proclaims in the Qur'an.

Reynolds notes that Christian commentators do not tend to discuss Abraham's contemplation of heavenly bodies, arguing rather that Abraham's conversion took place on the basis of faith alone. Indeed, Eusebius goes so far as to suggest that Abraham encounters the preincarnate Christ, stating,

> It was by faith toward the Logos of God, the Christ who had appeared to him, that he was justified, and gave up the superstition of his father and his former erroneous life, and confessed the God who is over all to be one; and Him he served by virtuous deeds, not by the worship of the law of Moses, who came later (*Ecclesiastical History* 1:4:13)

Reynolds explains that Eusebius has based his argument on God's appearance to Abraham, as recounted in Genesis 15. Eusebius believes that it is the Logos, not the Father, who is revealed to Abraham, a concept common in early Christianity and applied to all appearances of God in the Old Testament. Reynolds adds that Abraham is a particularly attractive figure to Christians, as he lived before Jacob, who became Israel, and before Moses, who was given the law. Paul argues in Romans 10 that Abraham was justified before he was circumcised, emphasizing the importance of faith, a topic I will return to below. As Reynolds explains, by claiming Abraham, Christians were asserting the ancient origins of their faith. It was not simply a recent innovation of Judaism, but a practice rooted in the patriarchs. This claim is important background for the Qur'anic presentation. The point is that Jews, Christians and Muslims are all claiming Abraham as their own, and interpreting his story and origins in the light of their own theological preferences and agenda.[24]

The disputation cluster provides Christians and Muslims with at least two key topics to discuss. First, what does it mean to claim that Abraham was the first monotheist? How was that message given to him, how did he receive it and how did he share it? In Jewish legends, such as the *Apocalypse of Abraham* cited above, Abraham preaches only to his father. But in the Qur'an, he preaches to his people (*ash-Shu'ara'* 26:69–93). Second, what does it mean for Muslims or Christians to say they are children of Abraham? This is a complex question, and the annunciation cluster sheds light on the different perspectives.

The Annunciation Cluster

The Qur'an has four accounts of the annunciation of Isaac, of which the most prominent is *Hud* 11:69–72 (the others are *al-Hijr* 15:51–56; *al-'Ankabut* 29:31–35; *ad-Dhariyat* 51:24–34). Reynolds points out the connection between the declaration of the messengers in verse 70 and the destruction of Lot's people in *Hud* 11:77–83, as well as arguing for the topos of annunciation (via the verb *bashshara*, meaning revelation of good news), linked to *al-Hadid* 57:12 and the Qur'an's self-description as a *bushra* (revelation, *al-Baqarah* 2:91; *al-Ahqaf* 46:12). Reynold's third point is that the divine voice, in the first-person plural, delivers the message of the birth of the son. So, God is somehow present. Fourth,

24. Reynolds, *Qur'an and Its Biblical Subtext*, 77–81.

comparison can be made with the annunciation in *Al-Imran* 3:39–40, the angels announcing to Zechariah that he will have a son. The other two references to Abraham's son come in *al-Hijr* 15:51–60, which is much more succinct, omitting both the meal and Sarah. The third reference, *al-Hijr* 51:24–34, has more details.[25]

Reynolds notes that there is a particular problem with the account in *surah Hud*. The order of events is: (1) messengers refuse to eat; (2) Abraham is afraid; (3) messengers reveal their mission to Lot's people; (4) Abraham's wife laughs; and (5) messengers announce she will conceive Isaac. Why does she laugh? *Al-Hijr* suggests she laughs at the news of the annunciation, but *Hud* takes a different view. Reynolds explains that some interpreters argue that her laughter was her reaction to Abraham's fear. That is, she did not recognize the visitors as being of divine origin, and so her husband's fear seemed humorous to her. Other interpreters suggest that the laughter came when the guests did not eat, or when they explained their mission to destroy Lot's people, that is, laughter with pleasure that God will punish the wicked. A further proposal is that she did not laugh, but rather menstruated. Finally, another view is that her laughter was in relief that her own family would not be destroyed when Lot's people were destroyed. Reynolds argues that the Qur'an follows the biblical order of events, but adds that it does not reproduce the account in full, nor does it give an alternative account. Rather, it presumes the audience is familiar with the story and develops a homily that refers to the account as it does so. For Reynolds, it is therefore entirely reasonable that in *Hud* the laughter comes before the annunciation as the facts are presumed. Furthermore, the rhyming poetry of the Arabic is preserved if the order of laughter then annunciation is used.[26]

Reynolds adds that the Qur'an does depart from the biblical story in a manner that reflects Jewish and Christian exegetical tradition. His first example is the fact that in Genesis 18:2 Abraham's three visitors are referred to as men, yet in *Hud* 11:69 they are described as messengers (*rasul*), who in the Qur'an could be either men or angels (see *al-Hajj* 22:75). Both Josephus (*Antiquities* 1.196) and Ibn Kathir describe the visitors as angels, with Ibn Kathir naming them as Gabriel, Michael and Israfil.[27] The exhortation to hospitality in Hebrews 13:1 may make a similar

---

25. Reynolds, *Qur'an and Its Biblical Subtext*, 87–89.
26. Reynolds, *Qur'an and Its Biblical Subtext*, 89–97.
27. Wheeler, *Prophets in the Qur'an*, 96.

identification, although there is no direct reference to Abraham's visitors. The early church father Ambrose argued that Abraham,

> who was glad to receive strangers, faithful to God and tireless in his service and prompt in fulfilling his duty, saw the Trinity typified. He added religious devotion to hospitality, for although he beheld three, he adored one, and, while keeping a distinction of persons, yet he called one Lord, thus giving honor to the three but signifying one power.[28]

Second, the messengers' refusal to eat contradicts the statement in Genesis 18:8 that they did eat. Later exegetical tradition, however, concurs that they did not eat. Ibn Kathir explains,

> According to the People of the Book, the fatted calf was roasted and served with three rolls, fat and milk. And, according to them, the angels ate, but this is not right. It is also said that they just appeared to be eating but that the food evaporated into the air.[29]

This is also true of Jewish, and indeed Christian, understanding of angels. Thus, when the angel Raphael reveals his true identity, he adds that he has only appeared to eat, when in fact he did not (Tobit 12:19). Likewise, in Judges, when an angel visits Manoah and foretells Samson's birth, the angel refuses to eat (Judges 13:15–16). Similarly, Philo (*De Abrahamo* 118) and Justin Martyr (*Dialogue with Trypho* 57) all argue that the angels who visited Abraham did not actually eat. Josephus (*Antiquities* 1.197–98) explains that the visitors made *a show of eating* until *they concealed themselves no longer, but declared that they were angels of God*.

But there is a clear difference on Sarah's laughter. For Genesis, the laughter is "a clear etiology for the name of their son," although the wordplay only works in Hebrew, not in Greek or Syriac.[30] Christians thus came up with alternative explanations. For Ephraem the Syrian, her laughter was related to the birth of Christ, a parallel to John the Baptist leaping in his mother's womb. Thus, Christians establish a Sarah/Mary typology, which is also found in the Quran. Reynolds adds:

> In Hud (11) 71 the Qur'an has God proclaim, "*We gave [Sarah] the good news of Isaac.*" In al Imran (3) 45 the angels foretell the birth of Jesus to Mary with the report, "*God gives you good news*

---

28. Sheridan, *Genesis 12–50*, 61.
29. Wheeler, *Prophets in the Qur'an*, 96.
30. Reynolds, *Qur'an and Its Biblical Subtext*, 95.

of a Word from him." Both women react in amazement. Sarah shouts, *"Woe is me. Shall I give birth in my old age, when my Lord is aged? This is an amazing thing"* (Q 11:71; cf. Q 51:29). Mary wonders, *"O My Lord, am I to have a child when no man has touched me?"* (Q 3:47).[31]

Reynolds therefore proposes that this Sarah/Mary typology holds the exegetical key to understanding Sarah's laughter. The Qur'an holds Mary in highest esteem, as one born without sin (*al-Imran* 3:36–37), the perfect woman (*al-Imran* 3:42), a sign for the worlds (*al-Abiya'* 21:91). Sarah's laughter is not understood as a wordplay. Rather, the laughter, and indeed the whole annunciation, is an anticipation of the annunciation to Mary.[32]

Lodahl discusses the conversation over the fate of Sodom that takes place between God and Abraham. He points out that while in the Genesis account Abraham debates with and challenges God, this type of holding God to account is "theologically uncomfortable for the Qur'an," and so "where Genesis offers one of the great bartering-for-justice stories in the history of human narration, the Qur'an is silent," or more accurately, Abraham is told to be silent and submit to God's judgment.[33] Lodahl suggest the Qur'anic account is cleaned up, crisper and more straightforward that the Genesis account, but he also points out that subsequent speculation on this story, as evidenced by the version in *Genesis Rabbah*, the retelling by Jewish rabbis, is also a bit more circumspect and does not have Abraham challenge God so directly.[34]

A final point that Lodahl makes in reference to Genesis 18 is the way in which Christian interpreters began to see the presence of the Trinity in the text. Abraham has three visitors, yet only the Lord speaks; as seen in the quote from Ambrose above, for many Christians this was a tantalizing hint of the Trinity. Lodahl references Rublev's famous icon, which depicts the three visitors each sitting at one of the three sides of a table. The fourth side, empty and facing the viewer of the icon, invites the Christian in, making God the host at the meal, inviting the believer into the divine life of the Trinity.[35]

---

31. Reynolds, *Qur'an and Its Biblical Subtext*, 96.
32. Reynolds, *Qur'an and Its Biblical Subtext*, 89–97.
33. Lodahl, *Claiming Abraham*, 17.
34. Lodahl, *Claiming Abraham*, 17–20.
35. Lodahl, *Claiming Abraham*, 22–24.

The annunciation cluster raises at least three further topics for Muslims and Christians to discuss in relation to Abraham. First, who visited Abraham, and how important is the identity of the visitors? Second, what resonances are there in the Sarah-Mary typology identified above? How convincing is it, and what impact does that have on Christian and Muslim devotion? Third, can you barter with God for justice, or must you always submit unquestioningly to his will? The sacrifice cluster explores this third question in more detail.

The Sacrifice Cluster

One account of the command to Abraham to sacrifice his son is found in *as-Saffat* 37:99–113. There is disagreement amongst Muslim exegetes as to which son Abraham offers in sacrifice. Reynolds cites *Tafsir al-Jalalayn*, which comments on *as-Saffat* 37:107, *Then We ransomed him, the one whom he had been commanded to sacrifice, namely Ishmael or Isaac*, demonstrating the ambiguity of some early interpretations.[36] Galadari argues that the majority of early companions of the Prophet confirm that it was Isaac who was offered in sacrifice, citing Abdulla ibn Mas'ud, al-'Abbas, Ibn 'Abbas and 'Ali ibn Abi talid, as examples of this trend. Thus, it seems likely that the early Muslim community recognized that Isaac was the son who was offered, but subsequent generations of Muslims, wanting to distinguish themselves from Christians and Jews, decided it was Ishmael.[37] Galadari subsequently adds that al-Tabari, one of the earliest commentators, suggests the son offered was Isaac, while later commentators, such as Ibn Kathir, discuss the different opinions amongst Muslims and eventually conclude it was Ishmael. Galadari cites the work of Reuven Firestone, which shows there were two groups, one supporting the idea of Isaac, the other of Ishmael, and that the writings of the former group can be dated earlier than the latter grouping.[38]

Firestone explains that the Qur'an never actually identifies the son who is almost sacrificed. The account comes in *as-Saffat* 37:99–113, and although Isaac is mentioned in 37:112, the reference is ambiguous and may be an announcement of his birth rather than an identification of him as the sacrificial victim. The lack of identification is problematic for Islam,

---

36. Reynolds, *Qur'an and the Bible*, 681.
37. Galadari, *Qur'anic Hermeneutics*, 64.
38. Galadari, *Qur'anic Hermeneutics*, 148.

as Arab descent from Abraham is traced via Ishmael, not to mention the issue posed for exegesis of the Qur'an.[39] Firestone explains that during the first two hundred years of Islam, two schools of thought developed amongst exegetes. He terms the first the "biblicist" school, who argued that the almost-sacrifice took place near Jerusalem and the intended victim was Isaac. The second group was the "Arabian" school, who believed Ishmael was the intended victim and the act took place somewhere near Mecca. For many scholars, this was a historical, geographical and textual debate, but for some it became polemical. Firestone cites Ibn Kathir as an example of this latter trend:

> That boy is Ishmael. He is the first son announced to Abraham in revelation. The Muslims and the People of the Book agree that he was older than Isaac . . . According to them, God commanded Abraham to sacrifice his only son, but according to another version, [he commanded him to sacrifice] his oldest son. They dishonestly and slanderously introduced Isaac here by forcing him in.[40]

While the biblicist school argued their understanding was based on the authority of the Companions of the Prophet, the Arabian school denied this, arguing instead that the biblicists had been deceived into believing the spurious tales of the *Israeliyatt*, the Israelite tales that circulated around the time the Qur'an was compiled, adding in detail to the sparse narratives of the Qur'anic text. The issue becomes one of intercommunity polemic, with the Muslims arguing that the almost-sacrificial victim was always Ishmael, but that the Jews had corrupted the text in order to bolster their own standing. In contemporary exegesis, Muslims almost universally assume the intended victim was Ishmael, while Jews and Christians take a similar position in favor of Isaac.

Reinink discusses an intriguing unpublished manuscript that documents an exchange between a Syriac Christian monk and an Arab Muslim emir that took place in the early eighth century. The pair begin by discussing their different understandings of Genesis 22. The monk explains that the sacrifice of Isaac was ordered to provide a typological example of the passion of Christ. Thus, the two unnamed boys that go with Abraham and Isaac (Genesis 22:3, 5) are understood to represent typologically the two robbers crucified with Christ (Matthew 27:44;

---

39. Firestone, "Merit, Mimesis and Martyrdom," 95–98.
40. Firestone, "Merit, Mimesis and Martyrdom," 99–100.

Luke 23:39–43). The wood that Isaac carries (Genesis 22:6) is a type of the wood of the cross. The binding of Isaac (Genesis 22:9) is contrasted with Christ's divinity, limited by incarnation yet unharmed, and the ram (Genesis 22:13) with his humanity, which died. Reinink argues that the monk understood Islam as a form of Abrahamic monotheism, which was inadequate in contrast with faith in Christ, and hence he defined his own faith over against the Islam of his conversation partner.[41]

Leemhuis examines early post-Qur'anic tradition. He begins by observing how sparse the narrative of *as-Saffat* 37:100–113 is in contrast with Genesis 22, focusing particularly on the fact that the son who was offered in sacrifice is not named. Leemhuis explains that, as cited above, Ibn Kathir forcefully made the case for identifying the unnamed son as Ishmael, arguing any reference to Isaac betrayed the corrupting influence of *Israeliyyat*, the stories of the Jews. But other commentators, including ak Fakhr al Razi, (1149–1210), al-Qurtubi (d. 1272) and al-Mahalli (1389–1459), mention both options, without necessarily indicating a preference. This indicates an ongoing debate during the first few centuries of Islam. Turning to the early sources, Leemhuis notes that the earliest *tafsir*, of Muqatil b. Sulaiman (d. 767), identifies the victim as Isaac and the place as Jerusalem. By contrast, in the *tafsir* of al-Thauri (d. 777) and al-Farra (d.822) only Ishmael is mentioned. Subsequent commentaries, for example, of al-Tabari (d. 923) and al-Nahhas (d. 949), mention traditions that include both possibilities, but opt for Isaac and Jerusalem. Leemhuis concludes that the debate was for many years a purely academic one; it was only when political necessity advocated polemic against the Jews that opinions favoring Ishmael as the intended sacrificial victim became dominant.[42]

Two obvious points of discussion flow from this. First, which son was almost sacrificed? Second, what does this episode teach us about Abraham, about God and about ourselves?

The Sanctuary Cluster

The sanctuary cluster links closely to the accounts of Hagar found in Genesis 16 and 21, discussed above. As Kaltner and Mirza note, one story that is unique to the Qur'an is the account of Abraham and Ishmael

41. Reinink, "Lamb on the Tree."
42. Leemhuis, "Ibrahim's Sacrifice."

building a structure in which worship of God can take place (*al-Baqarah* 2:124–29). This is understood as a reference to the Ka'ba, which eventually became a polytheistic site before Muhammad returned it to its original purpose. The text describes ritual practices of circumambulation and prostration still practiced by Muslims today, and includes prayers that Muslims would still pray, asking God to accept their worship.[43]

Muslim tradition holds that the Ka'ba is located directly below the Inhabited House of God in the heavens, where Ibn Kathir explains seventy thousand angels worship God daily, and never the same angel twice. He adds also that there are legends of the Israelites that the location of the Ka'ba is a place where Adam had pitched a tent and Noah's ark circumambulated for forty days, although Ibn Kathir is clear that these reports cannot be verified.[44]

Suddi tells the legend of the Black Stone that is the foundation stone:

> Abraham said to Ishmael: "My son, bring me a good rock so that I might place it here." Ishmael said: "My father, I am tired." So Gabriel brought the Black Stone from India. It had been white emerald, but when Adam fell with it from Paradise it became black from the sins of the people.[45]

The Black Stone of the Ka'ba is held in high regard within Islam; there are also reports of how Muhammad ensured it was treated with due honor when the Ka'ba was rebuilt. The tribal leaders in Mecca were arguing over who should have the honor of holding the Black Stone. Muhammad solved the problem by ordering the stone to be placed on a sheet. Each leader held on to the sheet, so they all had the same honor of transporting the Black Stone, before Muhammad himself placed it in its final position.

The sanctuary cluster also links with the story of Hagar in the desert; pilgrims on the *hajj* re-enact her desperate search for water and recognize the gift of God in preserving Ishmael's life. These stories have little direct connection to Christian tales of Abraham. This will shape the discussion that can take place, with the focus shifting to Muslim explanations of their beliefs and practices and Christians focusing on appreciative enquiry. Reynolds's discussion of *al-Baqarah* (2:125–28) notes that the issues are complex. He recognizes that Islamic tradition understands reference

---

43. Kaltner and Mirza, *Bible and the Qur'an*, 13.
44. Wheeler, *Prophets in the Qur'an*, 99–101.
45. Wheeler, *Prophets in the Qur'an*, 100.

to the house as indicating the Ka'ba in Mecca, but explains that the language is reminiscent of biblical references to Jerusalem. Moreover, the Syriac Christian tradition links the altar of Genesis 22 with the sanctuary in Jerusalem. This leads him to propose that the Qur'an is transferring this Syriac Christian understanding of Jerusalem to an Islamic understanding of Mecca.[46] Unal explains that the Ka'ba was the first building in the world to be built, by Prophet Adam; it was subsequently rebuilt by Abraham and Ishmael.[47] Nasr adds that Abraham's role was to purfty the Ka'ba, making a suitable site for monotheistic worship.[48]

The Muslim View: Abraham as a Friend of God and as a Hanif

For Christians and Muslims there is a particular advantage in going back to a figure who existed before Moses, that is, before the covenant ceremony and law-giving took place at Mount Sinai. Thus, the Qur'an selects and modifies pre-existing tradition, modifying it to support its own view. One example of this trend is seen in how the covenant episode of Genesis 15:9–21 is modified in *al-Baqarah* 2:260 to show divine power to resurrect the dead. The Qur'an states:

> Remember when Abraham said: "My Lord, show me how You give the dead life." He said, "Have you not believed?" He said, "Yes indeed! But (show me) to satisfy my heart." He said, "Take four birds, and take them close to you, then place a piece of each of them on each hill, (and) then call them. They will come rushing to you. Know that God is mighty, wise."

In this way Abraham is reconfigured from a biblical patriarch to a Qur'anic Prophet, in the mould of Noah. Reynolds explains that in both Genesis and *al-Baqarah* Abraham has already demonstrated his faith in God, and this is simply confirmation. But only in the Qur'an does he show interest in the resurrection.[49] Kaltner and Mirza comment that in the Qur'an Abraham is presented as a true believer, a prototype Muslim because of his complete submission to God. In *al-Imran* 3:67 (and elsewhere) he is described as neither a Jew nor a Christian, but as one who

---

46. Reynolds, *Qur'an and the Bible*, 69–70.
47. Unal. *Qur'an*, 113–14.
48. Nasr, *Study Qur'an*, 58.
49. Reynolds, *Qur'an and the Bible*, 102.

submitted himself to God. The logic is that since he lived long before either of those two religions existed he cannot be identified with them; he is an upright monotheist, and so an example to all true believers. Much of this story reflects Muhammad's own situation, especially his early prophetic career, although, of course, Muhammad was an orphan from a young age. Kaltner and Mirza suggest that Abraham's story is told to conform with the "prophetic paradigm" established by the Qur'an. That is to say, the lives of prominent Prophets are retold in a way that conforms their story with Muhammad's own story. Abraham is thus a paradigmatic believer, a prototypical Muslim. In *The Stories of the Prophets* Abraham is a precocious child, standing as a newborn to proclaim, *There is no god but God, Who has no partner*, a phrase he repeats as he grows up. Many of the stories concern Abraham's conflict with the local ruler Nimrod, who proclaims himself to be a deity and refuses to accept Abraham's message, resisting and ultimately dying. The local people also attack Abraham, at one point throwing him into a raging fire that is too hot for anyone to approach. God preserves Abraham, who walks out of the fire unscathed. Another tradition tells a story in which Abraham pretends his wife Sarah is his sister, in a fashion similar to the accounts of Genesis 12 and 20. The dispute between Hagar and Sarah, which is not discussed in the Qur'an, is taken up in *The Stories of the Prophets*. Abraham takes Hagar and Ishmael to Mecca, where the Ka'ba lay in ruins. He leaves them there, returning after Hagar has died, and rebuilds the Ka'ba together with Ishmael. Finally, the story in which Abraham dismembers birds is discussed. According to *The Stories of the Prophets*, the bird parts came together, reconstituting themselves, thus teaching Abraham about the resurrection of the dead.[50]

In the Qur'an, Abraham is described as a *hanif*, not of the idolaters (*mushrikin*). This, Reynolds proposes, is a way of distinguishing him from Jews and Christians (see *al-Baqarah* 2:135; *al-Imran* 3:67, 95; *al-An'am* 6:79, 161; *an-Nahl* 16:120, 123). He notes some leave the term untranslated, whilst others suggest *upright, firmly and truly, an upright man* or *a true believer*. Those who offer no translation are, Reynolds proposes, possibly following an Islamic exegetical tradition whereby *hanif* is regarded as a proper name for those who reject polytheism but do not become a Christian or a Jew. Those who do translate it are basing their interpretation on the idea that it indicates one who is faithful or one who has performed pilgrimage to Mecca, or one who followed the command

---

50. Kaltner and Mirza, *Bible and the Qur'an*, 10–14.

of God, specifically in relation to circumcision, or even that it means a Muslim.[51] Thus Ibn Kathir says, *God kept his friend from being a Jew or a Christian, and made clear that he was Hanif, Muslim, and not one of those who associate things with God.*[52] Devin Stewart discusses the meaning of *hanif*, proposing that the term is used to create a relationship between Abraham's monotheism and Islam, implying the two are identical. He adds a few references to those cited by Reynolds (*an-Nisa'* 4:125; *al-Hajj* 22:31) and explains that *hanif* stands in contrast with *shirk*, which he translates as *polytheism*.[53] In a later work, Reynolds makes three further points. First, Abraham is described in *an-Nahl* 16:120 as an *ummah*, a *nation* (see also Genesis 18:17–18 on this point). Second, he gives some further possible translations of *hanif*, including *by nature upright*, or *true in faith* or *man of pure faith*. Third, Reynolds explains that a *hanif* is a *Gentile*, and that Abraham believed in God naturally, independent of Jewish or Christian revelation, and so is used by Muslims to confront and challenge Jewish and Christian practices.[54]

For Wessels, the statement that Abraham was not a Jew or a Christian but a Muslim (*al-Imran* 3:67) is not meant to say that Abraham cannot be claimed by Jews or Christians, but "that Abraham is the model, the example, of the true believer for all three." The key question the text asks of Jews, Christians and Muslims is whether they are a Muslim "in the true sense of the word Muslim, one who has surrendered completely to God."[55] Wessels also discusses the idea of Abraham as a friend of God, explaining that Abraham was, like Jesus, as a *proclaimer of the truth* (*sadiq*) (*Maryam* 19:41; *al-Ahzab* 33:7–8), as well as being a *righteous man* (*salih*) (*an-Nahl* 16:122). The Qur'an portrays Abraham as a *humble man* (*halim*) as well (*at-Taubah* 9:114; *Hud* 11:75). Finally, God made Abraham his *friend* (*khalil*) (*an-Nisa'* 4:125, Isaiah 41:8; James 2:23). Wessels comments that "the famous mystic Ibn al-'Arabi (d. AD 1240) sees this title of friend as expressing a 'mutual penetration' between Abraham and God."[56]

---

51. Reynolds, *Qur'an and Its Biblical Subtext*, 75–76.
52. Wheeler. *Prophets in the Qur'an*, 106.
53. Stewart, "Notes on Medieval and Modern Emendations," 238.
54. Reynolds, *Qur'an and the Bible*, 429–30.
55. Wessels, *Torah, the Gospel and the Qur'an*, 54.
56. Wessels, *Torah, the Gospel and the Qur'an*, 188.

Muslims, Christians and of course Jews all claim Abraham as their own. To what extent are these claims mutually exclusive? Can they be held in tension, or even in unity, with one another?

The Christian View: Abraham in the New Testament

For the Christian, Abraham teaches us about faith. Thus, for example, Augustine explains:

> The right thing to do, brothers and sisters, is to believe God before he pays up anything, because just as he cannot possibly lie, so he cannot deceive. For he is God. That's how Abraham believed him. There's a faith for you that really deserves to be admired and made widely known. He had received nothing from him, and he believed his promise.[57]

There are at least six references to Abraham in the Gospels and Acts. These will only be discussed briefly. The main focus of the discussion is on Paul's use of Abraham in Galatians and Romans, before brief mention is made of reference in Hebrews 11 and James 2.

Abraham in the Gospels and Acts

First, in the Synoptic Gospels, Abraham features in the genealogies of Matthew (1:1, 2, 17) and Luke (3:34). Second, there are also disputes between Jesus and the Pharisees in which Abrahamic descent is evoked. Thus, John the Baptist says, *Do not presume to say to yourselves, "We have Abraham as our ancestor"; for I tell you, God is able from these stones to raise up children to Abraham* (Matthew 3:9). Hagner argues that John's comments depend on an Aramaic wordplay between *stones* (*'abnayya*) and *children* (*benayya*), and that the force of the argument is against presuming spiritual relationship with God on the basis of physical lineage.[58] Keener concurs that Jewish people believed they were chosen in Abraham, citing Nehemiah 9:7 and Micah 7:20 to support his case.[59]

Elsewhere, Jesus evokes the tradition of the God of Abraham, Isaac and Jacob in his dispute with the Sadducees over the possibility of

---

57. Sheridan, *Genesis 12–50*, 2.
58. Hagner, *Matthew 1–13*, 50.
59. Keener, *Matthew*, 124.

resurrection from the dead (Matthew 22:32; Mark 12:26; Luke 20:37). France explains that the force of Jesus' argument here is that if the living God identifies himself with Abraham, Isaac and Jacob, then these patriarchs cannot be truly dead, and so must be alive with God after their earthly life is finished. He concedes this is an argument premised on faith rather than logic, and so it may not have convinced the Sadducees.[60] Nolland concurs that "God will not have continued to advertise himself as God of the Patriarchs if he had long ago finished with them and abandoned them to the grave!"[61]

Fourth, familiarity with the stories of Abraham is seen in the parable of the rich man and Lazarus in Luke 16:19–31. The parable itself appears to have two messages: a warning of the dangerous corrupting influence of wealth and the reality of death as the point of final judgment. The fact that Lazarus, the poor man who dies destitute, is carried by the angels to *Abraham's bosom* (16:22) "is likely to express close intimacy."[62] Abraham's presence in paradise confirms the view that Lazarus is now in the most exalted place of blessedness it is possible to reside. As with earlier discussions of Abrahamic patronage, the parable makes the point that the only legitimate claim to have Abraham as father comes from lives that reflect repentance. Green suggests that not only do the rich man's actions show he cannot have Abraham as his father, his request that Lazarus runs errands for him further emphasizes his lack of comprehension of his own situation, as Abraham was "a model of hospitality to strangers, a model that this wealthy man has manifestly not followed with regard to Lazarus."[63]

Fifth, in John's Gospel, reference to Abraham comes primarily in chapter 8, where Jesus disputes origin and authenticity with his opponents. They claim Abrahamic descent (John 8:33, 39), a claim that Jesus simultaneously does not deny (8:37) but also refutes (8:39–40) on the basis that true descendants of Abraham would not behave as they do. The crux of the debate is that Jesus claims both temporal and spiritual superiority to Abraham in the powerful phrase, *Before Abraham was, I am!* (John 8:58). The Jews understand this as a claim to divinity, and regarding Jesus' words as blasphemy. They pick up rocks to stone him with, the prescribed punishment for blasphemy. Keener suggests this whole

---

60. France, *Matthew*, 840–41.
61. Nolland, *Luke 18:35—24:53*, 968.
62. Nolland, *Luke 9:21—18:34*, 829.
63. Green, *Luke*, 608.

exchange is rooted in a debate about the true nature of freedom and spiritual parentage; Jesus emphasizes that spiritual descent from Abraham comes only via faith in Jesus himself.[64] Jesus bases his claim to spiritual superiority on the testimony of both God (8:54–55) and Abraham himself (8:56); the claim that Abraham foresaw Jesus' day is a claim to divinity (8:56), a point that it takes Jesus' opponents a while to understand.

Sixth, Stephen recounts basic details of the life of Abraham in his speech in Acts 7:2–8, and refers to the God of Abraham as he develops his argument (Acts 7:16, 17, 32). Bruce explains that one key point Stephen makes throughout Acts 7 is that God's presence and activity is not restricted to one land; thus, Abraham meets God in Mesopotamia, not Canaan.[65] God's revelation of himself was so glorious that Abraham had no choice but to follow where he was called. He was given nothing tangible on which to build his faith: "he believed the bare word of God, and acted upon it."[66] Witherington concurs that Stephen's initial focus on Abraham receiving his call in Mesopotamia is part of Stephen's rhetorical route to his conclusion that God is at work outside the confines of the Jerusalem temple. Witherington also points out that there is no real mention of Abraham's faith; rather, Stephen's case is that God is at work, through Abraham, as through the other patriarchs and figures of history, whom Stephen will claim are all precursors to the faith of Jesus Christ.[67]

Paul's Use of Abraham in Galatians 3

Galatians is probably Paul's most polemical letter. In essence his argument is that pagans who have decided to follow Jesus do not first have to become Jews in order to follow their new faith. Reference to Abraham is crucial for Paul's argument because he is an example of a pagan who chose to follow God's call.

Longenecker explains that within the rabbinic writings, "Abraham is often affectionately called 'a bag of myrrh,' for 'just as myrrh is the most excellent of spices, so Abraham was the chief of all righteous men' (*Cant. Rab.* 1.13)." He adds that within Jewish thought, two points are constantly made about Abraham: first, that he was counted righteous because of his

---

64. Keener, *John*, 746–74.
65. Bruce, *Acts*, 130–35.
66. Bruce, *Acts*, 135.
67. Witherington, *Acts*, 266–67.

faith under testing, and second, that the faith mentioned in Genesis 15:6 must be linked with the covenant and circumcision in Genesis 17:4–14. Therefore, Abraham is seen as having anticipated and vicariously kept the full law revealed to Moses on Mount Sinai through his acceptance of circumcision and his willingness to offer Isaac on the altar of Mount Moriah.[68]

Philo argues that Abraham became the first monotheist because of divine revelation. Discussing the statement in Genesis 12:7 that God appeared to Abraham, he explains that it was *not that the wise man saw God but that God appeared to the wise man; for it was impossible for any one to comprehend by his own unassisted power the true living God, unless he himself displayed and revealed himself to him* (*De Abrahamo* 80). Josephus has a similar view, describing Abraham as

> a person of great wisdom both for understanding all things and persuading his hearers, and no mistaken in his opinions; for which reason he began to have higher notions of virtue than others had, and he determined to renew and change the opinion all men happened to have concerning God; for he was the first to publish this notion, that there was but one God, the Creator of the universe; and that as to other [gods], if they contributed anything to the happiness of men, that each of them afforded it only according to his appointment, and not by their own power. (*Antiquities* 1.154–55)

Paul operates within this thought world, but also seeks to redefine it, drawing a distinction between works of the law and faith. This allows Paul to argue that descent from Abraham is demonstrated by obedient faith. Paul also cites the promise related to Abraham's seed (in the singular, Genesis 13:15; 17:8), and takes it as a reference to Christ. Paul allows the normal collective meaning of *seed* only in the context of being *in Christ*. Thus, by means of union with Christ (Galatians 3:26–28), "Christians are joined with the single seed of Abraham and thereby find themselves to be collective 'descendants of Abraham.'"[69] One enters into true Abrahamic descent solely by participation in Christ.

Witherington adds, "Paul uses Abraham to make the positive point that the Galatians already have and will continue to receive the divine benefits they need on the basis of faith, just as Abraham did." But Paul also wants to make a negative point: that following the law can have

---

68. Longenecker, *Galatians*, 110–11.
69. Longenecker, *Triumph of Abraham's God*, 133.

dangerous consequences. In his discussion of Paul's quotation of Genesis 15:6 in Galatians 3:6, Witherington explains that it was important for Paul to be able to cite a text that showed Abraham's faith and his being reckoned as righteous and receiving a promise of blessing before there was any mention of circumcision as a sign of covenant (see Genesis 17) or of Abraham's faithful obedience in relation to offering Isaac as a sacrifice in Genesis 22. Although Paul redefines Jewish thinking about Abraham, he does seem indebted to the view that Abraham was "the prototype of the first proselyte and first convert to Jewish monotheism who abandoned idols at the call of God."[70]

The Analogy of Hagar and Sarah

Witherington notes parallels between how Paul and Philo use the story of Hagar and Sarah. Philo likens Hagar to preliminary learning, in grammar, geometry, astronomy, rhetoric and music, while Sarah represents virtue, a godly life (*De Congressu* 11). Philo goes on to explain the benefits of these minor subjects. Grammar gives intelligence and abundant learning through the study of history. Music teaches appreciation of harmony and rhythm. Geometry teaches one to appreciate equality and by extension also justice. Rhetoric sharpens the mind and trains a man to speak well. Finally, dialectic science enables one to distinguish truth from falsehood (*De Congressu* 15–18). All this learning is a profitable precursor to the acquisition of true virtue, just as a baby is fed milk before moving on to solid food (*De Congressu* 19). Philo goes on to argue that Hagar symbolizes that which is earthly, temporary and changeable; Sarah that which is heavenly, permanent and fixed. This is not to reject Hagar, or the learning she represents, but rather to ensure it is put in its proper place (*De Congressu* 20–24).

Witherington suggests that within Galatians, the analogy of Hagar and Sarah is used by Paul to equate Hagar with the agitators in the Galatian church, that is, those who are arguing Christians must obey the Mosaic law as part of their faith in Christ. Just as Abraham cast Hagar out of his family, so the Galatian Christians must cast the agitators from their church. The logical corollary of this is that Paul is the "woman" who bore the Galatians in freedom, which is why Galatians 4:19–20 refers to

---

70. Witherington, *Grace in Galatia*, 217.

Paul as the mother in labor until Christ is formed in the converts. Paul's main focus in discussing Sarah and Hagar is to contrast two covenants.[71]

Longenecker notes that while charges of idolatry are often leveled against Ishmael in the rabbinic writings, they are more ambivalent about Hagar, with some according her higher status. According to the rabbis, it was Ishmael's idolatry that led Abraham to expel him and his mother from his family (*Exodus Rabbah* 1.1) as well as the fact that he persecuted his younger brother.[72] Jewish tradition holds that Isaac was willing to offer himself in sacrifice:

> Ishmael said to Isaac: "I am more righteous that you in good deeds, for you were circumcised at eight days [and so could not prevent your circumcision], but I at thirteen years [and so accepted circumcision willingly]." "On account of one limb would you incense me?," he [Isaac] replied. "Were the Holy One, blessed be He, to say unto me: 'Sacrifice yourself before me,' I would obey." Straightaway, "God did tempt Abraham." (*Sanhedrin* 89b)

Longenecker adds that we cannot know whether this tradition was clearly developed by the time Paul wrote Galatians (although it was doubtless extant by the time the Qur'an was compiled), and that Paul has his own interest in the story of Hagar and Sarah, namely, using it as a way of attacking his opponents within the Galatian church. Longenecker concurs with Witherington that there are similarities between Paul's and Philo's usage of the Hagar-Sarah story. Both contrast the slave and the free; both note the two sons, that Hagar and Ishmael are banished while Sarah and Isaac are favored. In both, Hagar and Ishmael are the preparatory, preliminary stage, superseded by something greater. But he concludes that this indicates nothing more than both men read the Genesis account and used it for their own purposes.[73]

Paul's Use of Abraham in Romans 4

Moo argues that Paul has a particular purpose in citing Genesis 15:6 in Romans 4:3. This is the first time that faith is mentioned in the Bible, and one of the few where it is connected with attaining righteousness. Moreover, if Genesis 15:6 is understood in the sense that the *reckoning of*

---

71. Witherington, *Grace in Galatia*, 325–27.
72. Longenecker, *Galatians*, 201–2.
73. Longenecker, *Galatians*, 203–5.

righteousness to Abraham means *accounting to him a righteousness that does not belong to him*, then Paul's argument is a fair one.[74]

Kruse concurs with Moo's argument, referring to contemporaneous Jewish arguments that linked Abraham's righteousness with his willingness to offer Isaac and his acceptance of the covenant of circumcision. Paul, Kruse explains, has to define Abraham's faith according to Paul's own understanding, namely, that it precedes any form of action, a point Paul expands upon in Romans 4:9–12.[75]

Abraham in James 2

Bauckham explains that James uses Abraham as the premier example of one who was justified by his faith (James 2:23), but also by his works, because those were "the product and completion of his faith."[76] James does not make a particular distinction between faith and faithfulness; it is Abraham's faithful obedience when faced with the divine test of being asked to offer his son that demonstrates he has faith in God. For James, action demonstrates faith; Abraham's love for God is shown through his actions.[77]

McKnight concurs that Abraham was the "weightiest argument that James could find."[78] McKnight suggests that for the community to whom James writes, being called righteous means that life and behavior conformed to the Torah as interpreted by Jesus. James uses Abraham as a paradigm of hospitality, who accepts divine provision of the perfect sacrifice in place of his own son Isaac. This challenges James' audience to likewise put their faith into action through how they welcome and care for others.[79]

Abraham in Hebrews 11

Lane notes that in the list of heroes of the faith in Hebrews 11, Abraham occupies the most space (11:8–12, 17–19). Abraham illustrates faith in four ways. First, he sets out on a journey, trusting the ultimate

74. Moo, *Romans*, 261–62.
75. Kruse, *Romans*, 204–11.
76. Bauckham, *James*, 122.
77. Bauckham, *James*, 122–24.
78. McKnight, *James*, 245.
79. McKnight, *James*, 245–51.

destination to God. Second, he lived in a foreign land expectant that God would provide his ultimate home. Third, he fathers a child in his old age, and fourth, he offers that very son back to God, confident that if needs be, God can raise his son from death.[80]

DeSilva explains that when Hebrews introduces the example of Abraham offering Isaac, the focus of the discussion of faith in chapter 11 shifts to emphasize two points: first, that "the promise of God is more powerful than death," and second, that those who have faith look beyond death to the fulfilment of those promises. Indeed, Hebrews 11:17–18 seems to imply that Abraham expected God to raise Isaac to life after the sacrifice; thus, Abraham is an example of one who trusts in "the irrevocability of God's promise" rather than one who simply loves and obeys God.[81]

Conclusion

For the New Testament, Abraham is a paradigm of pure faith that trusts unflinchingly in the promises of God. In a sense this makes him a type of Christ, who was fully obedient to the Father, in a fashion that even Abraham could not match. In another sense, Abraham is the forefather of the Christian, the one who does not count the cost of obedience, but simply trusts in the promises of God and lives accordingly.

Claiming Abraham

Carol Bakhos describes the figure of Abraham as "at once a uniform and divisive figure" with respect to Judaism, Christianity and Islam.[82] Bakhos argues that the three faiths conceptualize Abraham differently. For Jews, he is the father of a people "with whom God makes an everlasting, exclusive covenant, the Jews." But for Christians, he is the father of all who believe; thus, his descendants have a spiritual, not a biological relationship with him. For Muslims, Abraham is the first monotheist, father to Ishmael and Isaac, a *hanif*.[83]

The discussion in this chapter has brought out at least five points for Christians and Muslims to discuss. First, Abraham was the first

80. Lane, *Hebrews 9–13*, 347–66.
81. DeSilva, *Hebrews*, 403–4.
82. Bakhos, *Family of Abraham*, 1.
83. Bakhos, *Family of Abraham*, 9.

monotheist. But how did he share this belief, and with whom did he share it? Second, the birth of his son Isaac was heralded by an angelic annunciation. But what does the birth of Isaac signify, and what is to be made of the manner in which it is announced? Third, Abraham almost sacrificed a son in obedience to the commands of God. But which son was offered, where was he offered, and what is the significance of Abraham's act of obedience? Fourth, what does it mean for Abraham to be described as a friend of God? Can Abraham argue with God, as Genesis records him doing over the fate of Sodom and Gomorrah? Does friendship with God mean Abraham is sinless, or does he still fear for his own life, and lie or otherwise scheme to protect himself? Finally, Abraham is understood typologically, but as a type of whom? Is he a prototypical Muslim? A precursor to Christian faith? A type of Muhammad or a type of Christ?

Joseph

THE STORY OF JOSEPH is one of divine control over history, the sovereign direction of events that seem bad in order to accomplish God's good purposes for his people. The precise understanding of these events and their interpretation differs between the Qur'an and the Bible. While in the Qur'an Joseph functions as a type of Muhammad and a paradigm for all believers to imitate, in the Bible he is a patriarch whose flaws are as instructive as his triumphs.

The Qur'anic story of Joseph is all found in *surah Yusuf*, the twelfth chapter of the Qur'an. Although there are two other brief references (*al-An'am* 6:84–87; *Ghafir* 40:34), this chapter will focus entirely on *surah Yusuf*. The story of Joseph in the Qur'an stresses monotheism. It makes Joseph and Judah the central characters; others are unnamed. Joseph acts as a type of Muhammad. Tottoli describes the parallels between their life stories: both are in danger for their lives because of their teaching, both suffer, yet both triumph in the end, and are generous to their brothers (which in Muhammad's case means the Meccans) who have rejected and despised them.[1]

Surah Yusuf skillfully combines a range of sources, including Samaritan materials, disputing and challenging the dominant Jewish interpretation. Thus, as Haleem explains, while the basic story is the same in the Qur'an and the Bible, the function of the story differs, and so "the tone, the time span, the characterization and the artistic forms" are also different. In Genesis, the account of Joseph is part of a historical narrative of origins, while in the Qur'an it is a discrete account that is written "to strengthen the Prophet and the believers and give them guidance."[2]

---

1. Tottoli, *Biblical Prophets*, 31.
2. Haleem, *Understanding the Qur'an*, 142.

Haleem adds that the Qur'anic account is much more compact in comparison with the verbose biblical story. He illustrates this point by noting that the Qur'an's account of Joseph is a mere one hundred verses, ten pages of Arabic, while the Arabic Bible's narrative of Joseph runs to four hundred and fifty verses, taking twenty-six pages. He further explains that while the biblical account is often regarded as a novel, the Qur'an is not a story or a national history. Rather, it is written solely for religious purposes. Thus, both Jacob and Joseph in the Qur'an are Prophets, models to be followed (*al-Ahzab* 33:21). Joseph is a universal, permanent guide whom believers are supposed to imitate. Haleem concludes that because we read the text with the presuppositions of the account with which we are more familiar (Muslims the Qur'an, Jews and Christians the Bible), the other account is dissatisfying because we feel it misses the point. But, Haleem argues, we must understand the different purpose of each text and read them accordingly.[3] In what follows I will first work though the story, contrasting the Qur'anic and biblical accounts, before discussing the significance of some of the differences identified. The third area of discussion is how the story of Joseph has been used elsewhere in the Old Testament, in extrabiblical literature, in the New Testament and in Christian Syriac sources. The concluding section asks what the story of Joseph teaches us today.

Significant Differences in the Story of Joseph in the Bible and the Qur'an

Arguably the greatest difference between the narrative of Joseph's life in the Bible and the Qur'an is whether divine control is explicit or implicit. In the Bible it is not until the very close of the story that Joseph explains that God has been in sovereign control, and that although his brothers intended to do him harm, God was working for the good of Joseph and his people (Genesis 50:19–20). By contrast, in the Qur'an God speaks regularly; the text is full of "interpolations that urge believers to see the hand of God in human affairs."[4] The difference in focus is seen clearly in the foreknowledge that Jacob has in the Qur'anic account, an understanding that is wholly lacking in the biblical narrative.

---

3. Haleem, *Understanding the Qur'an*, 156–60.
4. Wessels, *Torah, the Gospels, and the Qur'an*, 103.

Second, Joseph himself is characterized differently in the two texts. In Genesis he is introduced as an arrogant and brash young man, boasting of his ability to interpret dreams and subject to his brothers' jealousy. Over the time of his slavery and imprisonment he changes, but he still appears scheming in his treatment of his brothers once he has been elevated to second in command of Egypt. When Joseph eventually reveals himself to his brothers, Genesis describes him as being overcome with emotion, a reference not found in the Qur'an. Finally, the closing episodes in Genesis, where Joseph enslaves the people of Egypt in return for grain, Jacob blesses his children, and Joseph gives instructions about the burial of his bones, are all missing from the Qur'an. There are other details that are different from the account found in Genesis. To give two further examples: in the Qur'an Joseph's mother is alive at the end of the story, and in *Yusuf* 12:80 the brother who speaks is the eldest (that is, Rueben, not Judah as in the Genesis account).

A further significant omission is the interruption of the story of Judah and Tamar, which is found in Genesis 38 but nowhere in the Qur'an. The relationship between Genesis 38 and other biblical texts has engendered considerable academic speculation. Some scholars focus on potential connections with the story of Tamar and Amnon in 2 Samuel 13. The basis of the arguments is the similarity in name, as these are the only two biblical episodes featuring a woman named Tamar. Ho establishes a dozen parallels between the two texts, and Leuchter argues that the author of Genesis 38 knew the story found in 2 Samuel 13, although he also notes significant differences between the two accounts.[5]

Leuchter also notes that there are sound reasons for understanding Genesis 38 as part of the wider literary unit of Genesis 37–50. One of these is the theme of recognition; as Tamar is initially not recognized but later recognized by Judah, so Joseph is initially not recognized but then recognized by his brothers.[6] While the concept of recognition does establish a relationship between Genesis 38 and the wider unit, this motif is insufficient to argue for literary unity. But Wenham proposes further connections. First, by placing the episode immediately after Joseph is sold to slavery, the narrator creates suspense. Second, it illustrates key theological principles also at work in the wider story, notably the righting of injustice, and divine preference for the younger child. Third, there is

---

5. Ho, "The Stories of the Family Troubles"; Leuchter, "Genesis 38."
6. Leuchter, "Genesis 38", 210–11.

a striking contrast between Jacob's grief upon hearing Joseph has died, and Judah's absence of grief when his two sons die. Wenham argues that Genesis 37–50 should be understood as the story of Jacob, not of Joseph, as the narrative introduction, *This is the story of the family of Jacob* (Genesis 37:2), makes clear. Thus, the narrator does not just tell Joseph's story, but also a tale of another son. Finally, Genesis 38 deals with the theme of childlessness, a topic that is integral to the overall focus in Genesis on God's promises of land, nationhood and blessing to the nations. Without children, these promises cannot be fulfilled; and since Judah is the ancestor of King David, it is important that we understand his family tree.[7] For Hamilton, inserting the story of Judah and Tamar in its present location is the "only logical place" for it to appear. Judah is young and single in Genesis 37; and putting it much later would disrupt the flow of the Joseph narrative. Hamilton also identifies thematic and linguistic parallels that make this the best place. There is the examination of a robe—Joseph's torn and bloody one, and Judah's, which he leaves with Tamar. There is the use of the blood of a kid, and the offer of a kid. There is a contrast between Jacob who would not be consoled (Genesis 37:35) over Joseph, and Judah, who was consoled (Genesis 38:12) over his wife's death. There are parallel themes of deception (the brothers, Tamar) and of seduction (Potiphar's wife, Tamar), as well as grief or its absence, as Jacob mourns the apparent loss of one son, but Judah is unmoved by the loss of two.[8]

The Qur'an does not share any of these concerns, and so it is understandable why the story of Judah and Tamar does not feature in the Qur'anic account of Jacob and Joseph. The omission is significant for the comparative exercise this chapter undertakes, as it underlines the fact that the biblical and Qur'anic accounts have very different objectives. The main characters may have the same names and experience the same issues, but they are not necessarily exactly the same people. The purpose of the narratives differs between the texts, a point that becomes clear in the comparison below.

7. Wenham, *Genesis 16–50*, 363–65.
8. Hamilton, *Genesis 18–50*, 431–32.

A Read Through Surah Yusuf (12) in Contrast with Genesis 37–50

This section works through *Yusuf*, noting particularly the passages that strike me, a Christian reader, as being distinct from the account in Genesis. The first of these is *Yusuf* 12:4–6, where Joseph goes to his father Jacob, and tells Jacob of the dream he has just had, of eleven stars, the sun and the moon prostrating before him. There is no dream about sheaves of wheat (as in Genesis 37:5–8). Jacob warns Joseph not to tell his brothers of this dream to his brothers, because if he does, the brothers will hatch a plot against him. Jacob warns that *surely Satan is a clear enemy of mankind* (*Yusuf* 12:5), indicating that the whole of Joseph's experience should be interpreted as a sign of Satan attacking humanity. This is confirmed in verse 7, which explains that the story of Joseph is full of signs for inquirers; that is to say, it provides guidance for believers on how to live.

The differences with the account in Genesis are readily apparent. First, Joseph speaks only to Jacob of his dream, not the whole family, and he tells of only one dream. There is no mention of the bundles of wheat that are found in Genesis 37:5–8. More significantly, Joseph's arrogance that is clear in Genesis is missing in *Yusuf*. Similarly, Jacob in *Yusuf* is a wise and discerning Prophet, who warns Joseph to keep the dream to himself, as he foresees potential spiritual attack. By contrast, in Genesis we see a man who is outraged as his son's impudence, but at the same time he has a real soft spot for him, treating him as the clear favorite amongst his twelve sons, fueling his other sons' bitterness and jealousy, which explode in murderous rage.

In the Qur'an, Joseph's brothers discuss what they want to do with him; Reynolds[9] notes that this conversation takes place before Joseph's brothers leave the house, in contrast with the Genesis account where the plot to dispose of Joseph is a spur of the moment reaction to seeing him in the field. None of the brothers are named in the Qur'an, but they decide that they will not kill him, just throw him into a well and hope a passing caravan takes him. They ask Jacob to allow them to take Joseph with them, presumably while they pasture the sheep. Jacob is reluctant to do so, citing his fear that a wolf will eat Joseph (*Yusuf* 12:13). Yet Jacob consents to the brothers' wishes, and they take Joseph away and throw him in a well. God speaks to Joseph while he is in the well, telling him that he will have the chance to challenge his brothers over their behavior,

---

9. Reynolds, *Qur'an and the Bible*, 363.

although they will not know who he is (*Yusuf* 12:15). The brothers return to Jacob with Joseph's shirt covered in *fake blood*, and tell him that a wolf has eaten Joseph. Jacob refuses to believe this, saying they have made the story up and that *God is the one to be sought for help against what you allege* (*Yusuf* 12:18). Meanwhile, Joseph is found in the well, and is sold in Egypt *for a few dirhams* (*Yusuf* 12:20), that is, a small sum, to a man who is unnamed, but presumably is Potiphar, one of Pharaoh's officials. This man treats Joseph well, regarding him as someone who may be adopted as a son (*Yusuf* 12:21). God's sovereign control over the situation is clear:

> In this way We established Joseph in the land, and (this took place) in order that We might teach him about the interpretations of dreams. God is in control of His affair, but most people do not know (it). (*Yusuf* 12:21)

This truncated episode also has significant differences from the Genesis account. One important disparity is that in Genesis Jacob sends Joseph to bring supplies to his brothers. Joseph cannot find them, and asks a man for directions (Genesis 37:12–17). Exegetical tradition has debated the identity of this individual, with some interpreters arguing that he was an angel, sent by God to ensure Joseph is captured and sent to Egypt so he can eventually save his family. The conception of divine control is implicit in the Genesis account, but much more explicit in *Yusuf*, as illustrated by the quote above. The Qur'an wants the hearer to be in no doubt who is in control, while in Genesis matters are not so clear cut.

There are other differences in detail that may be significant. In Genesis there is a more protracted debate about what to do with Joseph, and the brothers do not agree, with some wanting to kill him and others content to sell him. Reuben is not present when Joseph is sold for twenty pieces of silver. By contrast, the Qur'an makes no mention of the brothers profiting financially from Joseph's capture. This may be because the early church identified Joseph as a type of Christ; his being sold for twenty pieces of silver is an echo of the price Judas was paid for betraying Jesus. By omitting this detail, the Qur'an can thus deny the plausibility of this typological reading.

The clothing that is torn and lie told to Jacob also differ. In Genesis it is a richly ornamented robe that is dipped in the blood of an animal from Jacob's own flock, identified as simply being from a *wild animal* (Genesis 37:31). In the Qur'an it is a shirt, and the blood is alleged to be that of a wolf. In Genesis Jacob is convinced, tearing his clothes and mourning the death of his favorite son for many days, refusing all comfort. But in *surah Yusuf* Jacob sees straight through his sons' lies and rebukes them, declaring his faith in God as sovereign. The stories thus take on a different narrative trajectory. In Genesis we have a foolish but grief-stricken father, while in *Yusuf* we see Jacob as a wise and godly man who recognizes the divine ordering of events. These differences continue as Joseph establishes himself in Egypt.

Although it is not explicitly stated in the Qur'an, the presumption is that Joseph prospers in Potiphar's house. But all is not straightforward, as Potiphar's wife has taken a shine to Joseph, and attempts to seduce him. He resists her attempts; God is using this episode to strengthen Joseph. The Qur'an states this all took place *in order that We might turn evil and immorality away from him* (*Yusuf* 12:24). Joseph is a paragon of virtue. When he is alone with Potiphar's wife, she again tries to seduce him, and he runs from her. As they both run to the door, she tears his shirt from behind. They meet Potiphar at the door; the wife declares Joseph the sexual predator; he protests his innocence. Potiphar sits in judgment between them, proposing that if Joseph's shirt is torn at the front, he is guilty, but if it is torn at the back, he is innocent. The shirt is duly examined and found to be torn at the back, and so Joseph is declared innocent. Potiphar rebukes his wife, warning her of the dangers of her plotting and the need to repent (*Yusuf* 12:25–29).

This version is very different from how the story plays out in Genesis. The attempt at seduction is the same, and in both texts Joseph makes a speech declaring he will not give in to temptation. In the Qur'an he states, *God's refuge! Surely he is my lord, and he has given me a good dwelling place. Surely the evildoers do not prosper* (*Yusuf* 12:23), referring to the generosity Potiphar has shown him. Similarly in Genesis Joseph says to Potiphar's wife, *Look, with me here, my master has no concern about anything in the house and he has put everything that he has in my hand. He is not greater in this house than I am, nor has he kept back anything from me except yourself, because you are his wife. How then could I do this great wickedness, and sin against God?* (Genesis 39:8–9).

Thus in both texts Joseph recognizes the generosity of his master, and refuses to abuse his position of power, primarily because of his faith in God. The difference comes, first, in the fact that *Yusuf* 12:27 records that there was a witness, and second, in the clothing associated with Potiphar's wife's attempt to persuade Joseph to have sex with her. While in the Qur'an Joseph's shirt is torn from behind, in Genesis Joseph leaves behind his garment in Potiphar's wife's hand, and so is found guilty by Potiphar and thrown into prison for attempted rape of Potiphar's wife. Arguably this exposes a significant difference between the Bible and the Qur'an. While the former is happy for even prophetic role models to be declared guilty, the Qur'an endeavors to ensure that those who are a guide for godly living are always vindicated and shown to be pure.

There follows in the Qur'an a story that is not in the Genesis account (*Yusuf* 12:30–34). Joseph is still in Potiphar's house at this point. The women of the city are gossiping about Potiphar's wife and her obsession with Joseph. She decides to demonstrate to them why she has become so besotted, and invites them all to eat at her house. They duly accept, and join her. Partway through the meal, she orders Joseph to come out and wait on the women. As Joseph comes out, the women are reclining with knives in their hands, probably to cut fruit. Yet one look at Joseph's beauty is so dazzling that the women forget they are holding the knives, and cut their hands, declaring that Joseph cannot be mortal but must be an angel (*Yusuf* 12:31). Joseph declares that he will never give in to his master's wife's scheming, stating he would rather be imprisoned that comply. He is eventually imprisoned, although there is no statement that his captors presumed him guilty, as the Genesis account records. *Yusuf* 12:35 implies that Joseph is seen as a threat to the women of the city, because of their obsession with his beauty.

The origin of this story is difficult to ascertain. Kugel cites a similar account found in *Midrash Tanhuma* and *Midrash ha-Gadol*, which he dates to a similar time period as the composition of the Qur'an.[10] Kugel then also attempts to argue that there is, in fact, a reference to the incident of the women with the knives in the account of Joseph's life in Genesis. The crucial phrase for his argument is the phrase *after a time* (which could also be translated *after these things*) in Genesis 39:7. For Kugel, this is a reference to this incident,[11] but this is at best an argument from silence that is perhaps, as Bal notes, driven more by an ideological commitment to the primacy and truth of the Bible than by any strong evidence to support it.[12] I see no reason to argue that this passage is biblical. Indeed, the argument of this chapter is that the Qur'an and the Bible

---

10. Kugel, *In Potiphar's House*, 29–30.
11. Kugel, *In Potiphar's House*, 41.
12. Bal, *Loving Yusuf*, 125, 166–73.

recount the story of Joseph for very different purposes, and so reference to different specific incidents in his life is unsurprising.

In the Qur'anic account, Joseph is imprisoned for an unspecified time before two young men enter the prison. There is no account of Joseph finding favor in the eyes of the chief jailer, nor does Joseph take charge of the prison. Moreover, the two new prisoners are not named as the cupbearer and baker to Pharaoh, but they have the same dreams as found in the Genesis account, and the interpretation given is the same. The cupbearer is restored to his position in Pharaoh's court in three days, while the baker is executed in three days (hanged in the Genesis account, crucified in the Qur'an). In both the Bible and the Qur'an, Joseph asks to be remembered by the cupbearer, but in both cases he is forgotten. The significant difference is that in the Qur'an it is clearly stated that this was because Satan made him forget (*Yusuf* 12:42). The other main contrast between the two accounts is that the narrative of the dreams is much longer in Genesis, with more interest in the emotional experiences of all involved. *Surah Yusuf*, by contrast, pays little attention to this, concentrating instead on a speech in which Joseph extols the virtues of monotheism, of faith in the God of Abraham, Isaac and Jacob, including recognition that God alone is sovereign and that he alone is judge. This is *the right religion, but most people do not know it* (*Yusuf* 12:37–40). In the Genesis account, Joseph is clear that only God gives the interpretation of dreams, but he makes no mention of the importance of monotheism (Genesis 40:8).

In both the Qur'an and the Bible, the ruler of Egypt then has dreams he cannot understand. In *Surah Yusuf* he is termed *king*, while Genesis calls him *Pharaoh*, but either way he dreams of seven fat cows followed by seven thin cows, and of seven fat ears of corn followed by seven thin, dry ears of corn. The exposition of the dreams is much longer in Genesis than in *Surah Yusuf*, but in both cases the cupbearer suddenly remembers Joseph and suggests he will be able to interpret the dream. The order of events then differs.

In Genesis the cupbearer tells Pharaoh that Joseph can interpret his dream. Joseph is duly summoned from prison, and after shaving and changing his clothes, he comes before Pharaoh, explaining that while he cannot interpret it, God can, and then hears the dream and duly gives the interpretation (Genesis 41:1–32). By contrast, in *surah Yusuf* Joseph gives the interpretation while still in prison. The king summons Joseph to him, but Joseph refuses to go until all those who have slandered Joseph admit their guilt. Joseph tells the messenger to return to the king and ask him about the women who cut their hands; they admit their attempts to seduce Joseph, and then Potiphar's wife does the same. Joseph is duly vindicated, declaring that he has not pronounced himself innocent, but rather that God has done so (*Yusuf* 12:53).

There is also a difference in how Joseph is exalted. In Genesis he simply offers advice to Pharaoh, that he should find a *discerning and wise man* and put him in charge of Egypt (Genesis 41:33). Having consulted with his officials, Pharaoh concludes that Joseph is the best candidate and duly appoints him to the role. But in the Qur'an Joseph gives the king a simple instruction: *Set me over the storehouses of the land. Surely I am a skilled overseer* (*Yusuf* 12:55), a move that is immediately interpreted as the sovereign hand of God ensuring Joseph is put where God wants him to be (*Yusuf* 12:56). The lesson this teaches is a generic one for all believers, as God explains:

> We smite whomever We please with Our mercy, and We do not let the reward of the doers of good go to waste. But the reward of the Hereafter is indeed better for those who believe and guard (themselves). (*Yusuf* 12:56–57)

The biblical account then explains how Joseph established his rule in Egypt, and used the seven years of plenty to prepare for the famine that was coming. It also records the origin of the two tribes of Manasseh and Ephraim, which is of crucial importance to the people of Israel (Genesis 41:46–52). The Qur'an has no interest, and so makes no mention of this, jumping immediately to the appearance of Joseph's brothers, looking for food.

In the Qur'an, the first episode of the brothers coming for grain is incredibly compressed. There is no dialogue about having a brother who has not come, yet Joseph asks for him to be brought next time. The retelling clearly presumes knowledge of the story, although whether that is the Genesis text or another retelling is a moot point. There are common features, such as the brothers' merchandise or money being returned to them, although it is in different places: in the Qur'an it is in Canaan in Jacob's presence, while in Genesis one brother finds his money on the return journey (*Yusuf* 12:59–65; Genesis 42:25–28). There are other differences. One notable one is that in Genesis 42:22–23 Reuben rebukes his brothers, reminding them of his earlier plea that they not kill Joseph, and suggesting their current difficulties are divine punishment for their earlier actions.

In the Qur'an, when the brothers return to Jacob, they immediately ask to be allowed to return again with their brother Benjamin (who is not named in the text), else they will not be able to get any more food. Jacob does not display the reluctance found in the Genesis account (Genesis 43:1–14). Rather, having seen the food, and extracted a promise from them that they will bring Benjamin back, he consents. He also gives them an instruction not found in Genesis, to enter by different gates. This presumably means the eleven brothers are not to travel as a single group, but rather to enter the city separately, perhaps to avoid drawing attention to themselves. This possibly has something to do with avoiding the punishment of God, but the Qur'an is clear that God's sovereign control is not something that can be avoided (*Yusuf* 12:68).

The way in which Joseph reveals himself is also markedly different. First, in the Qur'an he draws Benjamin aside as soon as the brothers reach Egypt; Joseph then explains, *Surely I am your brother, so do not be distressed at what they have done* (*Yusuf* 12:69). There follows the episode of the hidden drinking cup, without any reference to a meal or any other form of hospitality practiced by Joseph (Genesis 43). The brothers have presumably left Egypt and are stopped on their way back to Canaan, and asked to give account of the king's cup, which is missing (note that in Genesis 44:4, the cup is said to belong to Joseph). In the Qur'an, as in Genesis, the brothers agree that the one in whose sack the cup is found shall be held liable for the theft. The cup is duly found in Benjamin's sack, and a general moral lesson is drawn from the episode:

> In this way We plotted for (the sake of) Joseph. He was not one to take his brother, in (accord with) the religion of the king, unless God had (so) pleased. We raise in rank whomever We please, and above everyone who has knowledge is the One who knows. (*Yusuf* 12:76)

Thus *surah Yusuf* continues to expound its theme of divine sovereignty, making it clear that any actions that seem questionable are in fact part of God's plan. Joseph's brothers then blame Joseph for stealing, compounding their earlier sins against him, as they suggest Benjamin is just like his brother Joseph, a thief. Joseph keeps his counsel at this and does not reveal his true identity (*Yusuf* 12:77). The brothers do offer one of their number in Benjamin's place, but Joseph rebuffs the offer, and it appears that Benjamin is the one who stays in Egypt, while the brothers return to Jacob to tell him what has happened.

On their return to Jacob, he rebukes them, accusing the brothers of making up the story, and speaking of his own patient trust in God as well as his continued grief for Joseph. The brothers grumble at this continued attitude, but Jacob is resolute, sending the brothers back to Egypt to search out news of Joseph and his brother. The implication is that Jacob knows God is in control and is about to reveal his sovereign plan (*Yusuf* 12:83–87).

On their third visit to Egypt, the brothers again come to Joseph, and again ask him to be generous to them in giving food (*Yusuf* 12:88). He questions them, asking if they knew what they did with Joseph and his brother in their ignorance. The brothers respond with a question of their own, asking if their interlocutor is Joseph, and he reveals himself to them. This all stands in marked contrast with the account in Genesis, as the Qur'an displays no interest in Joseph's emotions; there is no mention of tears at all. Instead, Joseph simply states:

> I am Joseph, and this is my brother. God has bestowed favor on us. Surely the one who guards (himself) and is patient—surely God does not let the reward of the doers of good go to waste. (*Yusuf* 12:90)

In response to this revelation, the brothers immediately admit they are sinners, and Joseph tells them they will be forgiven. There are four notable differences with the account found in Genesis. First, Judah's speech in response to Joseph's stated intention to keep Benjamin prisoner. Judah speaks of the impact this will have on his father Jacob, and offers to become Joseph's slave instead (Genesis 44:18–34). Second, it is this offer that moves Joseph to tears, so that he at last reveals his true identity to his brothers. The emotional nature of this revelation is completely lacking in the Qur'an, which seems to have no interest in Joseph's emotional life. Third, the precise nature of God's plan in preserving Joseph seems to differ. In Genesis, Joseph reassures his brothers:

> And now do not be distressed, or angry with yourselves, because you sold me here; for God sent me before you to preserve life. (Genesis 45:5)

There is a contrast with the discussion in the Qur'an, where it is clear that Joseph has been preserved for a divine purpose, but that plan was not specifically the salvation of Israel (Jacob) and his descendants. Fourth, and finally, Pharaoh's joy and welcome of the news that Joseph's whole family will be coming to Egypt, not to mention his generosity toward them, is found only in Genesis, not in the Qur'an (Genesis 45:16–20).

In the Qur'an, once Joseph has revealed himself, the brothers are then instructed to take Joseph's shirt back to Jacob and put it on his face, which will restore his sight (*Yusuf* 12:91–93). As the caravan draws close to Jacob, he smells Joseph's scent, and when Joseph's shirt is put on his face it restores Jacob's sight, who then declares that he has received revelation from God that has allowed him to understand what has really been going on. The brothers then ask their father to intercede for their forgiveness, and Jacob does so, expecting God to forgive, as he is forgiving and compassionate (*Yusuf* 12:94–98). In Genesis, by contrast, Jacob does not believe the news until he sees the abundance of gifts that Joseph has sent, nor do his sons ask for his forgiveness. The text implies that even this may not have been enough, because God speaks to Jacob in a dream, reassuring him that he should go down to Egypt, and that when he dies there, Joseph will close his eyes (Genesis 46:2–4).

In *surah Yusuf* the whole family then return to Egypt and Joseph raises his parents onto the throne; and they prostrate themselves before him, an action that Joseph takes as the interpretation of the vision with which the *surah* began. This stands in contrast to Genesis 35:19, where Joseph's mother dies. Perhaps she is still alive at this point in the Qur'an's account to ensure that Joseph's first dream is fulfilled completely.[13] Joseph thanks and praises Allah for his mercy and grace, adding:

> My Lord, you have given me some of the kingdom, and taught me some of the interpretation of dreams. Creator of the heavens and the earth, You are my ally in this world and the Hereafter. Take me as one who has submitted [or "as a Muslim"] and join me with the righteous. (*Yusuf* 12:101)

The epilogue explains that the story is told for the benefit of believers in Muhammad's day, to call them from idolatry to worship of Allah (*Yusuf* 12:102–8), and the *surah* closes with a reminder that God sends only his messengers for the purpose of proclaiming his message (12:109–11). There are six notable omissions in contrast with the Genesis account. First, there is no dialogue with Pharaoh about where Joseph's family are to settle, a point that is crucial for the narrative in Exodus, but of no relevance to the Qur'anic account. Second, the genealogy of those who come to Egypt is not given. Third, Jacob does not bless his children.

---

13. Reynolds, *Qur'an and the Bible*, 384.

Fourth, Jacob does not die; indeed, his wife is still alive, contrary to the Genesis account. Fifth, the brothers do not come to Joseph, seeking reassurance that he will not take revenge on them now that their father has died. Sixth, Joseph does not give instructions regarding how his burial; in Genesis he orders his family to ensure his bones are not permanently buried, but are taken with the Israelites when they eventually leave Egypt, a command that is subsequently fulfilled during the Exodus.

Sources and Interpretations of the Story of Joseph

This section has five parts: an overview of the use of Joseph in extrabiblical material, a brief comment on how the *Stories of the Prophets* literature expands on *surah Yusuf*, the use of Joseph in the New Testament and by the church fathers, and a discussion of the influence of Christian Syriac texts.

Joseph in Jewish Sources

This section briefly discusses four extrabiblical Jewish references to Joseph. Kugel explains that ancient Jewish readers focused on Joseph as a paragon for resisting temptation, which is not necessarily the high point of the story from a modern perspective.[14] This is seen in 1 Maccabees 2, which lists examples of virtuous men who were faithful when tempted. Joseph is one such example, who *in the time of his distress kept the commandment* [the prohibition against adultery], *and became lord of Egypt* (1 Maccabees 2:53).

A second example is found in 4 Maccabees. Chapter 1 discusses the importance of abstinence and self-control, and then the second chapter introduces Joseph as an example of this virtue, specifically in relation to sexual temptation:

> And why it is amazing that the desires of the mind for the enjoyment of beauty are rendered powerless? It is for this reason, certainly, that the temperate Joseph is praised, because by mental efforts he overcame sexual desire. For when he was young and in his prime for intercourse, by his reason he nullified the frenzy of the passions. Not only is reason proved to rule over the frenzied urge of sexual desire, but also over every desire. (4 Maccabees 2:1–4)

---

14. Kugel, *In Potiphar's House*, 22.

Third, the book of *Jubilees* includes an extensive retelling of the story of Joseph, which includes his struggle to resist Potiphar's wife. Jubilees explains:

> And Joseph was good-looking and very handsome. And the wife of his master lifted up her eyes and saw Joseph and desired him. And she begged him to lie with her. And he did not surrender himself but he remembered the Lord and the words which Jacob, his father, used to read, which were from the words of Abraham, that there is no man who (may) fornicate with a woman who has a husband (and) that there is a judgment of death which is decreed for him in heaven before the Lord Most High. (*Jubilees* 39:5–6)

According to *Jubilees*, Joseph is tempted in this way for a whole year; eventually his master's wife locks him in the house with her and seizes him. He breaks free of her grasp, breaking the door of the house and fleeing naked. This is taken as incriminating him, and he is duly imprisoned.

Fourth, the *Testament of Joseph*, one of the *Testaments of the Twelve Patriarchs*, includes an extensive discussion of Joseph's struggles in resisting sexual temptation; of how he fasted, prayed, and pleaded with God for protection. The lesson brought out from this experience is the importance of trust and reliance on God in the fact of temptation.

Kugel remarks that the rabbis debated what it meant for Joseph to resist temptation. The crux of the argument is the Hebrew of Genesis 39:12. This reads, *And she caught him* bebigdo, *saying "Lie with me!"* The phrase *bebigdo* is traditionally translated *by his garment* but could also mean *in his betrayal*. From this alternative reading, some rabbis concluded that Joseph was genuinely tempted to have sexual relations with Potiphar's wife, and this moral wavering is argued to make him more human.[15]

In tractate *Sotah* of the Babylonian Talmud, the rabbis discuss Joseph's behavior, focusing especially on the verse, *And it came to pass about this time, that he [Joseph] went into the house to do his work* (Genesis 39:11).

> R. Johanan said: This teaches that both [Joseph and Potiphar's wife] had the intention of acting immorally. 'He went into the house to do his work'—Rab and Samuel [differ in their

---

15. Kugel, *In Potiphar's House*, 97–98.

interpretation]. One said that it really means to do his work; but the other said that he went to satisfy his desires. (*Sotah* 36b).[16]

Reynolds cites another section of the same passage, in which Joseph's father Jacob appears to him in a vision:

> That day was their feast-day, and they had all gone to their idolatrous temple; but she pretended to be ill because she thought, I shall not have an opportunity like today for Joseph to associate with me. And she caught him by his garment saying etc. At that moment his father's image came and appeared to him through the window and said: "Joseph, thy brothers will have their names inscribed upon the stones of the ephod and thine amongst theirs; is it thy wish to have thy name expunged from amongst theirs and be called an associate of harlots?" (*Sotah* 36b).[17]

Hamilton explains that it is possible that Joseph's proximity to Potiphar's wife, such that she can tear his clothing from him (Genesis 39:12), indicates he came very close to succumbing to her temptations.[18] This understanding is different from that of *surah Yusuf*, which presents Joseph as one who is completely unmoved by the charms of the woman who offers herself to him.

These developments of the account found in Genesis indicate the different ways the story can be read. Muslims and Christians can therefore discuss which account they find most convincing, and what the different accounts teach us about Joseph, ourselves and our relationship with God.

Stories of the Prophets

Kaltner and Mirza explain that further details about Joseph's story are added in the *Stories of the Prophets* literature. Various unnamed figures are identified: Rachel as Joseph's mother, Potiphar as his Egyptian master and Zuleikha as his wife. The youth Joseph is given a coat, and four other items are handed down to him from Abraham. There is a tradition that Joseph is sold in the slave markets dressed in fine clothes. An acquaintance of his father sees Joseph, and promises he will tell Jacob what has happened to his son. There are also traditions of appearances of Gabriel, both in the well that his brothers throw Joseph into and also once Joseph

16. Translation by Nashim, *Nazir, Sotah*.
17. Reynolds, *Qur'an and the Bible*, 368–69.
18. Hamilton, *Genesis 18–50*, 464–65.

is imprisoned. There is a tradition that Benjamin has three sons by the time he meets Joseph again. These three sons are named *Wolf*, *Blood* and *Joseph* as reminders of how Benjamin's full brother was taken from him.[19]

Wheeler recounts other traditions about Joseph. For example Sha'bi discusses the significance of Joseph's shirt:

> The shirt of Joseph has three verses: First, when they brought it to their father. They said, "A wolf ate him." He said to them, "If a wolf ate him, then his shirt should be torn." Second, when Joseph later rushed toward the door and the vizier's wife ripped his shirt from behind, the vizier knew that if Joseph had been stalking his wife, that the rip would have been in the front. Third, when Jacob cast the shirt over his face and became clear sighted."[20]

Ibn Kathir explains Joseph's beauty:

> In a report about the Prophet's Night Journey, he says: "I passed by Joseph and he had been given half the goodness." Suhayli and other scholars say that the meaning of this is that Joseph had half the beauty of Adam because God created Adam with his own hands, blew his breath into him, and he was the ultimate of human beauty. Because of this, the inhabitants of Paradise enter Paradise with the stature of Adam and beauty of Joseph.[21]

These Islamic accounts of Joseph's beauty raise an important point for discussion amongst Christians and Muslims. Was Joseph particularly handsome? Or was he just an ordinary man, with nothing particular to distinguish his physical appearance from that of his fellows? For Christians who develop their understanding of Joseph as a type of Christ, there is an attraction in arguing that he was simply an average person, with no beauty or majesty to attract people to him (Isaiah 53:2).

Joseph in the New Testament

Hamilton finds four uses of the Joseph story within the New Testament. First, it is part of Stephen's speech (Acts 7:9–16). Stephen's main point is to draw a distinction between Joseph and his brothers, challenging his audience as to who received divine grace and who did not. Moreover, Stephen draws parallels between the brothers and his own audience; as the brothers

---

19. Kaltner and Mirza, *Bible and the Qur'an*, 103.
20. Wheeler, *Prophets in the Qur'an*, 130.
21. Wheeler, *Prophets in the Qur'an*, 135.

wanted to kill Joseph, so his listeners want to kill him. Second, Jacob and Joseph are listed in Hebrews 11:21–22. Both are references to deathbed scenes, and in each case demonstrate a "future orientation, the deep conviction that God has a future for his people beyond the circumstances of the present."[22] Third, Hamilton proposes that in Matthew 1–2 the New Testament Joseph relives the experiences of his Old Testament counterpart. Both receive revelation in dreams; both go to Egypt. Both are involved with a king and children who become saviors and rescuers follow both. Finally, while he concedes there is no explicit parallel, Hamilton argues the words of the wicked tenant farmers in the parable of the vineyard—*Come! Let us kill him!*—parallel the brothers' desire to kill Joseph (Genesis 37:20; Matthew 21:33–46; Mark 12:1–12; Luke 20:9–19).[23]

Hamilton does not mention the reference to Joseph in the list of tribes in John's vision in Revelation 7:8, but this reference, together with the brief mention of Joseph in Stephen's speech in Acts 7:9–14, have little theological significance.

The reference in Hebrews is more substantial. The text states:

> By faith Joseph, at the end of his life, made mention of the exodus of the Israelites and gave instructions about his burial *[literally* his bones]. (Hebrews 11:22)

This instruction, given in Genesis 50:25, is fulfilled by Moses in Exodus 13:19. Lane explains that this command received relatively little attention in Jewish exegetical tradition; he cites only two mentions: *Nor was anyone ever born like Joseph; even his bones were cared for* (Sirah 49:15), and the instruction, *But you shall carry up my bones with you; for when my bones are being taken up, the Lord shall be with you in light* (*Testament of Joseph* 20:2). This stands in marked contrast with more frequent discussions of Joseph's faithfulness in the face of the trials he endured (Wisdom 10:13–14, as well as those texts discussed above). Lane argues that for Hebrews, Joseph's instruction about his bones is as an example of faith in the face of death; Joseph trusted in God's promise to his people, and wanted to remain part of it even after he had died.[24] Hebrews therefore takes Joseph as an example of faith, which recognizes that even a position of power is not a permanent home but a temporary tent, and

---

22. Hamilton, *Genesis 18–50*, 714.
23. Hamilton, *Genesis 18–50*, 713–15.
24. Lane, *Hebrews 9–13*, 366.

commends such an attitude to its audience.²⁵ The Christian understanding of Joseph is thus that he is an example of faith more than of piety; it is his trust in God, not his holy living, that Christians seek to emulate. The nature of Joseph's example to believers is therefore a further question for Christians and Muslims to discuss

The Church Fathers' Views of Joseph

One notable feature of the church fathers' views of Joseph is that they find typological and allegorical references to Christ within Joseph's story. For example, Cyril of Alexandria compares Joseph's splendid robe with the way Christ was clothed in his Father's glory:

> And Joseph was loved by his father a great deal. And he gave him a multicolored garment as an excellent gift and a proof of the love with which he accompanied him. And this was an incentive to envy for his brothers and a cause of hatred, as the following events demonstrate. In fact, the Pharisees were inflamed with anger against the beloved, that is, Christ, because he had been clothed by God the Father with a multiform glory.²⁶

Similarly, Caesarius of Arles contrasts Joseph wandering in the desert searching for his brothers with Christ wandering the world seeking out the lost:

> Jacob sent his son to manifest solicitude for his brothers, and God the Father sent his only-begotten Son to visit the human race, which was weak from sin and like lost sheep. When Joseph was looking for his brothers he wandered in the desert. Christ also sought the human race, which was wandering in the world; he too as it were, wandered in the world because he was seeking the erring.²⁷

Ambrose saw a parallel between Joseph being stripped of his splendid robe and Christ being stripped before his crucifixion. He also finds symbolic significance in the price paid for Joseph. Ambrose also developed a correspondence between the blood of the goat and Jesus, the Lamb of God:

---

25. DeSilva, *Hebrews*, 405.
26. Sheridan, *Genesis 12–50*, 231–32.
27. Sheridan, *Genesis 12–50*, 236.

> Now the fact that they sprinkled his tunic with the blood of a goat seems to have this meaning, that they attacked with false testimony and brought into enmity for sin him who forgives the sins of all people. For us there is a lamb, for them a goat. For us the Lamb of God has been killed, who took the sins of the world, whereas for them a goat piled up sins and amassed offences.[28]

Joseph's early experiences in Egypt are used primarily to exhort the Christian to a life of faithful obedience, rather than to draw any direct parallels with Christ. The main point the church fathers make is that it is important to remain faithful to God, even when experiencing trials. Those who endure to the end will be saved. Joseph's tests of his brothers are used to explain the trials and tests a Christian might face. Then when Joseph reveals himself to his brothers, comparison is once again made with Christ. Joseph's willingness to forgive his brothers prefigures the forgiveness that Christ offers. As Ambrose explains:

> Christ would even excuse his brothers' crime and say that it was God's providence and not humanity's wickedness, since he was not offered up to death by humans but was sent by the Lord to life.[29]

Ambrose also finds parallels between Jacob eventually believing that Joseph is alive and the Christian's faith in Christ. He argues:

> The first and greatest foundation of faith is belief in the resurrection of Christ. For whosoever believes Christ has been restored to life, quickly searches for him, comes to him with devotion and worships God with his inmost heart. Indeed he believes that he himself will not die if he has faith in the source of his resurrection.[30]

For the church fathers, Joseph was thus both a precursor to Christ and also an example of devoted faith. Joseph's instructions regarding his bones are taken as the supreme example of this faith. Chrysostom therefore links the instruction in Genesis 50:25 with the exposition in Hebrews 11:22, concurring that they are a challenge to the Christian to demonstrate a similar level of faith. This raises an interesting pointer for discussion: is Joseph primarily an example of piety and holy living, or an example of faith in God?

28. Sheridan, *Genesis 12–50*, 241.
29. Sheridan, *Genesis 12–50*, 291.
30. Sheridan, *Genesis 12–50*, 296.

Christian Syriac Sources

In what follows I will outline the argument of Witztum that *surah Yusuf* engages with the Syriac Christian retellings of the Joseph story. Witztum suggests that scholars focus overly on Jewish, not Christian antecedent texts; his argument seeks to rectify this by looking at Syriac sources. Witztum argues that the Qur'an shows "a strong affinity to Syriac poems which expand on biblical themes," since in his view the Syriac accounts and the Qur'anic accounts regularly depart from the biblical text in similar ways.[31] He gives some examples, explaining that the particularly striking instances are those that are different from Jewish sources. Thus, for example, both a Syriac lyric poem and the Qur'an omit the elements that are negative about Joseph and Jacob at the start of Genesis. Similarly, in both cases, Joseph first tells his dream to his father, not to his brothers as he does in Genesis. Jacob then warns Joseph not to speak to his brothers of his dreams. "Thus neither is Joseph arrogant nor Jacob ignorant."[32]

Witztum also discusses the Syriac texts' treatment of Potiphar's wife, and the parallels with *surah Yusuf*. He discusses *Yusuf* 12:52–53, arguing that if these verses record Potiphar's wife's speech, then she confesses her guilt. Witztum then cites a range of Syriac sources that include a scene where Potiphar's wife also confesses her guilt, albeit in a manner that is different from the Qur'anic account. Witztum proposes that the reason for these embellishments are curiosity about resolving loose ends, a desire "to create a neat chiastic pattern of events" and parallels with the story of Esther. The fact that there are literary parallels should not be confused with parallel intentions. As Witztum explains, although both the Syriac sources and the Qur'an establish Joseph's innocence, and Potiphar's wife's guilt, their purpose and timing in doing so is different. In the Syriac, it comes after his elevation with the aim of demonstrating Joseph's generosity and forgiving nature, while in the Qur'an vindication comes before his elevation, demonstrating his innocence and Potiphar's wife's repentance.[33]

Witztum's next focus is on how the Syriac sources and the Qur'an make similar adaptations of the biblical text. The example he gives is of the animal that is alleged to have killed Joseph. In Genesis 37:20, 33 we are simply told it was a wild animal. But the Qur'an states categorically that it was a wolf (*Yusuf* 12:13–14, 17). Witztum adds that he knows of

31. Witztum, "Joseph among the Ishmaelites," 426.
32. Witztum, "Joseph among the Ishmaelites," 430.
33. Witztum, "Joseph among the Ishmaelites," 431–32.

no rabbinic source that shares the designation of wolf, although there are Jewish sources that link a lion's whelp (identifying with Judah) or a bear with Potiphar's wife. But there are wolves in the Christian retelling of the story. Utilizing Joseph-Jesus typology, Joseph becomes a lamb, and his brothers wolves. Although the Qur'an itself does not describe Joseph's brothers as wolves, later Qur'anic exegetical tradition did do so.[34]

Witztum's second example is of how the news of Joseph's survival in Egypt is communicated to Jacob. In Genesis, it is seeing the wagons that Joseph has sent that revives Jacob's spirits (Genesis 45:27). But in the Qur'an, it is a shirt of Joseph's, which is placed on Jacob's face, restoring his sight (*Yusuf* 12:93–96). The Syriac sources are closer to the Qur'an than the Bible. In the Syriac sources, Jacob's sight is dimmed when he sees the bloodstained garment that is alleged to prove Joseph's death, and Jacob's eyes are enlightened when he sees Joseph again. Similarly, Syriac sources have Joseph sending garments to Jacob. Furthermore, all the brothers, but especially Benjamin, use the luxurious garments that Joseph has given them to convince their father Jacob that Joseph is still alive. Witztum notes the symmetry in this retelling: a garment brought by the brothers convinces Jacob that Joseph is dead, then other garments convince him he is alive. The Qur'an, Witztum proposes, "sharpens this symmetry" by referring to only one garment in each instance, which in both cases belongs to Joseph.[35]

Witztum argues there is also a correspondence between the literary form of *surah Yusuf* and the Syriac poems in contrast with Jewish midrash. While midrash makes discrete comments on individual verses, Syriac poems and *surah Yusuf* both have an uninterrupted retelling of the story; the former as verse, the latter as rhyming prose. Witztum expands on this point, illustrating how both Syriac poetry and *surah Yusuf* break down biblical dialogue into more discrete, pithy units. Moreover, in both *Yusuf* and one Syriac source, the brothers ask Jacob's forgiveness once their crimes against Joseph have been revealed. Furthermore, Witztum identifies lexical links, proposing that *Yusuf* "displays linguistic similarities to the Syriac sources on several levels; it includes cognates of words found in the Syriac texts, Syriac loanwords, and expressions that have a Syriac substratum."[36] This is not that surprising, given that a very similar story is told in two

---

34. Witztum, "Joseph among the Ishmaelites," 433–34.
35. Witztum, "Joseph among the Ishmaelites," 435–37.
36. Witztum, "Joseph among the Ishmaelites," 444.

Semitic languages, but Witztum does develop a case that suggests the correspondences do actually indicate a close literary relationship.[37]

Witztum's three points are that, first, the Qur'an retells biblical stories in order to encourage Muhammad and inform him that he will finally triumph. Second, the Qur'an also wants to warn Muhammad's people to avoid the fate of earlier generations. Third, the stories establish Muhammad as a true heir to the biblical tradition. Thus, the Qur'an is aware of extrabiblical Christian and Jewish traditions, and while it may draw on those traditions in retelling the stories, it is not simply derivative of them. Rather, it has its own particular purposes.[38]

Wessells also argues that there are elements of Muhammad's experience in the Joseph narrative: Muhammad was accused of seeking superiority over others for personal reasons, as Joseph was by his brothers. Muhammad believed he was given his leadership position in order to save his own people, just as Joseph was. Furthermore, Muhammad followed Joseph's example in forgiving his brothers who had wronged him. This is seen in Muhammad's triumphant return to Mecca in 630 CE. Hence *Yusuf* 12:92, which come toward the end of the Joseph narrative, are in fact words spoken by Muhammad as he enters Mecca as victor.[39]

What Does the Story of Joseph Teach Us?

The feminist biblical critic Mieke Bal discusses the story of Joseph at some length. Her Christian heritage means she first heard the story told from a Catholic Christian perspective; the main thing she took from that initial experience was the danger that women pose to men.[40] Bal echoes the point made by Haleem at the start of the chapter; that we all hear the story of Joseph from our own perspective. Her aim in writing is to challenge some of those presuppositions and attempt to hear the story afresh.[41] One of the key points Bal makes is that some characters remain nameless; Potiphar's wife is, she proposes, more property than person. The challenge that comes from this observations is whether, in our desire to see Joseph vindicated, we neglect the agency and value of other

---

37. Witztum, "Joseph among the Ishmaelites," 442–45.
38. Witztum, "Joseph among the Ishmaelites," 446–48.
39. Wessells, *Torah, the Gospel and the Qur'an*, 111.
40. Bal, *Loving Yusuf*, 2.
41. Bal, *Loving Yusuf*, 13.

characters in his story.[42] To use language that she turns to later in her argument, do we read this story with ethical indifference?[43]

For the Qur'an, Joseph is a prototypical believer, a type of Muhammad, who is himself a type of the perfect Muslim. Joseph is therefore an example of a pious Muslim who does not sin, as indeed the epilogue to *Yusuf* states (12:101, cited above). In the Bible, Joseph does not have that same moral authority, although he nevertheless is a figure Christians look to and learn from, and arguably is a type of Christ. There is a particular fascination with the Joseph story amongst Christians who are in a minority and who are experiencing persecution. As with the biblical book of Daniel, Joseph's experience demonstrates that faithfulness to God does receive reward and vindication in due time. The story of Joseph provides Muslims and Christians with a lot to talk about. Three particular topics are: first, how we respond to temptation; second, our understanding of the sovereignty of God; and third, what we can learn (and put into practice) from the story of Joseph's life.

---

42. Bal, *Loving Yusuf*, 31
43. Bal, *Loving Yusuf*, 192.

Moses

THIS CHAPTER IS DIVIDED into four main sections. The first is a discussion of the place of Moses in Islam and Christianity. The second section examines the differences between the biblical and Qur'anic stories of Moses, giving eight examples. These are the birth narrative, Moses the murderer, Moses' call, Haman's tower, the plagues and the magicians, Pharaoh, Moses on the mountain, and Moses as a type of the one to come. The third main section outlines a story of Moses found only in the Qur'an. The fourth, final section sets out pointers for further discussion, in particular opening up the question as to whether Moses is a precursor of Muhammad or of Jesus.

Moses in Islam and Christianity

As Kaltner and Mirza note, "with 115 mentions of his name in the text," Moses is the most frequently named person in the Qur'an.[1] The Qur'an contains many parallels with biblical traditions about Moses, but the details vary between the Qur'anic and biblical texts. Moreover, sometimes the Qur'an tells the same story of Moses multiple times. Moses features in more than thirty *surahs*; the longest section is nearly ninety verses long (*Ta Ha* 20:9–97). In what follows I will discuss this and other relevant passages, utilizing the observations in Kaltner and Mirza to guide the discussion.[2]

In the Qur'an, both Moses and his brother Aaron are identified as prophetic messengers:

> And remember in the Book Moses: Surely he was devoted, and he was a messenger, a prophet. We called him from the right

---

1. Kaltner and Mirza, *Bible and the Qur'an*, 125.
2. Kaltner and Mirza, *Bible and the Qur'an*, 125–32.

side of the mountain, and We brought him near in conversation. And We granted him some of Our mercy: his brother Aaron, a prophet. (*Maryam* 19:51–53)

The reference to *the mountain* indicates Mount Sinai, where Moses receives the law (Exodus 19). The *right side* is the western side. This passage also mentions the intimate relationship between God and Moses, which is also found in the Bible (Exodus 33:11), and Aaron's role in supporting Moses (Exodus 4:10–17). In this, and other passages, the Qur'an emphasizes Moses as recipient of a book from God; Moses is the first of three prominent Prophets who each receive a divinely authored written text that is authoritative for their own community (*Al-Isra* 17:2). This status means Moses, Jesus and Muhammad have a particular standing among the Prophets of God.

For Christians, Moses is one of those who points toward Jesus of Nazareth as the Christ, the Son of God. The accounts of Jesus' transfiguration in the Synoptic Gospels all include reference to Moses meeting with Jesus. John's Gospel opens with a reference to the fact that while the law was given through Moses, grace and truth came through Jesus Christ (John 1:17). The Apostle Paul is clear in his writings, especially his letter to the Galatians, that the law given to Moses was a temporary teacher until the fullness of God's grace was revealed in Jesus Christ. The story of the Passover, including the sacrifice of a lamb whose blood marked those households who were protected from God's wrath, is a key one for Christians, who understand the episode as pointing figuratively toward Jesus' own death on the cross. Moses is given the law, and while Christians still recognize the force of the ethical commands of God, they also teach that no human being is capable of completely fulfilling God's law, and as such we all depend on Christ for our salvation.

By contrast, for Muslims, Moses is the first recipient of a book from God, but his time has passed. Moses is understood as a type of Muhammad. Yet despite this difference in understanding, the Qur'anic account of Moses is very similar to the biblical one. Kaltner and Mirza list the following other parallel traditions: the killing of a man in Egypt, which causes him to flee (*al-Qasas* 28:14–28; Exodus 2:11–22); the exodus from Egypt (*al-A'raf* 7:134–40; *Yunus* 10:90–92; *Ta Ha* 20:77–79; *ash-Shu'ara'* 26:52–67; Exodus 14); events associated with the wandering in the wilderness (*al-Baqarah* 2:57–61; *al-Ma'idah* 5:21–26; Exodus 16:4–36;

Numbers 13–14); and Moses' meeting with God on a mountain (*al-A'raf* 7:142–46; Exodus 33:18–23).

The *Stories of the Prophets* literature has other traditions about Moses that are not in the Qur'an. These include the fact that Moses was miraculously conceived in Pharaoh's household; when he was brought home he escaped detection by being hidden in a hot oven that did not harm him. An alternative story says that Pharaoh only killed boys in alternate years, and Moses was born in the year when killings were not taking place. Moses' faith during his journey to Midian is stressed, because his only companion was God. His wife Zipporah gives birth to their child on the night when Moses encountered God in the burning bush. She returned to her father while Moses went to confront Pharaoh. Although the *Stories of the Prophets* has a lengthy discussion of the plagues that afflict Egypt, neither the Qur'an nor the *Stories of the Prophets* mention the killing of the firstborn, which is the final plague in Exodus. This shift of emphasis is probably due to the different focus in the retelling of the story. While for the Jewish nation the exodus is their foundational miracle, and the death of the first born a key moment within that story, for Islam the flight from Egypt is only a minor point. The Qur'an's focus is primarily on Moses as a precursor, and type of Prophet, whose legacy and image Muhammad fulfills. These differences are explored in more detail in the next section.

Contrasting the Biblical and Qur'anic Views of Moses

There are at least eight significant differences between the biblical and Qur'anic accounts of Moses' life. First, details in the birth narrative. Second, after Moses has killed the Egyptian, he repents (*al-Qasas* 28:15–17), a motif not found in Exodus. Third, in the Qur'an Moses' call is less dramatic. He goes to the bush for warmth, not because of the bush is burning but not being consumed. During the call narrative, there is also a merging of the timeline; the messenger recedes to the background as the conversation focuses on Pharaoh and God. This merging of timelines is a key feature in the Qur'an. Fourth, Pharaoh has Haman build a tower, a motif that does not occur in Exodus, although Haman plays a prominent role in the Esther narrative. Fifth, the plagues are not emphasized; the final plague, the death of the firstborn, does not occur at all in the Qur'an. Does this mean the theology of substitutionary atonement is replaced by a theology of a divine messenger? Moreover, the magicians lose the magic conflict with Moses and then repent and convert, while in the Exodus account they simply drop out of the story. For the Qur'an, winning is not the point; conversion is. Sixth, in the Qur'an Pharaoh repents as he dies, which is very different from the biblical motif of God hardening Pharaoh's heart to make an example of him. Seventh, the Qur'an sees the sins of the people in the wilderness wanderings as paradigmatic, both of how Jews and Christians behave and also as a warning for the *ummah* of the consequences of their failure. The shift is thus from discourse to discipline. Thus, the Qur'an rereads and retells the story for its own purposes. Finally, the role of God in the narrative differs, and with it the nature of Moses' prophethood; for Exodus he is the leader of the nation of Israel, while the Qur'an sees him as a precursor to Muhammad, a type of the Final Prophet who is to come.

Before examining these eight motifs is more detail, I will briefly discuss a further perceived difference, namely, the apparent Qur'anic conflation of Miriam (Mary) the sister of Moses and Mary (Miriam) the mother of Jesus. As Samir explains, in 1 Chronicles 5:29 the children of Amran are Aaron, Moses and Miriam (Mary). In Exodus 15:20, Miriam is described as the sister of Aaron. The Qur'an appears to confuse Mary the mother of Jesus with Mary the sister of Aaron. Thus, in *Maryam* 19:28 Mary is called the sister of Aaron, and in *at-Tahrim* 66:12 she is called the daughter of Imran. But this conflation is not limited to Qur'anic sources. Samir explains that the church fathers, such as Gregory of Nyssa and Aphraates, both well known to Syriac Christians, often compared Mary sister of Aaron with Mary mother of Jesus. Moreover, Muslim commentators note the issue, explaining that "sister of Aaron" can mean "descendant relative of Aaron."[3] Thus, this conflation cannot be explained as a unique feature of the Qur'an, and so will not be discussed in more detail here, although there is a fuller discussion in the chapter on Mary. The confusion over Miriam and Mary provides an important reminder for Christians to be careful to understand Muslim interpretations of the text before developing accusations of inconsistency or inaccuracy. Both the Bible and the Qur'an contain passages that are difficult to understand. Jumping to quick conclusions about inaccuracy or confusion does not help dialogue or the development of deeper understanding.

---

3. Samir, "Theological Christian Influence of the Qur'an," 143.

The Birth Narrative

The Qur'an has two passages that explain the story of Moses' birth. The account in *Ta Ha* 20:37–40 comes at the end of a discussion of the burning bush, in which God reminds Moses that his mother followed the divine command to put Moses in a basket and float him on the river, and that he was restored to his mother with his sister's help. The second account, in *al-Qasas* 28:3–13, describes the same episode in more detail. There are some similarities with the account in Exodus 2:1–10. Both accounts set out the threat from Pharaoh, who, fearful for his own power, gives orders for the sons of the Hebrews to be killed. Moses' mother therefore puts him on the river, and a member of Pharaoh's household finds Moses and rescues him. Moses' sister Miriam offers to find a wet nurse for the baby. This means Moses is restored to his mother, who cares for him.

There are also significant differences between the biblical and Qur'anic accounts. First, in *al-Qasas* there is no explicit mention of a basket or container (although this is mentioned in *Ta Ha*). Second, it is Pharaoh's wife who finds Moses, not his daughter as in Exodus 2. Third, the Qur'anic account does not mention Moses being returned to Pharaoh's household or his being brought up to follow Egyptian ways. Kaltner and Mirza suggest that the most significant difference is in the role God plays in the story. In Exodus 2 there is no mention of a divine command. The account is simply of a Levite woman conceiving, giving birth to a son, hiding him for as long as she could in her house and then after three months hiding him in a basket in the reeds, where he is found by Pharaoh's daughter. But in the Qur'an, Moses' mother receives direct divine intervention, instructing her to put the baby on the river (*al-Qasas* 28:7), strengthening her when her faith wavers (28:10). God also ensures Moses will receive no wet nurse except his own mother (28:12), so that God can return him to his mother (28:13). Thus, the Qur'an makes God's role in care for Moses much more explicit than in Exodus, where divine care may be implied but is never discussed plainly. Kaltner and Mirza refer to this as the "Islamization" of the tradition, exemplified by the fact that Moses is referred to as one of those who are sent, that is, a messenger, a word that has theological weight in the Islamic tradition.[4]

In the Qur'an, it is Pharaoh's wife, not his daughter, who finds the boy. Ibn Kathir narrates that when she opened the ark, *she discovered a boy, the most beautiful of creation. God put love for Moses in her heart when*

---

4. Kaltner and Mirza, *Bible and the Qur'an*, 126.

she saw him. When the Pharaoh saw him, he wanted to kill him, afraid that it was one of the Israelites. But the Pharaoh's wife convinced him.[5] While the rescuer differs between the Qur'an and the Bible, in both cases it is Moses' sister who offers to find a wet nurse and duly returns Moses to his mother. Reynolds also suggests that the fact that Pharaoh's wife adopts Moses means there is a father-son relationship between Moses and Pharaoh.[6] By contrast, some early Christian interpreters saw Pharaoh as representing the devil. Thus, Methodius argues, *it has been said that the Pharaoh of Egypt was a type of the devil, in that he cruelly ordered the males to be cast into the Nile and permitted the females to live.*[7]

Alexander points out that while the reader may presume that divine providence lies behind Moses' salvation from death, those who save him are in fact women: his mother, his sister and Pharaoh's daughter. In these opening chapters of Exodus, women are portrayed positively, something not that common in biblical texts.[8] Childs finds connections between Moses' birth story and the account in Matthew of the visit of the magi and Herod's attempts to kill the promised Messiah. In both, a young male child is born under threat of death from a ruling monarch. This child is rescued in the nick of time, while innocent others are slaughtered. Matthew's quote from Hosea 11:1, *Out of Egypt I have called my son* (Matthew 2:15), strengthens the parallel.[9]

While some may want to focus on the discrepancies in details about Moses' birth, the main point for Christians and Muslims to discuss in relation to the birth narrative is that of divine sovereignty and care for those who are suffering. How does God provide for us and what expectations do we have of his care?

Moses the Murderer

In both the Qur'an and the Bible, Moses strikes an Egyptian in anger and kills him. But the circumstances of the murder are much clearer in Exodus. Moses sees one of his own people being oppressed, kills the oppressor and then hides the body. It is only when he is challenged by another

---

5. Wheeler, *Prophets in the Qur'an*, 175.
6. Reynolds, *Qur'an and the Bible*, 597.
7. Lienhard, *Exodus, Leviticus, Numbers, Deuteronomy*, 4.
8. Alexander, *Exodus*, 63–64.
9. Childs, *Exodus*, 21.

Hebrew the next day that he realizes his actions are public knowledge, and so flees to Midian for safety. Childs points out that in Acts 7 Stephen understands Moses' actions in killing the Egyptian as a failed attempt at delivering his people, which he links to "prophecy and fulfilment within a redemptive history." Philo also explains Moses' actions in this way but he understands them in the context of the need to be patient as fortunes change over time.[10] Alexander proposes that the reference in Exodus 2:11 to *his brothers* indicates that despite being brought up in Pharaoh's court, Moses considers himself to be a Hebrew. He adds that Moses' upbringing by the compassionate woman who saved him has given him a heart for justice. But the fact that he resorts to deadly violence in his search for justice means he is not yet qualified to be a national leader.[11]

The early church fathers also look for positive interpretations of Moses' actions. Thus, Basil the Great explains that *He who, possessing naturally a love of justice, on one occasion even before the government of the people was entrusted to him was seen inflicting on the wicked punishment to the extent of death because of his natural hatred of villainy.* Ambrose likewise comments that Moses would not have killed the Egyptian if *he had not first destroyed in himself the Egypt of spiritual wickedness.*[12]

The Qur'an blames Moses' actions on Satan, and Moses himself prays in repentance, *My Lord, surely I have done myself evil. Forgive me!* (al-Qasas 28:15–16). As Haleem explains, this is the same prayer of repentance that is prayed by Adam and Eve (*al-Baqarah* 2:37).[13] The *Enlightening Commentary* explains that "certainly Moses did not commit any sin here," but he nevertheless asked for forgiveness, which he received from Allah. The commentators conclude that Moses' actions were not really criminal, because the Egyptian he kills was one of those who had *cut the head of thousands of newborn sons from the Children of Israel and refused to commit no crime against the Children of Israel.*[14]

In Exodus, Moses first kills an Egyptian who is beating a Hebrew, and then intervenes in a fight between two Hebrews. They rebuke him, asking if he wants to kill one of them as he killed the Egyptian the previous day. Moses is described as being afraid, and he flees from Pharaoh to

10. Childs, *Exodus*, 33–34.
11. Alexander, *Exodus*, 66–70.
12. Lienhard, *Exodus, Leviticus, Numbers, Deuteronomy*, 7.
13. Haleem, *Understanding the Qur'an*, 138.
14. https://www.al-islam.org/enlightening-commentary-light-holy-quran-vol-13/section-2-moses-saved-allah-being-murdered#surah-al-qasas-verse-14.

live in Midian (Exodus 2:11–15). Nowhere is he described as repenting. The Qur'an also records the same two fights, but the repentance comes between the two (*al-Qasas* 28:15–21).

The difference between whether Moses repents or not is an important one for understanding the status and function of a Prophet, and by extension, our own relationship with God. Can we be useful to God even if we are sinful, or must we first purify ourselves before we can serve his purposes?

Moses' Call

There are at least four accounts of Moses' encounter with God at the burning bush in the Qur'an (*Ta Ha* 20:9–36; *ash-Shu'ara'* 26:10–22; *an-Naml* 27:7–12; *al-Qasas* 28:29–35). Kaltner and Mirza's discussion focuses on the first of these, which they contrast with the biblical account found in Exodus 3:1—4:17. They note that the biblical account is almost four times as long as the Qur'anic one, primarily because Moses is much more reluctant to obey the divine command in the Bible than in the Qur'an. In Exodus there are seven exchanges between God and Moses, as Moses comes up with increasingly desperate excuses as to why he should not return to Egypt and confront Pharaoh. Moses tries strategies including averting his eyes, questioning God's authority, self-depreciating language and hypothetical scenarios. By contrast, in *Ta Ha* 20:9–36 Moses listens until God has finished, and then when he does speak, it is to enlist divine help to carry out divine commands. Thus, "the resistant protestor of the Bible has been replaced with a receptive partner in the Qur'an."[15] *Tafsir al-Jalalayn* explains that Moses cannot speak because of a live coal that he accidently placed in his mouth as a child, a tradition that is associated with Isaiah 6:6–7 and referred to in Jewish sources.[16]

In Exodus, Moses goes to the bush because he sees it is on fire but not burning up; the fire is clearly no ordinary one (Exodus 3:2–3). God speaks, ordering Moses to take off his shoes, for he stands on holy ground (a point also made in *Ta Ha*). God explains to Moses that he has seen the suffering of his people, and has come to deliver them, to bring the Israelites to a land flowing with milk and honey. Moses doubts his ability

---

15. Kaltner and Mirza, *Bible and the Qur'an*, 127.
16. Reynolds, *Qur'an and the Bible*, 490.

to fulfill the charge that God has laid upon him, and the first question he asks is who is this God who is speaking to him.

> God said to Moses, "I AM WHO I AM." He said further, "Thus you shall say to the Israelites, 'I AM has sent me to you.'" God also said to Moses, "Thus you shall say to the Israelites, 'The LORD, the God of your ancestors, the God of Abraham, the God of Isaac, and the God of Jacob, has sent me to you': This is my name for ever, and this my title for all generations." (Exodus 3:14–15)

Generations of Jewish and Christian scholars have debated and discussed the meaning of this revelation of God. Clement found a typological symbolism between the burning thorn bush and Jesus' crown of thorns, explaining that the Word appeared *first in the bush of thorns and later being surrounded with thorns that he might show that all was the work of one and the same power*. Eusebius explains that the divine name indicates that *everything that has ever existed or now exists derives its being from the One, the only existent and pre-existent being*. Hilary of Poitiers argues that *there is nothing more characteristic of God than to be*.[17] Turning to modern views, Wessels suggests that it describes a God who is present and active, who is involved in the world with the intention of liberation and salvation.[18] Weinandy proposes it reveals a God who is One, Savior, Creator, and All Holy.[19] Bray describes a God who is personal, eternal and "sovereign over everything that exists because he made it and sustains it in being."[20] It describes a God who is Pure Act, a God who is Pure Love, understanding love as primarily active, as a verb rather than as a noun.

In his discussion of the divine name, Alexander describes it as "somewhat enigmatic," explaining that while the Hebrew is normally translated *I am who I am*, it could equally be *I shall be who I shall be*. The translator's dilemma stems from the fact that the Hebrew verb is in the imperfect verbal form, which often has a future sense, indicating "a recurrent or continuing action or state," sometimes rendered as a 'timeless present" in English or, especially in poetry, referring to the past. This does not tell us exactly who God is. The etymology indicates unchanging eternity and divine transcendence. Alexander proposes the main message is

---

17. Lienhard, *Exodus, Leviticus, Numbers, Deuteronomy*, 12, 20.
18. Wessels, *Torah, the Gospel and the Qur'an*, 36.
19. Weinandy, *Does God Suffer?*, 40–63.
20. Bray, *God Has Spoken*, 71.

the unchanging nature of God, who has rescued his people in the past, and will do so again.[21]

Childs notes that when Jesus debates the possibility of the resurrection of the dead with the Sadducees (a group which denied this could take place), Jesus cites Exodus 3:6 as part of his argument, explaining that God described himself to Moses as the God of Abraham, Isaac and Jacob, that is, *God not of the dead but of the living* (Matthew 22:32 and parallels). Childs adds that this method of citing texts from the Torah in defense of the resurrection of the dead was an attested rabbinic practice of Jesus' day.[22]

What is particularly striking from the perspective of this chapter is that while Exodus 3 includes this discussion of divine identity, elements of which are repeated in Exodus 6:1–9, it is not discussed at all in the Qur'an. This is a significant difference between the two texts, and reveals their different purposes in recounting the story of Moses. In the Bible, the story of Moses, foundational to the identity of the people of Israel, includes disclosure of the character of the God who calls them as his people. In the Qur'an, the fact of God's existence and interest is a given, and the focus is on Moses as a type of Muhammad. Moreover, Muslims and Christians will find there is much food for thought in trying to understand who God discloses himself to be in the burning bush. What exactly does *I AM* mean?

Haman's Tower

The fourth topic that I will discuss is found in the Qur'an but not in the Bible. Pharaoh has Haman build a tower to heaven, in order to reach high enough to look down on the God of Moses, most probably because Pharaoh thinks Moses is a liar (*al-Qasas* 28:37–38). Ibn Kathir explains that in building the tower, *Pharaoh wanted to show to his people that Moses was a liar concerning what he alleged about a god other than Pharaoh.*[23]

Haman appears to be a partner to Pharaoh, and elsewhere a third figure is added in, Qarun (*al-'Ankabut* 29:39). These three torment Moses and his people, but are themselves in turn destroyed by God. There is a problem in establishing the identity of Haman; in the Bible he features in

---

21. Alexander, *Exodus*, 88–91.
22. Childs, *Exodus*, 80–81.
23. Wheeler, *Prophets in the Qur'an*, 189.

the Esther narrative, and so is in Iran, acting as vizier to Xerxes, not in Egypt serving Pharaoh. In the Qur'an there are also stories of the tower that Pharaoh and Haman construct, including one of how it became too high for people to climb. An alternative construction, of an ark that is born aloft by four eagles, is also narrated, but neither this effort nor the tower building enable Pharaoh and Haman to reach heaven.

Although the text of Exodus does not mention Haman, Childs suggests that Pharaoh in the opening two chapters of Exodus thinks he is acting shrewdly, but he is in fact "the wicked fool who is duped by the clever midwives", drawing a comparison with the way Haman is duped by Esther.[24] The biblical subtext of this story is the tower of Babel; later Jewish tradition does include the aspiration to enter heaven, just as Pharaoh espouses. Thus, *Jubilees* 10:19 has the people build a city and tower with the express aim of entering heaven. Similarly, the *Targum Neofilti* on Genesis 11:4 has the people in Shinar say, *Come let us build ourselves a city, and a tower whose top will reach to the heavens, and let us make for ourselves at its top an idol and we will put a sword in its hand, and it will make war against Him* [that is, against God].[25] Jewish exegetical tradition argued that this assault on heaven was planned and led by Nimrod, whom Genesis 10:9 describes as a mighty hunter before the Lord. Josephus says that Nimrod was *a bold man, and of great strength of hand*, also stating he *gradually changed the government into tyranny, seeing no other way of turning men from the fear of God, but to bring them into constant dependence on his power*. Having gained control of the populace, Nimrod then forced them to build the tower, which would be *too high for the waters to be able to reach* should God chose to flood the world again. God thwarted their plans by confusing their speech, so they could no longer communicate with each other (*Antiquities* 1.113–19). Nimrod's attempt at self-exaltation is argued by some to be reflected in Isaiah 14:13–15, which recounts how one who tried to exalt himself has been flung down into Shool.

Reynolds explains that the image of building monuments and towers appears in the Bible as a symbol of human rebellion against God. He further proposes that the Qur'an combines the actions of Nimrod and Pharaoh in its account of the instruction to Haman to build a tower. But, he notes, the Qur'an does appear to refer to Nimrod in association with

---

24. Childs, *Exodus*, 13.
25. Cited in Reynolds, *Qur'an And Its Biblical Subtext*, 101.

Abraham. That is to say, the king with whom Abraham argues is probably Nimrod (*al-Baqarah* 2:258). Thus "Nimrod and Pharaoh in the Qur'an represent the same type, the ruler who challenges God's sovereignty."[26] Finally, while some may question how and why the Qur'an conflates stories that are clearly separate within the biblical narrative, Reynolds points out that within the Talmud there is a tradition that Pharaoh had helpers, including Jethro, Balaam and Job. Thus, he proposes, the Qur'an merely continues in the same vein, adding in Haman and Qarun. Reynolds argues that the historical confusion in this conflation is irrelevant, as the Qur'an is not trying to reproduce an accurate historical account of the biblical story, but rather to reshape the information for its own rhetorical purposes. The interesting question is thus not why are the historical details wrong, but what is the aim of connecting Haman and Pharaoh? For Reynolds, the link comes in the trope about human conceit and rebelliousness that is met with divine punishment. The point is not to narrate history but to warn against the consequences of rebellion against God.[27]

The Plagues and the Magicians

Alexander explains that Exodus 7:8—11:10 is usually called the *ten plagues* in Christian tradition, or the *ten strikes* in Jewish tradition. He argues that of the two, "'strikes' conveys better than 'plagues' the precise nature of what is narrated here."[28] He also points out that often there is a reference to a hand or a staff being used to initiate the divine action, which ties in with describing them as strikes.[29] Isidore of Seville commented that while the plagues *were carried out corporally among the Egyptians; they are now carried out spiritually in us, for Egypt is a figure of this world.*[30]

There are at least four accounts of the plagues in the Qur'an (*Ta Ha* 20:42–73; *al-A'raf* 7:103–37; *Yunus* 10:75–89; *ash-Shu'ara'* 26:16–51). The focus is quite different from the account in Exodus. First, although there are multiple accounts, each account is quite brief and all are fairly similar in the content they discuss. Second, the focus in the Qur'an is on the competition between Moses and Pharaoh's magicians. Thus, the Qur'an

26. Reynolds, *Qur'an and Its Biblical Subtext*, 103.
27. Reynolds, *Qur'an and Its Biblical Subtext*, 97–105.
28. Alexander, *Exodus*, 146.
29. Alexander, *Exodus*, 147.
30. Lienhard, *Exodus, Leviticus, Numbers, Deuteronomy*, 44.

concentrates on the two miracles that Moses performs, namely, turning his staff into a snake that eats the magicians' staff-snakes, and making his hand leprous and then clean again. Third, in the Qur'an the magicians convert as a result of seeing these signs, professing faith in the God of Aaron and Moses. Pharaoh is furious, threatening dire punishments; cutting off hands and feet and crucifixion. But even this intimidation does not sway the magicians, who respond:

> We shall not prefer you over the clear signs which have come to us, nor (over) Him who created us. So decree whatever you are going to decree. You can only decree for this present life. Surely we have believed in our Lord, so that He may forgive us our sins and the magic you forced us to (practice). God is better and more lasting. (*Ta Ha* 20:72–73)

Nasr explains that at this point the magicians have come to "such a high degree of certainty in God that they come to see the trials and pleasures of this life as merely passing," and therefore prefer allegiance to Allah over against loyalty to Pharaoh.[31]

The Exodus account (8:19; 10:7) also intimates that Pharaoh's officials start to believe, but they are not as clear as in the Qur'an. In Exodus 8:19 Pharaoh's officials refer to the *finger of God* at work, which Isidore of Seville takes to indicate the Holy Spirit, who, *when he is opposed, stirs up disquiet against the merciless and the proud.*[32] The sentiments expressed within the Qur'an are very similar to the warning that Jesus gives to his followers to fear God, the one who can cast both body and soul into hell, rather than being worried about the punishments that human rulers can inflict on the physical body (Luke 12:5). But these are not views found in the Qur'an; the magicians here appear to be speaking as much out of the experience of the first companions of Muhammad as they do to the situation of Egypt under Pharaoh.

A fourth striking feature of the Qur'an's discussion of the plagues is the compressed nature of the account. This means there is no back-and-forth between Moses and Pharaoh, where time and again Pharaoh initially relents, agreeing to let the people go into the desert to worship, and then changes his mind. The Qur'an does not have this build-up, and although it does list the increasingly severe plagues that demonstrate the divine punishment that comes with rebellion against the will of God, it

---

31. Nasr, *Study Qur'an*, 799.
32. Leinhard, *Exodus, Leviticus, Numbers, Deuteronomy*, 47.

does not dwell on them (*al-Aʿraf* 7:133). Indeed, the number of plagues mentioned varies. Thus, *al-Aʿraf* 7:133 refers to five *plagues*, while *Al-Isra* 17:101 refers to nine *signs*. Most significantly for both Jewish and Christian understandings of the exodus, there is no plague on the firstborn. The Qurʾan does not have any atonement theology, arguably because it does not have a theology of sinfulness that requires atonement. Hence, it has no need of sacrifices as the Jewish and Christian understandings of the human situation do. While the Passover is the culmination of the Exodus narrative, it is not even mentioned in the Qurʾan.

Alexander discusses the status of Passover as a sacrificial rite, adding that through it all Israelites obtain a holy status, although firstborn sons were already consecrated to God. The Passover marks freedom from bondage and also consecration as a holy nation, the first stages of entering into covenant relationship with God. This means, Alexander proposes, that Passover must have historical origins in an actual escape from slavery, not simply in the practices of wandering shepherd-nomads. It marks God's sovereign choice of Israel as the nation through which he will act; it is only later that divine mercy is extended to all nations. Even this extension of mercy is modeled on Passover. Thus, the New Testament utilizes Passover as a means of understanding the death of Jesus Christ. In the Synoptic Gospels, Jesus' final meal with his disciples is a Passover meal (Matthew 26:17; Mark 14:12; Luke 22:7–8), and in John, Jesus' bones are unbroken, just like a Passover lamb (John 19:36).[33]

The New Testament appropriates and uses Passover imagery for its own purposes; thus, in John's Gospel, John the Baptist describes Jesus as *the Lamb of God who takes away the sin of the world* (John 1:29, 36). Moreover, in John, Jesus dies at the very moment Passover lambs are being sacrificed. This symbolism is a clear indication of the way in which the Fourth Gospel reinterprets Jewish religious festivals and imagery for its own theological purposes. Similar imagery occurs in 1 Corinthians, where Paul exhorts his audience to *Clean out the old yeast so that you may be a new batch, as you really are unleavened. For our paschal lamb, Christ, has been sacrificed* (1 Corinthians 5:7). First Peter talks of *the precious blood of Christ, like that of a lamb without defect or blemish* (1:19). Finally, the image of Jesus as a lamb occurs frequently in the book of Revelation (5:6, 8, 12–13; 6:1, 16; 7:9–10, 14, 17; 8:1; 12:11; 13:8, 11; 14:1, 4, 10; 15:3; 17:14; 19:7, 9; 21:9, 14, 22, 27; 22:1, 3).

---

33. Alexander, *Exodus*, 230–34.

The early church fathers also utilized Passover imagery to speak of Christ. Isidore of Seville saw the firstborn of the Egyptians as representing *the principalities and powers and rulers of this world of darkness. Or they are the originators and inventors of the false religions that existed in this world*.[34] Discussing the blood that marked the Israelites' doorposts, Augustine adds that *our foreheads are marked with the blood of Christ*, a sign that *drives the destroyer away from us insofar as our hearts receive the Savior*. Origen notes that the Passover meal was eaten with unleavened bread and that Jesus described himself as the Bread of Life that came down from heaven.[35] Finally, Caesarius of Arles explains that *original sin could not have easily been forgiven, if a victim had not been offered for it, if that sacred blood of propitiation had not been shed*, understanding the sacrificial lamb as a type of Christ.[36]

Muslims and Christians therefore have very different understandings of the functions of the plagues within the Exodus narrative. For Christians there is great typological significance, especially in the final plague on the firstborn, which has no real meaning for Muslims. The fact that this plague is missing from the Qur'an is, of course, a significant point in and of itself and worthy of further exploration and discussion. Second, the status of Pharaoh's magicians, in particular the question of whether they convert, is also an important one that deserves deeper examination.

Pharaoh

In the Exodus account, Pharaoh regularly relents and appears willing to let the people of God leave Egypt to worship in the desert; but each time he then rescinds his offer, refusing to allow the people the freedom they ask for. This is because God has decided to make an example of him; even when Moses is called, God explains to him that *I know, however, that the king of Egypt will not let you go unless compelled by a mighty hand*, adding that he will strike Egypt, performing miracles that force Pharaoh to comply (Exodus 3:19). God later adds that he is the one who will harden Pharaoh's heart (Exodus 4:21; 7:3), and the same motif occurs sixteen times throughout the story (Exodus 7:14, 22; 8:15, 19, 32; 9:7, 12, 34, 35; 10:1, 20, 27; 11:10; 14:4, 8, 17). The result of Pharaoh's hardness of heart is

---

34. Leinhard, *Exodus, Leviticus, Numbers, Deuteronomy*, 55.
35. Leinhard, *Exodus, Leviticus, Numbers, Deuteronomy*, 60.
36. Leinhard, *Exodus, Leviticus, Numbers, Deuteronomy*, 63.

that he chases after Moses and the people, determined to recapture them. Eventually he and his whole army are drowned in the Red Sea (Exodus 14:26–31). Ambrose describes Pharaoh as *a man given to vain, empty thoughts*,[37] while Augustine argues that *with God there is no injustice*. Augustine cites Paul's argument in Romans 9, understanding the point to be that God *shows mercy out of his great goodness; he hardens out of no unfairness at all*.[38]

Some readers have found this description of Pharaoh troubling, understanding the text as implying God wills Pharaoh's destruction. Alexander points out that the Hebrew word *leb*, normally translated *heart*, indicates the whole of a person's inner life. Therefore, we must understand the reference as much to Pharaoh's will or mind, that is, to any aspect of his inner disposition. Moreover, the text uses three different verbs in relation to Pharaoh's heart, which are translated as *strengthened*, *hardened* and *made heavy*. Furthermore, a *hard heart* does not indicate a lack of compassion, but rather determination, being resolute in purpose. Similarly, a *heavy heart* is one that is fixed on a previously decided course of action. Pharaoh's decision to keep the Israelites as slaves, come what may, raises ethical concerns for some commentators. Alexander argues that God does not deny Pharaoh free will or choice. Rather, he leaves Pharaoh to suffer the consequences of his choices, since Pharaoh's stubbornness comes from within himself.[39] Moving on to discuss Pharaoh's final actions, Alexander suggests that despite all he has seen, including the death of the firstborn Egyptian males, Pharaoh does not grasp the truth about God. Therefore, he regrets freeing his slaves and pursues them. His arrogance leads to his own death, as well as that of his army; they are punished for their pursuit of unarmed civilians, as they follow the desire of Pharaoh's heart.[40]

The Qur'anic account strikes a different tone. Moses is instructed that when he goes to Pharaoh he is to *speak to him a gentle word. Perhaps he may take heed or fear* (Ta Ha 20:44). Pharaoh does drown and is guilty of leading his people astray (Ta Ha 20:77–79; see also al-Qamar 54:41–42, which Reynolds argues echoes Psalm 136:13–15).[41] In one account,

---

37. Lienhard, *Exodus, Leviticus, Numbers, Deuteronomy*, 46.
38. Lienhard, *Exodus, Leviticus, Numbers, Deuteronomy*, 51.
39. Alexander, *Exodus*, 163–71.
40. Alexander, *Exodus*, 280–81.
41. Reynolds, *Qur'an and the Bible*, 794.

Pharaoh repents as he dies, saying, *I believe that (there is) no god but the One in whom the Sons of Israel believe. I am one of those who submit* (*Yunus* 10:90). God responds with a rebuke at the tardiness of Pharaoh's repentance, but agreeing that *Today We rescue you with your body so that you may be a sign for those who succeed you. Yet surely many of the people are indeed oblivious of Our signs* (*Yunus* 10:92). It is noticeable that while *surah Yunus* has Pharaoh repenting, the other three accounts make no mention of this fact, and indeed perhaps presume that he drowns an unbeliever. Reynolds proposes that even the references in *Yunus* actually reinforce the Qur'anic doctrine that God does not accept the repentance of a sinner at the moment of death.[42] Nasr concurs, explaining that Allah's response is a rhetorical question with the force that repentance at this late stage is unacceptable.[43]

This raises an interesting discussion about the mercy and purposes of God. What do we as Muslims and Christians reading these texts together discern about our own relationships with God? What do they teach about repentance, predestination and the fate of humanity? What is the example of Pharaoh supposed to teach us?

Moses on the Mountain

Bede argues that only Moses was able to ascend Sinai to meet with God because only *the more perfect know how to grasp and observe the deeper and most secret mysteries of the law*.[44] Likewise, in his discussion of Exodus 24:18, Ambrose explains that if anyone wishes to see God, *he must love God so as to be loved by him, no longer as a servant, but as a friend who observes his commandments, that he may enter the cloud where God is*.[45]

The story of golden calf (Exodus 32) occurs twice in the Qur'an (*al-A'raf* 7:148–54; *Ta Ha* 20:86–98). The broad outline is the same in both texts, but there are nevertheless significant differences in detail. Kaltner and Mirza focus on the different portrayal of the Israelites. In Exodus, they have two lines of dialogue, both times demonstrating they have forgotten that it was God who brought them out of Egypt. They first say that it was Moses who rescued them, and second that it was the golden calf

---

42. Reynolds, *Qur'an and the Bible*, 339.
43. Nasr, *Study Qur'an*, 562.
44. Lienhard, *Exodus, Leviticus, Numbers, Deuteronomy*, 99.
45. Lienhard, *Exodus, Leviticus, Numbers, Deuteronomy*, 121.

that they have made. They never express regret for their actions, and the text is critical of them (Exodus 32:6, 25). In the Qur'an, by contrast, the people speak only once, in repentance (*al-A'raf* 7:149). Discussing this incident, Ephrem the Syrian suggests that Moses was taken from the people so that their paganism might come out into the open and be exposed and punished.[46] Cassiodorus likewise sees God's hand at work:

> So these sinners undergo a contrary experience: their necks which they fatally raised against the Lord are subjected to his sweet yoke with the humility which brings salvation. We recall that this often befell persecutors, so that having earlier maintained their idols by the most sacrilegious compulsion, they became proclaimers of our most holy religion.[47]

Aaron is much less prominent in the Qur'an than in the Bible; he is not even named in the former text. His only appearance in the Qur'an is in connection with the golden calf. Moses comes down the mountain and angrily grabs his brother by the hair; Aaron responds by protesting his innocence, saying the people wanted to kill him (*al-A'raf* 7:150). But in Exodus Aaron takes more initiative: he fashions the calf, builds an altar for it and calls for a feast to honor it (Exodus 32:2–6). He is disingenuous and deceptive, protesting his innocence when confronted (Exodus 32:21–24).

Moses' response to the golden calf differs. In Exodus, he first defends the people, persuading God to not destroy them (Exodus 32:7–14). But when he comes down the mountain, he becomes increasingly angry with them. Moses smashes the two tablets that contain the Ten Commandments, which symbolizes the fractured covenant between God and his people. Then he burns the golden calf, grinds it into powder and forces the people to drink it. Third, he commands the Levites to go through the camp killing the disobedient, and three thousand die (Exodus 32:19–29). In the Qur'an, Moses descends the mountain full of rage, but, having pulled Aaron's hair, and heard him repent, Moses then appeals to God for forgiveness (*al-A'raf* 7:150–51). The people are not mentioned in the prayer because they have already repented; the focus of Moses' intercession is his, and his brother's, failure as Prophets.

Perhaps most significantly, in the Qur'an the tablets are not smashed, merely thrown aside. Moses is therefore able to retrieve them after he has prayed, and they continue to offer guidance and mercy to all who

---

46. Lienhard, *Exodus, Leviticus, Numbers, Deuteronomy*, 140.
47. Lienhard, *Exodus, Leviticus, Numbers, Deuteronomy*, 141.

fear God. Kaltner and Mirza comment that in the Qur'an the golden calf episode is associated primarily with divine mercy, peace and forgiveness, while in Exodus there is a much greater emphasis on punishment.[48]

Exodus 33:7–11 describes the regular meetings that took place between Moses and God in a tent outside the camp. Although it is a face-to-face encounter, the veil that separates them obscures God's features. This leads to Moses' request to see God's face (33:18), a request that is not granted, although Moses is able to see God's back and understand more of his character. God continues to make himself known, both through his relationship with Moses and also by disclosing his requirements of his people in greater detail.[49] For Clement of Jerusalem, Moses saw Christ as far as he was able to; when the Lord proclaimed his name, *the Lord, merciful and gracious*, this was the Father proclaiming the Son. Likewise, for Augustine, this incident was a prefiguring of the incarnation of Christ. Finally, Gregory of Nazianzus states:

> I was running to lay hold on God, and thus I went up into the mount and drew aside the curtain of the cloud and entered away from matter and material things. And as far as I could I withdrew within myself. And then when I looked up, I scarce saw the back parts of God, although I was sheltered by the rock, the Word that was made flesh for us.[50]

For Glaser and Kay, the contrasting approaches of the biblical and Qur'anic accounts demonstrate the fundamentally different understandings of the nature of God that the two texts hold. Glaser and Kay note that the most detailed account in the Qur'an of Moses on the mountain, which appears to respond to the account in Exodus 33:17—34:9, does not include a direct encounter between Moses and God:

> And when Moses came to Our meeting, and his Lord spoke to him, he said, "My Lord, show me (Yourself), so that I may look at You. He said, "You will not see Me, but look at the mountain. If it remains in its place, you will see Me." But when his Lord revealed his splendor to the mountain, He shattered it, and Moses fell down thunderstruck. And when he recovered, he said, "Glory to You! I turn to You (in repentance), and I am the first of the believers." (*al-A'raf* 7:143)

---

48. Kaltner and Mirza, *Bible and the Qur'an*, 129–30.
49. Alexander, *Exodus*, 631–50.
50. Lienhard, *Exodus, Leviticus, Numbers, Deuteronomy*, 149–51.

This leads to the observation that the Qur'an is clear that people cannot see God (see also *al-Baqarah* 2:55), a concern that is also found in the New Testament, which states clearly that God is invisible and cannot be seen (Colossians 1:15; 1 Timothy 1:17; Hebrews 11:27). Glaser and Kay suggest there are two elements to the problem of seeing God. First, it is impossible, as it is not in God's nature to be seen. Second, it is presumptuous of human beings to want to be seen by God. In the Qur'an, they explain, this results in the teaching that the mountains will fall down before a human being sees God, and so Moses repents of his request (*al-A'raf* 7:143). By contrast, in the Bible it is the holiness of God that means people cannot see him; that is to say, it is because of sin that people cannot see God.[51]

Glaser and Kay add that the Qur'an does state people will see God in the Day of Judgment (*al-Qiyamah* 75:22–23), and that seeing God is therefore a Muslim aspiration, reflected both in facing Mecca to pray and in some Sufi devotional practices. For Glaser and Kay, the story of Moses illustrates the clear difference in the Qur'anic and biblical understandings of God. In Exodus, and indeed the entire Bible, they argue that God's focus is on fulfilling his desire to live with human beings. But the Qur'an never tells us anything about God's feelings or intentions, although it does speak of the immanence of God. The most commonly cited verse in this regard is:

> Certainly We created the human, and We know what his own self whispers within him, (for) We are closer to him than (his) jugular vein. (*Qaf* 50:16, see also *al-Baqarah* 2:186)

Thus, although the Qur'an speaks of the immanence of God, it lacks the dialogue and covenantal relationship with God that are so characteristic of the Exodus narrative. Glaser and Kay go on to explain that in the Qur'anic account there is little detail about the laws that were given; there is no real discussion of the tabernacle, the priesthood or sacrifices; there is no covenant ceremony. They argue that this is because in the Qur'anic perspective God does not live with people, and so does not need a tabernacle.[52]

The Qur'an and the Bible thus give very different accounts of Moses' time on the mountain with God. These differences arguably expose the different theological presuppositions of the two texts. In particular, the

---

51. Glaser and Kay, *Thinking Biblically about Islam*, 124–25.
52. Glaser and Kay, *Thinking Biblically about Islam*, 194–95.

Moses as a Type of the One to Come

Many biblical scholars argue that Matthew's Gospel is written to establish Jesus as the new Moses. The gospel contains five blocks of teaching (Matthew 5–7, 10, 13, 18, 23–25), argued to parallel the five books of Moses. Jesus begins his teaching ministry on a mountain, much as Moses does, and he offers an interpretation of Mosaic law that goes to the heart of the teaching, on the basis of his own authority, thus establishing himself as one greater than Moses (Matthew 5–7). When Jesus feeds five thousand men (not to mention the women and children who were doubtless present), he does so in a desert place. John's Gospel makes a particular point of emphasizing the connections, including the time of year (Passover, John 6:4), and the fact that the men were divided into groups of fifty and one hundred, just as Moses does with the people in the desert on the advice of his father-in-law Jethro (Exodus 18:13–27). John's Gospel follows the feeding narrative with a long discussion about Jesus as the Bread of Life, the new and Living Manna that does not fade away in the morning.

There are numerous other places in the four Gospels that emphasize the notion that Jesus is the fulfillment of the Mosaic hope. John's Gospel begins with the observation that *the law indeed was given through Moses; grace and truth came through Jesus Christ* (John 1:17). As Keener explains, this is not to say that John rejects Moses or the Torah; rather, he wants his audience to realize that "Christ is the full embodiment of the law, the actual model of lived-out commandments, in flesh."[53] Michaels agrees that the focus is on continuity; the law was given through Moses as preparatory grace for the full gift of grace in Christ.[54] The repeated references to fulfillment of scripture, especially in Matthew and John, further reinforce the same point about Jesus' superiority to Moses.

Later, John contrasts Moses lifting up the bronze snake in the desert as a healing miracle for the people (Numbers 21:1–9) with Jesus being lifted up on a cross (John 3:14). Some commentators suggest Jesus' statement that *No one has ascended into heaven except the one who descended from heaven, the Son of Man* (John 3:13) is a reference to legends of

---

53. Keener, *John*, 421.
54. Michaels, *John*, 90.

Moses' ascent to heaven to receive the Torah. If this is the case, John's point is that not only is Jesus greater than Moses because he is the physical embodiment of the law, not simply its mediator, but Jesus' superiority to Moses is also seen in that he provides the instrument of salvation in contrast with Moses merely lifting it up.[55] Justin Martyr argues that Moses' actions must be understood as a foretaste and a type of the cross. He points out that Moses was commanded not to make any idol or graven image, yet he does so in making the bronze snake. This bronze snake is linked allegorically to the snake in Genesis 3, who first tempted Eve and so brought sin into the world. A connection is then made with the cross of Christ, who brought *salvation from the fangs of the serpent* by being lifted up on the cross (*Dialogue with Trypho* 94; see also chapters 91 and 112 and *1 Apology* 60).

The transfiguration narrative in the Synoptic Gospels also makes the clear point that Jesus is acting in fulfillment of the ministry of Moses and Elijah (Matthew 17:1–8; Mark 9:2–8; Luke 9:28–36). Lane points out the connections between Moses' vision of God on Mount Sinai (Exodus 24:12–18) and the transfiguration, where Jesus becomes the central figure, thereby demonstrating his superiority to Moses.[56] The fact that Moses' face shone with the reflected glory of God while Jesus' face shines with his own divine glory is, as Keener explains, a further claim to superiority. Jesus is the new Moses, but he is also far more than that.[57]

The Apostle Paul also speaks of the superiority of Jesus to Moses. Thus, he speaks of Moses' veiling of his face, because the glory was too much for the people of Israel to bear, contrasting this with the unveiled face of the believer, who is able to gaze on the glory of God in Christ (2 Corinthians 3:7–18). Martin entitles the section "life under two covenants" and explains that Paul's argument is that the law set a standard that it failed to attain, and its role as a temporary teacher has been fulfilled now that Christ has come.[58] The veil that Moses wore after speaking with God illustrates, for Paul, the barrier that blocks his Jewish contemporaries from seeing the full revelation of God in Christ. Witherington argues that Paul here develops an argument about the *glorious face*, describing the "greater glory of Jesus, which is the very mirror in which we see God and

---

55. Keener, *John*, 562–63.
56. Lane, *Mark*, 317.
57. Keener, *Matthew*, 437–38.
58. Martin, *2 Corinthians*, 56–76.

God's glory, since Jesus, unlike Moses, is the very image, the full human representation of God."⁵⁹ The sense of superiority is reinforced by the fact that while the Israelites could not bear to look upon Moses' face, Christians, who have the Spirit, are thereby enabled to look upon Christ, and so be transformed into his likeness.

Finally, the letter to the Hebrews makes two references to Moses. First, he is listed amongst the heroes of the faith:

> By faith Moses was hidden by his parents for three months after his birth, because they saw that the child was beautiful; and they were not afraid of the king's edict. By faith Moses, when he was grown up, refused to be called a son of Pharaoh's daughter, choosing rather to share ill-treatment with the people of God than to enjoy the fleeting pleasures of sin. He considered abuse suffered for the Christ to be greater wealth than the treasures of Egypt, for he was looking ahead to the reward. By faith he left Egypt, unafraid of the king's anger; for he persevered as though he saw him who is invisible. By faith he kept the Passover and the sprinkling of blood, so that the destroyer of the firstborn would not touch the firstborn of Israel. (Hebrews 11:23–28)

Childs argues that the interpretation of Moses in Hebrews 11 goes beyond the plain sense of the text of Exodus. Hebrews emphasizes Moses' choice to identify as an Israelite, not a son of Pharaoh's daughter, a point only implicit in Exodus. This is, of course, in line with the rhetorical thrust of Hebrews 11 as a whole. Childs regards the "boldest innovation" of this section to be the claim that this suffering was *abuse suffered for Christ*. Childs argues this refers not simply to typology (Moses' suffering was a type of Christ's suffering) but rather that it was participative; that is, Moses participated in Christ's suffering as the saints who follow Christ also share in it.⁶⁰

Lane proposes there is a connection with Psalm 89:51–52, where the Greek of the psalm echoes the Greek of Hebrews in using a word often translated as *reproach* (although the NRSV has *abuse*). The point, Lane suggests, is that like Christ, Moses put aside the joy he could have had to instead share in his people's suffering, a choice that was motivated primarily by faith.⁶¹

---

59. Witherington, *Conflict and Community*, 379.
60. Childs, *Exodus*, 36–37.
61. Lane, *Hebrews 9–13*, 373.

Second, Hebrews contrasts the fear of the people of Israel at the foot of Mount Sinai with the boldness that the believers in Christ can have, knowing they can come to the heavenly Jerusalem through Jesus, who established the new covenant with God by his blood (Hebrews 12:18–24). Lane explains that for Hebrews the "foundational experiences of Christians have been qualitatively different from those of Israel at Sinai." The old and new covenants are fundamentally different, and so the mediators of those two covenants are equally distinct, with Jesus far superior to Moses.[62]

The Qur'an's presentation of Moses arguably performs a similar function to these New Testament appropriations; with the obvious difference that the Qur'an's focus is on how Moses is a precursor and type of Muhammad. Thus, Glaser and Kay note that the aspects of Moses' life that are parallel to Muhammad's are given greater emphasis in the Qur'an. These include the confrontation with idolatry, leading people out of a place of insecurity, the formation of a people under a new law and the struggle with Jewish people who did not obey him. There is a clear emphasis in the Qur'an on Muhammad being a Prophet like Moses, to the extent that some Muslims would argue that even the Bible predicts this.[63]

In his speech to the people of Israel toward the end of his life, Moses explains that God has promised him: *I will raise up for them a prophet like you from among their own people. I will put my words in the mouth of the prophet, who shall speak to them everything that I command* (Deuteronomy 18:18). For many Muslims, this is a reference to Muhammad, signaling that he is the Final Prophet appointed by God. Thus, as Wessels explains,

> Moses and Aaron were commissioned to tell the good news (*bushra*, from which the Islamic word for "gospel, glad tidings" is derived) to the believers (Q 10:87). Jesus confirmed the Torah, which preceded him, and proclaimed the good news of a messenger whose name is to be praised (Q 61:6), which is see as the announcement of the coming of Muhammad.[64]

Discussing this verse from an evangelical Christian perspective, McConville proposes that *raising up* a Prophet does not necessarily indicate a single act or a single individual. Rather, he argues, it "envisages a succession of prophets" sent at times determined by God. There is no

---

62. Lane, *Hebrews 9–13*, 459.
63. Glaser and Kay, *Thinking Biblically about Islam*, 191–95.
64. Wessels, *Torah, the Gospel and the Qur'an*, 50.

dynastic or permanent office of Prophet in view here.⁶⁵ Millar adds that the context of this section of Deuteronomy is of divine guidance. Deuteronomy 18:9–13 discuss apostasy and warn against listening to false teachers. There follows a reassurance that God will continue to speak through his chosen mouthpiece, who must be heeded, and whose position must be neither usurped nor abused.⁶⁶

Christians and Muslims both see Moses as a type of one to come, but the identity of that later figure differs. For Christians, Moses points to Jesus Christ, while for Muslims, Moses is a precursor of Muhammad. The role we assign to Moses and the understanding of his ministry we develop depends on our own theological presuppositions. As we discuss how Moses prefigures other key figures in our faith, we must be aware of these ideas that we bring with us into the discussion.

A Story of Moses Found Only in the Qur'an

Al-Kahf 18:60–82 contains a story of Moses that does not have any direct biblical parallels. This account of Moses' journey to the end of the world has echoes in the Epic of Gilgamesh, the Syriac Christian *Alexander Romance* (an account of Alexander the Great) and the Jewish legend of Elijah and rabbi Joshua ben Levi. Since it does not have a biblical parallel, I will not discuss it at length, but merely make a few general observations.

In this striking story, Moses speaks to *his young man* that he will travel until he reaches the *junction of the two seas*, that is, the end of the world, where the waters of heaven and earth meet. The two set off and travel there:

> When they reached the junction of them, they forgot their fish, (for) it had taken its way into the sea swimming off. So when they had passed beyond (that place), he said to his young man, "Bring us our morning meal. We have indeed become weary from this journey of ours." He said, "Did you see when we took refuge at the rock! Surely I forgot the fish—none other than Satan made me forget to remember it—and it took its way into the sea—an amazing thing!" He [Moses] said, "That is what we were seeking!" So they returned tracing their footsteps. And they found a servant, one of our Servants to whom We had given mercy from Us, and whom We had taught knowledge from Us. (*al-Kahf* 18:61–65)

65. McConville, *Deuteronomy*, 303.
66. Millar, *Now Choose Life*, 129–30.

Commenting on this story, Wheeler explains that most Muslim exegetes identify *the servant* as al-Khidr, from whom Moses attempts to learn God's justice. In this account, God chides Moses for claiming to be the most knowledgeable of all people. God explains that al-Khidr has greater and more esoteric knowledge than any other person. Moses therefore sets out with Joshua (*his young man*) to find al-Khidr, following the sign of the fish, and then accompanying al-Khidr on a quest for knowledge recounted in *al-Kahf* 18:66–82.[67]

The rock at the junction of the waters is a marker for the spring of immortality, the waters of life. In the account found in the *Alexander Romance*, the fish is dead and comes to life when thrown into the spring, thus showing this is the water of life.

Wheeler also discusses *al-Qasas* 28:21–28, an account of Moses at Midian, pointing out that there are potential links with the Jacob story in Genesis 28:10—31:21. Wheeler argues that *al-Qasas* does not confuse the Jacob story, although he proposes that some Muslim interpreters of the text did so, for their own purposes of linking Jacob, progenitor of Israel, with Moses. His argument is that through conflating Moses and Jacob, Muslim exegetes retold the story of the redemption of Ishmael, Abraham's son, as well as that of Isaac, ancestor of the Israelites. This allowed them to claim Abraham as their ancestor, while assigning Moses the role of "father of the Jews."[68]

Wheeler's main argument is as follows. Just as Christianity needs a weak Judaism, that is, a Judaism that exists so that it can be fulfilled but at the same time is weak enough to be superseded, so Islam also needs a weak Christianity and a weak Judaism. That is, Islam needs both Judaism and Christianity to exist in order to fulfill them, but the two faiths must also be weak enough to be superseded. Theologically robust expressions of Judaism and Christianity are more problematic for an account of Islamic triumph. Thus, Muslim exegetes singled out and retold the stories of Moses in order tell their understanding of divine action within history. They do this by isolating key textual elements, forging links with widespread motifs, introducing new elements and stories and importing elements into different contexts. Wheeler explains:

> Not unlike the opposition of Jesus and Moses in the Gospel of John 1:17, the Muslim criticism of Moses is in contrast to the

---

67. Wheeler, *Moses in the Qur'an*, 10.
68. Wheeler, *Moses in the Qur'an*, 37–63.

image of the Prophet Muhammad, who is revealed in the Qur'an which repeals the curse of the law.[69]

Moses is mentioned so frequently in the Qur'an because in the Islamic understanding he has been superseded. He was given a revelation for a particular time, but that time has passed. Muhammad the Seal of the Prophets, has now come, and all should submit to him.

In Summary

Moses is the founding figure of Judaism, the one who led the people to freedom, received the Torah and guided the people of God through the desert to the edge of the Promised Land. He is arguably the most important figure within the Jewish faith. It is therefore unsurprising that both Christianity and Islam proclaim their own founding figures as being in the mold of Moses. Muslims and Christians will develop a deeper appreciation of their own faith—as well as the faith of others—as they explore this reality. How are Jesus and Muhammad types of Moses, what does it mean to argue they fulfill the precedents Moses set and what impact does this have on our faith and relationships with each other today?

---

69. Wheeler, *Moses in the Qur'an*, 125.

David and Solomon

This chapter examines the accounts of David and Solomon as found in the Bible and the Qur'an. It also refers to Jewish stories and legends of David and Solomon, primarily as a bridging exercise in connecting the biblical and Qur'anic accounts. The Qur'an has a detailed account of the Queen of Sheba's visit to Solomon, and so that is discussed in a specific section. The chapter is divided into two main parts, which focus on David and Solomon in turn. Each part is subdivided into four main sections, discussing the Old Testament, New Testament, extrabiblical and Qur'anic perspectives on the character in question.

David

David in the Old Testament

Limitations of space preclude a detailed engagement with David's whole life. He is introduced in 1 Samuel as a shepherd boy, whom Samuel selects and anoints as a future king of Israel. David defeats the Philistine giant Goliath, stunning him with a stone and then cutting off his head. David enters Saul's court, establishing a close friendship with Saul's son Jonathan. Saul and David have a tempestuous relationship; Saul fears David's growing reputation as a warrior and tries to kill him. David flees for his life, pursued by Saul. David refuses to raise a hand against God's anointed king and twice shames Saul into abandoning pursuit. Eventually Saul is killed in battle with the Philistines, and David is crowned king. He unites the twelve tribes behind him, establishing Jerusalem as his capital and himself as God's chosen king. The Hebrew scriptures record both good and bad incidents in David's life, including the fact that he committed adultery with Bathsheba and ruthlessly arranged for the murder of his enemies. David wants to build a temple for the Lord, but is told that job will fall to his son Solomon, so he merely prepares for the great task. David's succession is problematic; his sons quarrel and fight amongst each other. David even has to flee for his life, although he manages to retake control of the throne. David eventually dies, having appointed Solomon, Bathsheba's son, as his heir.

David is also reputed to have written many of the psalms. In his discussion of Davidic authorship, Eaton lists some of the texts that support this claim. David's playing the harp is said to have soothed Saul's spirit (1 Samuel 16:14). David composed songs of lament at national tragedies (2 Samuel 1:17; 3:33). God raised David up, anointed him and filled him with prophetic power, making him the sweetest singer in Israel (2 Samuel 23:1). David was recognized as one who made musical instruments (2 Chronicles 7:6; Nehemiah 12:36; Amos 6:5). A much later author, Jesus Ben Sira, writing around 190 BCE, summarized David's contribution as follows:

> In all that he did he gave thanks
>   to the Holy One, the Most High, proclaiming his glory;
> he sang praise with all his heart,
>   and he loved his Maker.
> He placed singers before the altar,
>   to make sweet melody with their voices.
> He gave beauty to the festivals,
>   and arranged their times throughout the year,
> while they praised God's holy name,
>   and the sanctuary resounded from early morning.
> The Lord took away his sins,
>   and exalted his power forever;
> he gave him a covenant of kingship
>   and a glorious throne in Israel. (*Sirach* 47:8–11)

Eaton explains that many modern scholars are unconvinced by claims that the psalms were written by David. Eaton himself counter-argues that the early monarchy was a time of psalm composition, and proposes that the concept of Davidic authorship should be respected. Eaton has three reasons for his claim. First, the connection with the royal figure: in many of the psalms the person praying is the king; why should this not be David? Second, the link with ceremonies of worship in the sanctuary; if David gathered Israel to worship the Lord in one place, it makes sense that he wrote songs to facilitate that worship. Third, the connection to prophecy: when he wrote psalms, David "saw and set forth deep things of

God by the power of the Spirit." Modern readers are invited to participate in the mysteries of relating to God through reading them.[1]

There are two accounts of David's life in the Hebrew scriptures, found in the books of Samuel and Chronicles. I will focus on three incidents: the defeat of the Philistine, the accounts of his becoming king and David's adultery with Bathsheba, including Nathan's parabolic rebuke.

David Defeats the Philistine (1 Samuel 17:1—18:5)

The story of David killing Goliath is only found in 1 Samuel, not in the account of David's life in Chronicles. Klein notes that placing the incident when David defeats the Philistine within the wider context of the narrative in 1 Samuel is problematized by the fact that the account displays no knowledge of David's anointing (16:1–13), nor his service as a musician, man of war and weapon carrier (16:14–23). Rather, in chapter 17 David is portrayed as an inexperienced shepherd boy; his brother Eliab is unconvinced that David can be a leader, yet he has witnessed David's anointing in chapter 16. For Klein, this indicates that the defeat of the Philistine "had a separate tradition history."[2] This may be the case, or it may be that the text simply indicates that Eliab remains unconvinced that his relatively untested young brother is really up to the task of killing the Philistine champion.

As Klein notes, Saul regards defeating the Philistine as a "man-sized" job, but with God's help a boy would be enough to do it. David is scornful of armor and weapons, trusting in the weapon he is used to, a slingshot. Having knocked Goliath unconscious, David then uses Goliath's own sword to cut off his head, causing the Philistine army to flee in panic. Interestingly, although Saul promised whomever defeated Goliath would receive his daughter's hand in marriage, this goes unmentioned at the end of this section. Once Saul finally offers Merab (18:17–19) and Michal (18:20–27) to David in marriage, it is not as a reward, but as a potential trap.[3]

David's actions were celebrated as an example of what could be accomplished by a person of faith. These verses from Jesus Ben Sira's reflection on David's life illustrate the point:

---

1. Eaton, *Psalms*, 6–7.
2. Klein, *1 Samuel*, 173.
3. Klein, *1 Samuel* 178.

> In his youth did he not kill a giant,
>> and take away the people's disgrace,
> when he whirled the stone in the sling
>> and struck down the boasting Goliath?
> For he called on the Lord, the Most High,
>> and he gave strength to his right arm
> to strike down a mighty warrior,
>> and to exalt the power of his people. (*Sirach* 47:4–5)

Although the New Testament itself does not make much of David's defeat of Goliath, the story remains a staple text for Christian preachers, who regularly use it to illustrate the point that faith in God is enough to overcome even the biggest obstacles. For the early church fathers, David's actions are seen as prefiguring Christ. For example, Caesarius of Arles explains:

> Both the lion and the bear typified the devil, for they had been strangled by the strength of David for having dared to attack some of his sheep. All that we read prefigured in David at that time, dearly beloved, we know was accomplished in our Lord Jesus Christ; for he strangled the lion and the bear when he descended into hell to free all the saints from their jaws.[4]

Maximus of Turin finds spiritual significance in the manner of Goliath's death:

> We read in the Scriptures that Christ is figuratively designated by the word *stone*, as the prophet says: "The stone that the builders rejected has become the head of the corner." [Psalm 118:22] Therefore, when Goliath was struck by a stone, he is struck down by the power of Christ.[5]

David Becomes King

Both 2 Samuel and 1 Chronicles record the fact that following Saul's death, it is David who becomes the next king. Dynastic succession should have passed to Saul's son Jonathan, but he too died. None of Saul's other relatives attain the throne; David becomes the next monarch. Second Samuel 2:1–4 stresses that the first thing David does on hearing of Saul's

---

4. Franke, *Joshua, Judges, Ruth, 1–2 Samuel*, 271.
5. Franke, *Joshua, Judges, Ruth, 1–2 Samuel*, 274.

death is to consult God; thus, the gift of the throne is from God himself.[6] Japhet points out that in 1 Chronicles 11 David is made king over the whole of Israel, not just the northern kingdom of Judah.[7] David does not automatically ascend the throne; he has to fight to attain it, fight to keep it and fight to pass it on to the son whom he chooses. The detail of this will not detain us here. Suffice to say that maintaining power means shedding blood. David is not a spotless and innocent king, but a crafty and cunning political operator.

David, Bathsheba and Uriah (2 Samuel 11:1—12:25)

The book of Chronicles does not record the incident in which David commits adultery with Bathsheba, but it is recorded in great detail in 2 Samuel. One spring, David does not go out to war with the army, which was the expected action of a king. He remains behind in Jerusalem. One afternoon, he sees a woman, Bathsheba, bathing, and decides he wishes to have sex with her. She is duly summoned to his bedroom. It is not clear from the text if this is a one-off or regular visit, but either way she becomes pregnant. David summons her husband, Uriah, from the battlefield, hoping he will sleep with his wife while on leave and thus explain her pregnancy. Uriah does not go home to her, choosing instead to remain in David's palace. David then sends him back to the battlefield, instructing Joab, the commander of the army, to arrange for Uriah's death in battle. Uriah duly dies, and David takes Bathsheba as his own. The Prophet Nathan then rebukes David using a judgment parable in which a rich man who owns many sheep steals a poor man's only lamb as a feast for a guest. David, initially outraged, is caught in the parable's trap as Nathan reveals that David's actions against Uriah make him the rich man who is the villain of the story. David duly repents, but the son born of adultery dies in childbirth.

Anderson asks whether Bathsheba was victim or accomplice to the adultery. She probably knew the king could see her bathing, but equally she could have resisted his advances to some extent. Anderson also argues that Uriah's death seems pointless; there would be no court that could convict David of sin. At best, it is an attempt to preserve David and Bathsheba's honor, but even that is dubious as there would have been at

---

6. Anderson, *2 Samuel*, 22.
7. Japhet, *I & II Chronicles*, 236.

least a two-month delay between the adultery and the marriage. Anderson concludes that David is more concerned with protecting his reputation that obeying God's law.[8]

This means David must experience God's judgment, as he does in Nathan's parable and its sequel (2 Samuel 11:27b—12:25). Anderson explains the purpose of this type of "judgment parable" is to disguise a real-life transgression of the law "as a parable told to the guilty person in order to lead him to pass judgment on himself." Examples of other judgment parables include 2 Samuel 14:1–20; 1 Kings 20:35–43; Isaiah 5:1–7. The basic message of the parable is that one who is rich and has everything takes the only treasured possession of a man who has nothing. To compound the situation, the rich man pretends to be "an outwardly generous and considerate host."[9] David admits his guilt, but the consequences of his sexual sin blight his family, as it is sexual infidelity that is their undoing.

Scholars speculate as to why Chronicles does not record this incident. As Japhet observes, the opening formula of 1 Chronicles 20 includes the statement that Joab and all Israel are fighting at Ammon, while David remains in Jerusalem.[10] In 2 Samuel 11, this introduces the episode in which David commits adultery with Bathsheba, but Chronicles omits the whole incident. We cannot be certain as to the relationship between Chronicles and Samuel, but Pratt is convincing in his suggestion that the incident with Bathsheba is omitted to recast the narrative in a positive light.[11] In essence, this second telling of the story of David wants to emphasize the great king, not the fallen sinner.

It is striking that some of the early church fathers interpret David's actions in a positive, allegorical light. Thus, Cassiodorus explains:

> Just as Bathsheba when washing herself unclothed in the brook of Kidron delighted David and deserved to attain the royal embraces, and her husband was slain at the prince's command, so too the church, the assembly of the faithful, once it has cleansed itself of the foulness of sins by the bath of sacred baptism, is known to be joined to Christ the Lord.[12]

---

8. Anderson, *2 Samuel*, 156.
9. Anderson, *2 Samuel*, 160–62.
10. Japhet, *I & II Chronicles*, 361–62.
11. Pratt, *1 and 2 Chronicles*, 164.
12. Franke, *Joshua, Judges, Ruth, 1–2 Samuel*, 355.

Here we see a clear example of how David is seen primarily as a type of Christ, and so even his apparently negative actions are understood in a positive light.

David as an Ideal King

The Old Testament regularly refers to David as the paradigmatic king, the one chosen and blessed by God to rule God's chosen and blessed people. There is a messianic prophecy in 2 Samuel 7:12–17 that states a Davidic king will remain on the throne of Israel forever. This idea was developed in later Jewish texts (Psalm 89; Jeremiah 23:5–8; Ezekiel 37:21–23; Zechariah 3:8–10; 12:17—13:1; Haggai 2:21–22; 4 Ezra 12:31–32; *Psalms of Solomon* 17–18; 1QM 11:1–18; 4Qflor 1:11–14; 4QTest 9–12). The early church fathers also made much of this prophecy, pointing to the connection with Jesus. Tertullian, for example, says:

> But is not Christ here designated the seed of David, as of that womb which was derived from David, that is, Mary's? Now, because Christ rather than any other was to build the temple of God, that is to say, a holy manhood, wherein God's Spirit might dwell as in a better temple, Christ rather than David's son Solomon was to be looked for as the Son of God.[13]

For the church fathers, the point was that the prophecy pointed primarily toward Jesus.

David in the New Testament

Overall, although the New Testament is interested in David, it is primarily focused on Davidic lineage, with the usage of the christological title *son of David* indicating particular understandings of Jesus. Christians interpreted the messianic prophecies about a *son of David* as referring to Jesus. Contemporary expectation was that this *son of David* would be a political leader who would defeat the Roman military occupation. Jesus thus engaged with, but also confounded, the messianic expectations of his peers. In Luke's birth narratives, Jesus' Davidic heritage is a key factor in establishing his legitimacy as the Messiah (Luke 1:27, 32, 69; 2:4, 11), as well as reference to David in genealogical records (Matthew 1:1, 6; Luke 3:31).

---

13. Franke, *Joshua, Judges, Ruth, 1–2 Samuel*, 351.

Moreover, when the angel tells Joseph in a dream that Mary is pregnant by the Holy Spirit, he addresses Joseph as *son of David* (Matthew 1:20). France explains this is a crucial part of the narrative, as Jesus' royal pedigree is established by having Joseph as his father, making Jesus also a "son of David."[14] Luke's Gospel accomplishes the same point via a different means. As Nolland explains, the reference to Joseph as being *of the house of David* (Luke 1:27) provides legal Davidic ancestry for Jesus.[15] The point is emphasized in Zechariah's song, where God is praised because *He has raised up a mighty savior for us in the house of his servant David* (Luke 1:69), using language reminiscent of David's prayer in 2 Samuel 7:26. Finally, when Luke tells us of the journey to Bethlehem, he again makes clear the connection between David and Joseph (and hence Jesus).

In Matthew's Gospel, the title *son of David* is associated with healing miracles (Matthew 9:27; 15:22; 20:30–31). France suggests the title is particularly important for Matthew, used both in relation to healing miracles, and also in discussing (Matthew 12:23) and proclaiming (Matthew 21:9, 15) Jesus' messianic status.[16] In an earlier volume, France discusses the title in more detail. He points out that Matthew uses *son of David* more than the rest of the New Testament. Luke and Mark share the reference in the story of the healing of Bartimaeus and the dispute over whether the Messiah is greater than David as well as being David's son. But the other uses of the term are unique to Matthew. While Matthew seems to expect the Messiah to be *son of David* and to have a healing ministry, there is no real evidence of this understanding in other texts of the time. France also proposes that since some of those who come to the *son of David* for healing are in fact Gentiles (the Syrophoenician woman and her demon possessed daughter, Matthew 15:22) or the socially marginalized, blind, dumb and oppressed (Matthew 9:27, 20:30–31), then Matthew is here reconfiguring messianic speculation away from Jewish preconceptions.[17]

Jesus, in dispute with the religious leaders, also sets out why he should be considered both David's son but also greater than David (Matthew 22:42–45; Mark 12:35–37; Luke 20:41–44). Mark's record of the incident is as follows:

---

14. France, *Matthew*, 53.
15. Nolland, *Luke 1:1—9:20*, 49.
16. France, *Matthew*, 366.
17. France, *Matthew: Evangelist and Teacher*, 284–86.

While Jesus was teaching in the temple, he said, "How can the scribes say that the Messiah is the son of David? David himself, by the Holy Spirit, declared,

> 'The Lord said to my Lord,
> "Sit at my right hand, until I put your enemies under your feet."'

David himself calls him Lord; so how can he be his son?" And the large crowd was listening to him with delight.

Gathercole explains that the basic argument is straightforward: since David recognizes the Messiah as Lord, then he cannot be the Messiah's forefather. Thus, Jesus implies he is not simply Son of David, but in fact Son of God. For Gathercole, this indicates Jesus hinting at his divine pre-existence, an argument supported by the rest of Psalm 110, whose opening verse Jesus cites here. The Greek version of the text, *From the womb, before the morning star, I gave you birth* (Psalm 110:3), would have been understood as indicating pre-existence. The next verse establishes the Messiah's priestly lineage: *The Lord has sworn and will not change his mind: "You are a priest forever, according to the order of Melchizedek"* (Psalm 110:4). This latter verse is picked up in Hebrews 16–17, which argue that the Messiah is an eternal priest in the order of Melchizedek. The point in the dispute in the Gospels, Gathercole concludes, is that Jesus argues the Messiah is David's Lord, not David's son. The citation of the first verse of Psalm 110 brings to mind the whole psalm, which supports this claim that the Messiah not simply Davidic, but in fact greater than David.[18]

David in the Qur'an

According to Kaltner and Mirza, there are sixteen mentions of David by name in the Qur'an, including instances where he is given powers that are not discussed in the Bible. Contrastingly, the story of his rise and reign are not featured in the Qur'an, while they are discussed extensively in the Bible (1 Samuel 16 to 1 Kings 2).[19] Both the Bible and the Qur'an tell the story of David killing Goliath, although the former does so in much more detail, and both associate David with the Psalms, with the Qur'an stating clearly that they were given to David by God (*an-Nisa'*

---

18. Gathercole, *Pre-Existent Son*, 236–38.
19. Kaltner and Mirza, *Bible and the Qur'an*, 34–36.

4:163; *al-Isra* 17:55). Reynolds comments that this attribution of the Psalms to David has both Jewish (*m. Avot* 6:9) and Christian precedent (Mark 12:36–37).[20]

The Qur'an also says that David received other gifts from God. This includes the gift of the throne and of wisdom (*al-Baqarah* 2:251), as well as knowledge from on high (*an-Naml* 27:15). David and his son Solomon are both associated with the natural world (*al-Anbiya'* 21:79; *Saba'* 34:10). David is also said to be skilled in metalworking and making weapons (*al-Anbiya'* 21:80; *Saba* 34:11). David and Adam are the only two people in the Qur'an who are given the title *khalifah* (*Sad* 38:26; *al-Baqarah* 2:30). Kaltner and Mirza suggest that in David's case the title *khalifa*, normally translated *vice-regent* or *successor*, indicates that his rule as king is temporary since only God is the supreme sovereign.[21] Wessels adds, "Thus, David is a good king insofar as he exercises kingship like a caliph."[22] Finally, Reynolds suggests the reference to David as king builds on Jewish and Christian tradition of David as the ideal king.[23]

The longest passage in the Qur'an that discusses David is *Sad* 38:16–28. This passage includes a scene where two men ask David to resolve a dispute between them. One man, who owns ninety-nine ewes, has taken the only ewe belonging to the other man. David criticizes the first man, but the realizes this is in fact a test from God for a sin he has committed. The Qur'an states, *And David guessed that We had (somehow) tested him, so he asked his Lord for forgiveness, and fell down, bowing, and turned (in repentance)* (*Sad* 38:24). This echoes the story in 2 Samuel 12 where the Prophet Nathan confronts David for his sins in committing adultery with Bathsheba and having her husband murdered. The Qur'an makes no explicit mention of this episode, but as Kaltner and Mirza comment: "Whatever its relationship to the biblical tradition might be, the episode is remarkable because it is a rare instance of a prophet seeking repentance in the Qur'an."[24] Reynolds argues that the Qur'an has made Nathan's parable into a "real" encounter.[25] Unal explains the incident as a test from

---

20. Reynolds, *Qur'an and the Bible*, 441.
21. Kaltner and Mirza, *Bible and the Qur'an*, 34–35.
22. Wessels, *Torah, the Gospel and the Qur'an*, 65.
23. Reynolds, *Qur'an and the Bible*, 691.
24. Kaltner and Mirza, *Bible and the Qur'an*, 35.
25. Reynolds, *Qur'an and the Bible*, 691.

God.²⁶ Nasr disputes the connection with the biblical Bathsheba incident, arguing that David as portrayed in the Qur'an is not an adulterer. Nasr proposes that David was in fact frightened when the two disputants entered his sanctuary, because he had given orders that no one should come in, and so thought the men had come to harm him. Thus, the request for forgiveness concerns David's fear, not his mistake in responding after only hearing one man. Moreover, the men are in fact angels, sent by God to test David.²⁷

Kaltner and Mirza note that the *Stories of the Prophets* traditions contain more background detail about the stories found in the Qur'an, including, for example, a more extensive account of the killing of Goliath and David's marriage to Michal daughter of Saul. According to *Stories of the Prophets*, David did not benefit financially from Saul's death, but rather made his living selling weapons. Tradition also records he divided his day in four: one quarter spent earning a living and resting, one quarter in prayer, one quarter in listening to his people's concerns and the final quarter giving sermons. He died suddenly, and was mourned by four thousand priests and thousands of people on a day so hot that Solomon ordered the birds to create shade for the crowd.²⁸

Wessels notes that neither David nor Solomon are called a *king* in the Qur'an, but rather referred to as *Prophets*. However, when David defeats Goliath, the Qur'an does state that he is given the kingdom, and God teaches him what to do (*al-Baqarah* 2:251).²⁹ Wessels also draws attention to parallels between Saul fighting with only a small army (*al-Baqarah* 2:249), and Gideon's army (Judges 7:5); both forces are deliberately minimized so that it is clear victory belongs to God. The defeat of Goliath by David is also woven into this story (*al-Baqarah* 2:251). Wessels argues this foreshadows the victory of the Muslims at the battle of Badr in 624, where they defeated a much larger army of Meccan opponents.³⁰

Finally, David receives the divine book of the *Zabur*, the Psalms. The content or teaching of *Zabur* is not discussed in detail in the Qur'an, which simply states that it was given to David as a gift of God. Thus, for example, Muhammad is told:

26. Unal, *Qur'an*, 876.
27. Nasr, *Study Qur'an*, 1106–7.
28. Kaltner and Mirza, *Bible and the Qur'an*, 35.
29. Wessels, *Qur'an and the Bible*, 64–65.
30. Wessels, *Qur'an and the Bible*, 120–21.

> Surely We have inspired you [that is, Muhammad] as We inspired Noah and the prophets after him, and as We inspired Abraham, and Ishmael, and Isaac, and Jacob, and the tribes, and Jesus, and Job, and Jonah, and Aaron, and Solomon, and We gave David (the) Psalms. (*an-Nisa'* 4:163; see also *al-Isra* 17:55)

Later Muslim tradition extols David's voice and music. For example, Awaza'i claims David's voice was so excellent that *the birds and wild animals used to stay with him until they died of thirst and hunger*. Similarly, Wahb. B. Munabbih explains that all who heard David had to skip as if they were dancing, and the *jinn*, as well as people, birds and animals, all stayed close to hear him.[31]

Later Islamic tradition holds up David as a model of piety. Thus, in the *hadith* of Bukhari and Muslim, the Prophet is recorded as saying:

> The most beloved prayer to God is the prayer of David. The most beloved fast to God is the fast of David. He used to sleep half the night, then keep vigil for another third of it, then sleep for another sixth. He used to fast for a day, then break the fast for a day. He did not flee when he met an enemy.[32]

Conclusion

David is therefore an important figure for Christians and Muslims, but the way in which he is understood and his role in the family of faith differs. What do we make of the accounts of David's moral failures and his repentance? What does that teach Muslims and Christians about their own relationship with God? How do we understand Davidic authorship of the Psalms? In what was is David a precursor for Jesus and does he have a similar relationship with Muhammad?

Solomon

The discussion of Solomon will focus on three areas: his wisdom, his building projects and his wives. A fourth, related area, the visit of the queen of Sheba, will also be discussed.

---

31. Wheeler, *Prophets in the Qur'an*, 261.
32. Wheeler, *Prophets in the Qur'an*, 260–61.

Solomon in the Old Testament

As well as the account of his life found in the books of Kings and Chronicles, the figure of Solomon is also present within the wisdom literature of the Old Testament. He is identified as *the Teacher* who tells his wisdom in the book of Ecclesiastes, and as the author of many of the Proverbs found in the book of that name.

King Solomon's Wise Acts of Justice, 1 Kings 3:16–28

The main Old Testament story that demonstrates Solomon's wisdom is found in 1 Kings 3:16–28. Two prostitutes come to Solomon demanding justice from him. They have both had a son, but one son has died in the night, and now both women are claiming the living son as their own. Solomon decrees that the only fair way of solving this problem is for the baby boy to be cut in half: each woman will then have half a son. One woman readily agrees to the solution, but the other renounces her claim. Solomon then explains his ruse. The one who relinquished her claim is the true mother, for any mother would rather her son be given to another than for him to die.

DeVires argues that the story of the two prostitutes and the argument over the fate of their children is not necessary especially Israelite; the situation could have occurred anywhere in the world. It is only the final word of judgment that makes it particular to Israel. The fact that they are prostitutes is crucial to the narrative, because it shows a wise king acting on behalf of the lowliest of his subjects. Moreover, a house of prostitution would lack a male authority figure to make decisions. Finally, the moral bankruptcy of prostitution forms the backdrop to the contrasting display of selfless love and heartless cruelty the two women display. While all this is true, the main focus of the anecdote is to demonstrate Solomon's wisdom.[33]

Wray-Beal argues that the focus is not simply on Solomon's wisdom, but on the fact that this wisdom is a gift of God, explaining that in passing judgment,

> Solomon indicates the true mother by stating, "Give to her the living child . . . she is his mother," which in no way indicates which of the two women he means . . . The Hebrew does not specify which

---

33. DeVires, *1 Kings*, 58–62.

woman Solomon indicates when he makes his pronouncement, nor how he reaches his judgment. But that it is acknowledged as "justice" by all is the whole point. Textually, the riddle remains unsolvable for the reader . . . The reader cannot resolve the dilemma; Solomon does so only by divine wisdom.[34]

Wray-Beal develops the point, stressing that the point the text is teaching is the importance of listening to God for guidance. The focus is thus less on Solomon and more on God.[35] This view is also taken by Ambrose, who says that the mind of God was in Solomon and that it *was therefore a sign of wisdom to distinguish between secret heart thoughts, to draw the truth from hidden springs and to pierce as it were with the sword of the Spirit not only the inward parts of the body but even of the mind and soul.*[36]

Solomon's Building Projects

DeVires explains that political reality meant Solomon had to build a temple, as recorded in 1 Kings 6:1–71: "One nation, one capital, one king demanded one temple for its one God."[37] Wray-Beal adds that the "length and detailed account of the temple's construction is not only the focal point of Solomon's reign, but is the high point of Israel's covenant history."[38] The elaborate ceremony when the building is consecrated and the presence of God established there is testament to the significance of this event.

But while the temple was a massive construction, built to last, the palace that Solomon builds for himself is in fact far bigger (1 Kings 7:2–12). Thus, Solomon did everything he could to show he was a great king, as he built a temple to show that the Lord was a great god. But Solomon's construction projects focus more on riches and honor than on wisdom. "His was undoubtedly the piety of worldly success."[39]

---

34. Wray-Beal, *1 & 2 Kings*, 88.
35. Wray-Beal, *1 & 2 Kings*, 89–91.
36. Conti, *1–2 Kings*, 16.
37. DeVires, *1 Kings*, 96.
38. Wray-Beal, *1 & 2 Kings*, 125.
39. DeVires, *1 Kings*, 103.

Solomon's Wives

First Kings 9:26—11:13 discusses Solomon's wealth, wisdom and wives, although, as DeVires states, the focus is on wealth, with mention of gold dominating the narrative.[40] Even the visit of the queen of Sheba is really a test of Solomon's riches and glory, not simply his wisdom. Solomon passes the test with flying colors.

Origen sees the visit of the queen of Sheba primarily in spiritual terms:

> The Scriptures express astonishment that the queen of Sheba came from "the end of the earth to hear Solomon's wisdom." When she saw his dinner, his furnishings and the attendants in his place, she was astounded and wholly in a state of wonder. If we do not embrace the great riches of our Lord, the great furnishings of his Word and the wealth of his teachings; if we do not eat the "bread of life"; we are not fed with the flesh of Jesus and do not drink his blood; if we disdain the banquet of our Savior, we should realize that God has both "kindness and severity" [Rom 11:22]. Of these, we should pray more for his kindness on us, in Christ Jesus our Lord.[41]

Thus, for Origen, the visit of the queen of Sheba has less to do with Solomon and more to do with the faith of the Christian disciple of Jesus.

Regarding Solomon's wives, DeVires identifies the many marriages as part of Solomon's political strategy. His many concubines were a demonstration of his wealth and virility. DeVires does not regard the numbers as historical or factual, but says they are "patently schematic (7x10x10 of queenly rank, 3x10x10 mere concubines)." He points out the problem of accommodating such numbers to support his case that the numbers are symbolic.[42]

Wray-Beal suggests that Solomon's horses, which are of great interest to the Qur'an, are indicative of military strength (see 1 Kings 10:25). Moreover, the queen of Sheba is an example of a prominent foreigner who praises the God of Israel. She is portrayed as a monarch who has status, wealth and wisdom, standing on equal footing to Solomon. It is therefore significant that she praises not only Solomon for his wealth, but also the god who provided that wealth and wisdom. Finally, Wray-Beal argues that the queen of Sheba's words "contribute to the ambiguous

---

40. DeVires, *1 Kings*, 138–39.
41. Conti, *1–2 Kings*, 68.
42. DeVires, *1 Kings*, 143.

portrait of Solomon" that the text presents. While she says that the Lord has placed Solomon on the throne to practice righteousness and justice, the text emphasizes his wealth, which is focused only on his court, not the people as a whole.[43]

The ambiguity of Solomon's reign is further emphasized by his many marriages. Wray-Beal suggests that Pharaoh's daughter (1 Kings 11) functions as a "cipher of Solomon's blemished rule."[44] Solomon transgresses Deuteronomy's commands to avoid foreign wives because of fear that they will turn Israel astray (Deuteronomy 17:17).

The Account in Chronicles

Pratt explains that Chronicles records neither Solomon's rise nor his fall. There is no account of Solomon's ruthless treatment of his political opponents (1 Kings 1:1—2:46). Although Solomon's Egyptian wife is mentioned once (2 Chronicles 8:11), there is no account of foreign wives bringing syncretism into the kingdom of Israel (as found in 1 Kings 11:1–25). Thus Chronicles does not recount Solomon's fall in the way Kings does.[45]

In Chronicles, Solomon is established as king, but recognizes his own inadequacy. Visited by God in a dream, he asks for the wisdom he knows he will need in order to rule over the people. God responds with the gift not just of wisdom, but also of riches and honor. Solomon's wisdom is assumed; there is no case of the two prostitutes in this account (2 Chronicles 1:7–13).

Regarding the queen of Sheba's visit, Japhet describes the account in 2 Chronicles 20:1–12 as having "a literary, even popular tone," explaining that the focus is on Solomon's "wealth, wisdom and international status," not on the political implications of the visit.[46] Japhet identifies three elements in the queen's speech to Solomon: wonder at Solomon's wisdom, blessing on the king's household and praise to the God of Israel for favoring the people with such a worthy monarch.[47] Pratt concurs that the Chronicler is here reinforcing his own perspective. The text has praised

---

43. Wray-Beal, *1 & 2 Kings*, 162–64.
44. Wray-Beal, *1 & 2 Kings*, 170.
45. Pratt, *1 & 2 Chronicles* 205
46. Japhet, *I & II Chronicles*, 634.
47. Japhet, *I & II Chronicles*, 636.

Solomon; now confirmation comes from the mouth of a skeptical foreign queen. International recognition bolsters Israelite praise of Solomon as a great king.[48]

The Wisdom of King Solomon

King Solomon has traditionally been believed to be the author of the two biblical wisdom books of Proverbs and Ecclesiastes. The former introduces itself as *The proverbs of Solomon son of David, king of Israel* (Proverbs 1:1), while the latter has *The words of the Teacher, the son of David, king in Jerusalem* (Ecclesiastes 1:1). As noted above, both Kings and Chronicles describe Solomon as wise, giving further support to the case that Solomon wrote these two books. While many readers of the text may take these statements as confirming the idea of Solomonic authorship, modern scholarship is less convinced. Murphy points out that Proverbs contains several collections, some of which are described as having different authors.[49] Koptak adds that of the seven superscriptions in Proverbs, three name Solomon (Proverbs 1:1; 10:1; 25:1), two name "the wise" (Proverbs 22:17; 24:23), one names Agur (Proverbs 30:1) and one Lemuel and his mother (Proverbs 31:1). No one really knows who Agur and Lemuel were. While Murphy is unconvinced that Solomon can be described as author of Proverbs in any meaningful way, Koptak proposes that "there is no reason to doubt that Solomon is to be associated with much of the book as author and patron." This does not mean Koptak thinks Solomon wrote the whole book, as he concedes there is no rigorous, scholarly method for distinguishing what may be Solomonic and what may be the product of a later wisdom tradition that carried on Solomon's work.[50]

Regarding Ecclesiastes, Longman explains that *the Teacher* (*Qohelet* in Hebrew) has traditionally been taken as a nickname for Solomon. The theory was that an older, wiser and repentant Solomon looked back at his life, especially his apostasy as recorded in 1 Kings 11:1–13, and wrote Ecclesiastes as a guide to a better way of life. Further support for this theory comes from 1 Kings 8, which records the dedication of the temple. Solomon *gathers* the people for the ceremony. The Hebrew verb has the

---

48. Pratt, *1 & 2 Chronicles*, 257.
49. Murphy, *Proverbs*, xx.
50. Koptak, *Proverbs*, 32.

root *qhl*, making Solomon the *assembler*, a possible intertextual reference to *Qohelet*.

While this convinces some, Longman makes a strong case that refutes the notion of Solomonic authorship. First, he suggests the pseudonym *Qohelet* indicates someone wanting to associate himself with Solomon, rather than Solomon the king. Second, regarding the use of the past tense where the author states, *I, Qohelet, was king over Israel in Jerusalem*, Longman argues this indicates a time when Solomon was alive but no longer king, yet 1 Kings 11 records that Solomon died while still king. Third, the association between Solomon and *Qohelet* lasts only for the first three chapters. By chapter 4, the author distances himself from those in power. Indeed, Ecclesiastes 5:8–9 is critical of how rulers oppress the poor for personal gain, the very thing Solomon did. Fourth, Longman cites external evidence that indicates the bulk of the book (Ecclesiastes 1:12—12:7) has a similar style and structure of other ancient Near Eastern texts that are classified as fictional autobiographies.[51] Murphy also supports the case against Solomonic authorship of Ecclesiastes, concurring that *Qohelet*'s attitude to royalty is "distant, if not critical, as in the observations about injustice in 3:16; 4:1–2; and 5:7."[52]

A third biblical book that is linked with Solomon is the Song of Songs, also called the Song of Solomon. It begins, *The song of songs, which is Solomon's*. Garett argues that this superscription could be translated as *belonging to Solomon* or *written by Solomon* or even *dedicated to Solomon*.[53] This could mean the text is anonymous but sponsored by Solomon or else that he wrote it. He further contends that the archaeological evidence supports the historicity of the accounts in Kings and Chronicles. That is to say, there is strong evidence that Solomon did indeed build the temple, which, while not proving Solomonic authorship of the text, does indicate it could have been written during that period. The main challenge to the case that Solomon wrote Song of Songs is Solomon's morality. His sexual appetites and marriages to foreign princesses drew him away from worshipping Israel's God. I personally am persuaded that this is a book written *for Solomon*, that is, as a rebuke to Solomon's sexual excesses. Garrett counterargues that virtuous lives and virtuous words

---

51. Longman, *Ecclesiastes*, 2–8
52. Murphy, *Ecclesiastes*, xx.
53. Garett, *Song of Songs*, 22–25.

do not go hand in hand. Perhaps it is true that Solomon wrote piously of monogamy while practicing polygamy.

Longman mounts a strong case against Solomon as author of Song of Songs. His main point concerns Solomon's lifestyle, his "dubious reputation in the area of love." While Song of Songs praises an exclusive, committed, monogamous relationship, Solomon had many wives and concubines. This is clearly judged as a moral failure within the book of Kings; indeed, it is argued to be the root cause of Israel's eventual exile from the Promised Land. Longman also argues that Solomon barely features in the text of Song of Songs. He only features on three occasions, and each time as object, not composer, of the poem. Finally, building on his argument that Solomon did not write Ecclesiastes, or the whole of Proverbs, Longman argues that Song of Songs is probably an anthology of love poems. Solomon may have written one or more poems, but there is no reason to presume he was responsible for the book as a whole.[54]

This section has briefly introduced three books of wisdom literature, all of which are associated with Solomon. Most modern scholars are unconvinced that Solomon actually wrote all of any of the three books, although some concede he may have written at least part of perhaps two of them (Proverbs and Song of Songs). For the purpose of our discussion, it does not really matter whether Solomon actually did write them, and indeed the question of authorship does not necessarily have a significant impact on how the three books are interpreted. Suffice to say that Solomon was, and still is, associated with wisdom, even if he is also recognized within the Old Testament as a flawed character, whose wisdom did not save him from apostasy to the living God.

Solomon in the New Testament

For the New Testament, Solomon is a minor figure, but Jesus does refer to the queen of Sheba as one who will rise up in judgment against the generation that saw Jesus but rejected him (Luke 11:31; Matthew 12:42). Green finds an element of ironic contrast in Jesus' statement in Luke. The visit of the queen of Sheba was a test that resulted in recognition and relationship; the crowd talking with Jesus tests him but then rejects him. Moreover, Jesus' audience is drawn from the people of Israel, while Solomon's visitor was a foreigner. God's own people ought, Jesus argues,

---

54. Longman, *Song of Songs*, 2–7.

to have recognized God's own messenger if a foreigner managed to do so.⁵⁵ Keener adds that the image of a foreign queen being resurrected to condemn Israelites would have horrified Jesus' audience, many of whom expected "Israel's final vindication against the nations at that judgment day."⁵⁶ The point of Jesus' reference to the queen is that her actions are condemnation for those who fail to emulate them.

Solomon in Extrabiblical Material

The Babylonian Talmud argues that Solomon had power over demons, which enabled him to build the temple. The head of the demons is called *Ashmedai*, through whom Solomon acquires a magical worm (the *shamir*), which is able to cut through stones:

> He said to the Rabbis, How shall I manage [without iron tools]?— They replied, There is the *shamir* which Moses brought for the stones of the ephod . . . He asked them, Where is it to be found? They replied, Bring a male and a female demon and tie them together; perhaps they will know and tell you. So he brought a male and a female demon and tied them together. They said to him, We do not know, but perhaps Ashmedai the prince of demons knows. He said to them, Where is he?—They answered, He is in such-and-such a mountain . . . Solomon kept [Ashmedai] with him until he had built the Temple. (*Gittin* 68a-b)⁵⁷

In its account of Solomon's wisdom, the *Targum Sheni* of Esther recounts how Solomon would summon *wild beasts, birds of the sky, reptiles of the earth, demons, spirits and screeching owls to dance before him, so as to show his greatness to all the kings who were hosted in his presence.* On one occasion, the hoopoe was missing; when he returned, Solomon summoned him to explain himself. The hoopoe explains that he has been travelling, and has visited the queen of Sheba. Sheba is described as a wealthy land, but one where the people do not know how to fight. The hoopoe proposes that he fly to the queen of Sheba with a letter ordering her to submit to Solomon's rule, as Solomon is the king ordained by God to rule over *the wild beasts, over the fowl of the heavens and over demons and spirits.* Solomon consents to the plan and the hoopoe flies

---

55. Green, *Luke* 464.
56. Keener, *Matthew*, 368.
57. Cited in Reynolds, *Qur'an and the Bible*, 654–55.

forth. The message instructs the queen to submit or face the armies of demons that Solomon will send against her. The prospect of invasion terrifies the queen, who duly sets out to see Solomon to determine if she should surrender. The journey is supposed to take seven years, but she does it in three.

When she arrives, the queen is conducted to Solomon, who is seated in a house of glass. This illusion deceives the queen, and she raises her dress, fearful she will get it wet, because she thinks Solomon is sitting in water. This movement exposes her hairy legs, which causes Solomon to comment, *Your beauty is the beauty of a woman but your hair is the hair of men. Now hair is beautiful for a man but shameful for a woman.* The queen of Sheba then sets Solomon three riddles to test his wisdom, the first of which is: *What is a wooden well, an iron pail which draws up stones and brings forth worth?* Solomon supplies the correct answer: a makeup box. Solomon answers all three riddles correctly, causing the queen to bless and praise God for giving Solomon the throne, as well as giving Solomon a large quantity of gold.[58]

In his account of the queen of Sheba in *Antiquities* 8.165–75, Josephus explains that she hears of his wisdom and virtue and resolves to visit him herself. *Accordingly she came to Jerusalem with great splendor and rich furnishings* (*Antiquities* 8.166). She gives Solomon many gifts and asks many questions, which Solomon answers easily. The queen is amazed by what she encounters, and in particular is impressed by the piety and devotion of the temple worship she sees. She tells Solomon that she blesses God for having made Solomon king and for all that he has given to the people.

Solomon in the Qur'an

Solomon is mentioned by name seventeen times in the Qur'an. Kaltner and Mirza note four sections that present his life in more detail (*al-Anbiya'* 21:78–82; *an-Naml* 27:15–44; *Saba'* 34:10–14; *Sad* 38:30–40).[59] Both Solomon and his father David are granted wisdom by God (*an-Naml* 27:15), which they demonstrate by resolving a dispute about sheep grazing in a field (*al-Anbiya'* 21:78–79). Solomon can also communicate with birds and ants and has authority over *jinn*:

58. Account taken from Grossfeld, *Two Targums of Esther*, 114–17.
59. Kaltner and Mirza, *Bible and the Qur'an*, 160–61.

> Solomon inherited (it) from David, and said, "People! We have been taught the speech of birds, and we have been given (some) of everything. Surely this—it indeed is clear favor." Gathered before Solomon were his forces—jinn, and men, and birds—and they were arranged (in rows)—until, when they came upon the Wadi of the Ants, an ant said, "Ants! Enter your dwellings, or Solomon and his forces will crush you without realizing (it)." But he smiled, laughing at its words, and said, "My Lord, (so) dispose me that I may be thankful for your blessing with which You have blessed me and my parents, and that I may be righteousness (that) pleases You, and cause me to enter, by Your mercy, among your righteous servants." (*an-Naml* 27:16–19)

While this passage describes Solomon as having authority over the *jinn*, these beings are elsewhere described as *satans* (*al-Anbiya'* 21:82, see also *al-Baqarah* 2:101–3, *Sad* 38:37), that is, a type of *jinn* who are in rebellion against the divine will. Solomon also has power over the wind (*al-Anbiya'* 21:81; *Saba'* 34:12; *Sad* 38:36). Thus, within the Qur'an, Solomon has control over the sky, the earth and the sea, and over human, animal and spiritual forces. Nasr comments that for Sufis, *the language of the birds* symbolized a higher state of consciousness, enabling the believer to understand the deeper significance of things beyond their outward form,[60] while Ibn Kathir explains:

> Solomon went out one day with his army of Jinn, people and birds. The Jinn and the people went with him and the birds flew overhead providing shade from the heat with their wings.[61]

In a similar vein, Zuhri tells of the time Solomon overheard an ant's prayer:

> Solomon went out with some of his companions to pray for water. He saw an ant standing and raising one of its legs toward heaven, praying for water. He said to his companions, "Return, for you will have rain. This ant has already prayed for rain, and it will be answered."[62]

Wessels explains that God gave kingship (*mulk*) to Solomon in a way that he did not do for any other ruler (*Sad* 38:35). Solomon also received the gift of knowledge (*'ilm*) and wisdom, just as his father David

---

60. Nasr, *Study Qur'an*, 931.
61. Wheeler, *Prophets in the Qur'an*, 267.
62. Wheeler, *Prophets in the Qur'an*, 267.

did (*an-Naml* 27:15; *al-Anbiya'* 21:79). Solomon became David's heir (*an-Naml* 27:16), growing to become more righteous than his father (*al-Anbiya'* 21:78, 79). Solomon also had other gifts, but was especially renowned for his divinely given great wisdom and esoteric, comprehensive knowledge of all things. He exceeded all people in the East and all Egyptians in his wisdom. This meant that many people, including the emissaries of rulers, came from the surrounding countries to listen to his wise words.[63] Thus, the Qur'an also records the visit of the queen of Sheba (*an-Naml* 27:20–44; compare 1 Kings 10:1–13), an episode discussed in more detail below.

Solomon is also recognized in the Qur'an as a builder (*Saba'* 34:13). The Qur'an makes no mention of Solomon following other gods (as found in 1 Kings 11), but it does say his skewed priorities meant he did not worship God properly (*Sad* 38:30–40). Wessels explains the incident as follows:

> One evening before sunset, Solomon has his racehorses paraded before him and becomes completely absorbed in admiring them. He strokes their legs and necks and becomes so preoccupied that he forgets about the time of prayer at sunset, so he thus neglects thinking about God. He loves his horses, the possession of worldly goods, more than he does thinking about God, until the sun is concealed behind the veil of night (*Sad* 38:32).[64]

The detail of the story is disputed, but Kalter and Mirza suggest that the main point is that Solomon's love of horses distracts him from devotion to God. Once he realizes his mistake and asks for forgiveness, he is restored in his relationship with God. This is "one of the few texts in the Qur'an to acknowledge that sometimes even prophets must repent of their shortcomings."[65] Reynolds suggests there are links with Deuteronomy 17:16, which argues that a king should not have excessive numbers of horses. There are also echoes of 2 Kings 23:11, where Josiah destroys statues of horses that have been dedicated to the sun.[66] As an aside, it is worth noting that Unal argues the verses teach that nothing, not even his superbly bred horses, distracted Solomon from remembrance of God.[67]

---

63. Wessels, *Torah, the Gospel and the Qur'an*, 131.
64. Wessels, *Torah, the Gospel and the Qur'an*, 141.
65. Kaltner and Mirza, *Bible and the Qur'an*, 161.
66. Kaltner and Mirza, *Bible and the Qur'an*, 692.
67. Unal, *Qur'an*, 878.

Finally, Solomon's death is also narrated in the Qur'an:

> And when We decreed death for him, nothing indicated his death to them except a creature of the earth devouring his staff. When he fell down, it became clear to the jinn that, if they had known the unseen, they would not have remained in the humiliating punishment. (*Saba'* 34:14)

The detailed meaning of this statement is obscure, but tradition holds that Solomon had enslaved the *jinn* and had them build the temple for him. They continued working even after Solomon died, because his body remained either standing or seating on his throne, propped up by his staff. Eventually a small creature, perhaps a worm or ant, ate its way through the bottom of the staff, causing it to collapse. This meant Solomon's body fell and the *jinn* realized he was dead, and that they had continued to work in apparent slavery, finishing the temple, when they could, in fact, have been free.

The Queen of Sheba in the Qur'an

There is one account in the Qur'an of the visit of the queen of Sheba to Solomon (*an-Naml* 27:20–44), which parallels the biblical account in 1 Kings 10:1–13. In both sources, she remains unnamed and her land is not precisely identified.

Wessels explains that Sheba, or Saba, is a country in the southern part of the Arabian Peninsula, a region where commerce flourished, and so the country became wealthy through trade. The people who lived there originally worshipped the sun, moon and morning star, and they had flourishing gardens. The Qur'an records that God punished the people for turning their backs on him, by breaking down a dam that flooded their gardens (*Saba'* 34:15–17), a tradition also found in Josephus' *Antiquities* 2.22. Wessels adds that the Ma'rib dam broke in 542 CE, twenty-five years before the birth of Muhammad. Ma'rib was the capital of the region of Saba, and sat on an important trade route, connecting to Jerusalem. The queen of Sheba, unnamed in the Bible or the Qur'an, but called *Balkis* in later Christian and *Bilqis* in later Islamic tradition, comes from this region to Solomon. Her journey was undoubtedly a commercial venture.[68]

In the Qur'an it is a hoopoe, a member of Solomon's retinue of birds, that reports on a visit to the queen of Sheba. The hoopoe explains that she

---

68. Wessels, *Torah, the Gospel and the Qur'an*, 133–35.

and her people have been deceived by Satan, and so do not worship God. Solomon dispatches the bird back to the queen, with a letter ordering her and her people to come to him in submission. The queen responds with a gift, but Solomon rejects it, regarding it as simply her flaunting her wealth.

Solomon then threatens to invade her land, but the queen instead visits him, and is tested twice. The first test involves her throne. Solomon has the *jinn* transport it to his palace, and disguised. It is presented to the queen, who is asked if it is hers. She responds that it seems to be. The second test involves her entering the palace, which she thinks has a pool of water in it, and so bares her ankles. Solomon explains that it is actually a crystal floor. The queen then admits her mistake, and surrenders to Solomon's god. Kaltner and Mirza note that the Qur'an and Bible have different purposes in telling the story. The former focuses on the queen and her conversion, while the latter aims to illustrate Solomon's God-given wisdom.[69] Wessels notes that the throne is the symbol of the power of a ruler, a point that he discusses in relation to Solomon's throne in the Qur'an (*al-Baqarah* 2:255), as well as the queen of Sheba's. But most significantly, the throne really belongs to God, the Lord of the throne (*al-Isra* 17:42; *al-Anbiya'* 21:22; *al-Mu'minum* 23:86, 116; *an-Naml* 27:26; *az-Zukhruf* 43:82; *at-Takwir* 81:20; *al-Buruj* 85:15).[70] Nasr argues for a spiritual interpretation of the text, proposing that the hoopoe represents an aspect of the soul, and Solomon the spiritual heart, which must control the soul and keep it devoted to Allah.[71]

Pointers for Discussion

Solomon is a complex figure in the Qur'an. He is both a paradigm of virtue and also a warning of the consequences of unbelief and moral failure. Solomon receives wisdom from God, which he uses to good effect in governing his kingdom, and his fame spreads far and wide. Yet at the same time, his wealth and his women take him away from his relationship with God. The Qur'an and the Bible treat Solomon differently, but both books do acknowledge his failures as well as his successes. This is an important reminder for Muslims and Christians as we discuss Solomon. Not only does he show us how to follow God, but he also indicates the

---

69. Kaltner and Mirza, *Bible and the Qur'an*, 152–53.
70. Wessels, *Torah, the Gospel and the Qur'an*, 136–37.
71. Nasr, *Study Qur'an*, 932.

consequences of disobedience. Finally, neither the Qur'an nor the Bible makes any typological claims about Solomon; he is more an example for the believer than he is a type of Muhammad or of Christ.

Mary

THIS CHAPTER FOCUSES ON the nativity and childhood of Mary and Jesus, as they are all interlinked within the text of the Qur'an. Other aspects of Jesus' life are dealt with in the next chapter. Mary is the only woman named in the Qur'an; there are thirty-four references. Twenty-three of these define her as Jesus' mother. A further six are found in *al-Imran* 3:35–47, which recounts Mary's birth and pregnancy. There are two verses that do not mention Mary by name, but describe her and Jesus as signs (*al-Anbiya'* 21:91; *al-Mu'minun* 23:50). But Mary is not considered a Prophet by most Muslims; that role is limited to men. This final point is potentially controversial, as both Mary and Jesus are addressed as *messengers* in *al-Mu'minun* 23:51. At any rate, Mary is regarded as "an exceptionally pious woman with the highest spiritual rank among women."[1]

The chapter is divided into four main sections. First is an examination of six key texts within the Qur'an; second, a discussion of the designation of Mary as *sister of Aaron*; third, a presentation of Christian understandings of Mary; and fourth, comparison of Mary in Christian and Muslim devotion.

Six Key Texts

The six key texts that this chapter discusses are: the conception and birth of Mary, Mary's childhood in the *mihrab*, the annunciation of Jesus' birth, Jesus' birth, Mary's defense of her virginity and the miracle of Jesus speaking as an infant.

---

1. Nasr, *Study Qur'an*, 763.

Conception and Birth of Mary (al-Imran 3:35–37)

In these verses, the unnamed wife of Imran promises the unidentified child in her womb will be dedicated in God's service once he or she is born, saying, *My Lord, surely I vow to You what is in my belly, (to be) dedicated into Your service). Accept (it) from me. Surely You—You are the Hearing, the Knowing* (al-Imran 3:35). Once the child is born and identified as a girl, Imran's wife gifts her to God, naming her Mary and seeking refuge for Mary and her descendants from Satan. She is placed in the care of Zechariah, as she lives in the temple.

In discussing this section of the Qur'an Reynolds suggests there are strong links to the *Protoevangelium of James*.[2] This text was written in Greek in the second half of the second century and translated into Syriac in the fifth century, and relates events before the ministry of Christ. As Elliott notes in his discussion of the text, there is little historical value to these stories, but the significance for this discussion is not historicity but literary connection with the Qur'an.[3]

The *Protoevangelium* describes Mary's mother Anna as barren, who is belittled when she goes to offer sacrifices to God. In her grief, she puts on mourning garments, and raises a prayer of lamentation to God. God hears her prayer and sends an angel who gives her a promise of a child. In response, Anna prays, *As the Lord my God lives, if I bear a child, whether male or female, I will bring it as a gift to the Lord my God, and it shall serve him all the days of its life* (Protoevangelium 4:1). This is just one example of how the Qur'an is "closely in conversation with the *Protoevangelium*," which was widely read and very influential in the Christian near East.[4] Both Christians and Muslims hold Mary in high esteem, but many evangelical Christians would not put much weight on extrabiblical texts. Nevertheless, they can discuss their understandings of Mary's birth and conception, as well as what these events teach us about our relationship with God.

Childhood of Mary in the Mihrab (al-Imran 3:37–44)

Mary grows up in the *mihrab*. Reynolds notes that the precise meaning of this word is subject to debate, but most assume it must indicate

---

2. Reynolds, *Qur'an and Its Biblical Subtext*, 140–44.
3. Elliott, *Apocryphal New Testament*, 51.
4. Reynolds, *Qur'an and Its Biblical Subtext*, 144.

a building, or part of a building.⁵ A common translation is *sanctuary*, suggesting that this is part of the Jerusalem temple. In his notes to his translation, Droge suggests *al-mihrab* is the place of prayer of a mosque, or in this case the Jerusalem temple.⁶ Droge himself uses the translation *place of prayer*. Nasr adds that many mosques have the relevant section. *Whenever Zechariah entered . . . Surely God provides for whomever He pleases without reckoning* inscribed above the *mihrab*.⁷

The Qur'an records that Mary grew up in the temple cared for by God. Whenever Zechariah entered the place where she lived, he found that food had already been provided for her. When he enquired as to the origin of this food, Mary responded, *It is from God. Surely God provides for whomever he pleases without reckoning* (*al-Imran* 3:37). There is a further tradition that Gabriel brought Mary fruit out of season, that is he supplied her with summer fruits in winter and winter fruits in summer; another tradition is that he brought grapes from heaven. The point is that Mary was fed from the garden of paradise.⁸

Zechariah, witnessing this, is then moved to pray for a child, despite his and his wife's advancing years. God answers his prayer, promising him the boy John the Baptist. As a sign of God's provision, Zechariah is then silent for three days. He is also reminded of Mary's obedience, presumably as a sign that he too should be obedient, in marked contrast with the account found in Luke, discussed below.

As with the section above, there are parallels with the *Protoevangelium of James*. In this text, Mary is kept in seclusion and purity for the first three years of her life, before her parents deliver her to the temple in fulfillment of her mother's vow. In the temple, Mary is under the charge of the high priest, Zechariah. *Mary was in the temple of the Lord nurtured like a dove and received food from the hand of an angel* (Protoevangelium 8:1). The next two chapters of the *Protoevangelium* record how Mary came to be married to Joseph, who is recorded as being much older than her. The parallels with the section of the Qur'an cited above indicate it is likely there is some kind of relationship between the two texts, although the exact nature of that relationship is unclear.

5. Reynolds, *Qur'an and Its Biblical Subtext*, 135.
6. Droge, *Qur'an*, 34n51.
7. Nasr, *Study Qur'an*, 142.
8. Reynolds, *Qur'an and Its Biblical Subtext*, 136.

Annunciation of Jesus' Birth to Mary
(al-Imran 3:45–47; Maryam 19:16–21)

Mourad proposes there are subtle differences between the two annunciation stories found in the Qur'an, arguing that the one in *surah Imran* (3:45–47) derives from the *Protoevangelium of James* while that of *surah Maryam* (19:17–21) comes from the Gospel of Luke. Both Luke and *Maryam* start with the annunciation of John to Zechariah before recounting the annunciation of Jesus to Mary, in which the angel tells Mary she will conceive a boy. By contrast, *Imran* and the *Protoevangelium of James* begin with the annunciation of Mary and her upbringing in the temple, before reporting the annunciation of Jesus, in which the angel tells Mary she will conceive the word of God.[9]

In Luke's Gospel, an angel appears to Mary, telling her she has received the favor of God. As she considers what this greeting means, the angel adds, *And now, you will conceive in your womb and bear a son, and you will name him Jesus. He will be great, and will be called the Son of the Most High, and the Lord God will give to him the throne of his ancestor David* (Luke 1:31–32). Mary questions how this will happen, and the angel explains that *the Holy Spirit will come upon you, and the power of the Most High will overshadow you* (Luke 1:35). A further sign of this miracle is the child whom Elizabeth has conceived. The account in *Maryam* is similar. Mary has withdrawn to *an eastern place* and God explains, *We sent to her Our spirit, and it took for her the form of a human being exactly* (*Maryam* 19:16–17).

In *Imran*, the annunciation story is a bit longer. The angels say to Mary, *Mary! Surely God has chosen you and purified you and He has chosen you over all other women. Mary! Be obedient to your Lord, and prostrate yourself and bow with the ones who bow* (*Imran* 3:42–43). As they continue to explain what will happen, the angels add, *Mary! Surely God gives you good news of a word from Him: his name is the Messiah, Jesus, son of Mary, eminent in this world and the Hereafter, and one of those brought near* (*Imran* 3:45). In the *Protoevangelium* Mary has gone out to draw water, and she hears a voice telling her she is blessed by God. She cannot see who is speaking, but when she returns home, an angel appears to her and says, *Do not fear Mary; for you have found grace before the Lord of all things and shall conceive by his Word*. Mary questions how

---

9. Mourad, "Mary in the Qur'an," 166.

this will take place, and the angel's reply almost quotes the Gospel of Luke verbatim (*Maryam* 3:45–47; Luke 1:31–35).

One common feature of both Qur'anic accounts is the way in which the angel responds to Mary's question. In each case, Mary asks how she will conceive a child without sexual intercourse, and both times the response is that it is simple for God to create out of nothing. Thus, the angel says, *when He decrees something, He simply says to it, "Be!" and it is* (*Imran* 3:47). The other account says, *It is easy for Me. And (it is) to make him a sign to the people and a mercy from Us. It is a thing decreed* (*Maryam* 19:21).

The New Testament accounts of the annunciation of Jesus' birth, and the birth itself are discussed in more detail later in the chapter. Suffice to say that there are many points of connection and contact with the Qur'anic accounts. Indeed, Muslim reverence for Mary is arguably greater than it is for some Christians, a point worthy of further discussion.

Birth of Jesus and Confrontation with Mary's People (Maryam 19:22–34)

Surah Imran does not really discuss the birth of Jesus in any detail; it moves swiftly from the annunciation of Jesus to his ministry. *Surah Maryam*, however, has a long birth narrative, albeit in a form that is very different from that found in the canonical Gospels of Matthew and Luke. Mourad identifies a further parallel account, of the birth of Jesus by a palm tree and the miracle that follows.[10] Here the parallel is between *Miriam* (19:22–26) and the gospel of *Pseudo-Matthew* 20.

In *Maryam* Mary conceives Jesus, and withdraws to a quiet place to give birth to him.

> The pains of childbirth drove her to the trunk of the date palm. She said, "I wish I had died before (this) and was completely forgotten!" And then he called out to her from beneath her, "Do not sorrow! Your Lord has made a stream beneath you. Shake the trunk of the date palm toward you, and it will drop on you fresh ripe (dates). Eat and drink and be comforted. If you see any human being say, 'Surely I have vowed a fast to the Merciful, and so I shall not speak to any human today.'" (*Maryam* 19:24–26)

Mary delivers Jesus next to a palm tree. A voice then speaks, offering her comfort. Some commentators say this is a divine messenger,

10. Mourad, "Mary in the Qur'an," 167–69.

while others that it is Jesus. The text does identify the voice as coming from below Mary—and so the claim is made that this is the first miracle of Jesus, speaking as soon as he left the womb.

The account in *Pseudo-Matthew* has both points of connection and also differences. In the first place, it is longer, and second, Joseph is present. Third, the Qur'an's account takes place when Mary is in labor, while the *Pseudo-Matthew* account occurs on the flight to Egypt. In *Pseudo-Matthew* 18–19 Joseph and Mary leave for Egypt; Joseph has three boys with him and Mary a girl. They take shelter in a cave, which is suddenly filled with dragons, terrifying the children. But Jesus gets down from his mother's lap and the dragons worship him, fulfilling the scripture, *Praise the Lord from the earth, dragons and all you ocean depths* (Psalm 148:7). Lions and panthers also worship Jesus, going before the travelers, showing the way and bowing in worship; they also walk among wolves as well as beasts of burden. Again Mary is afraid, but Jesus speaks to her, reassuring her that these animals have come to worship him. This also fulfills scripture: *Wolves shall feed with lambs; lion and ox shall eat straw together* (Isaiah 65:25).

Pseudo-Matthew 20 recounts a story similar to that in *Maryam*. On the third day of their journey, Mary is tired, and seeing a date palm, tells Joseph she would like to rest there. He duly leads her to the date palm, and while she is sitting in its shade she expresses a wish to eat the fruit of the tree. Joseph tells her the palm tree is too tall for them to get fruit, and that he is more concerned about their lack of water, as their water skins are empty and they have no water for themselves or for their animals.

> Then the child Jesus, reposing with a joyful countenance in the lap of his mother, said to the palm, "O tree, bend your branches and refresh my mother with your fruit." And immediately at these words the palm bent its top down to the very feet of Mary; and they gathered from it fruit with which they all refreshed themselves. (*Pseudo-Matthew* 20)

Once they had eaten, the tree awaits Jesus' order, and he tells it to right itself. Jesus then orders the palm to open from its roots a spring of water for all to quench their thirst. *And it rose up immediately, and at its root there began to gush out a spring of water exceedingly clear and cool and sparkling.* They all drank from it, both people and animals, and all were refreshed.

Mourad suggests that both accounts have a common source: the Greek myth of Leto's labor and the birth of Apollo. "Leto, who was desperately trying to hide herself from the angry Hera, sought the remote island of Delos. Aggrieved and distressed, she sat by a palm tree alongside the Inopos River and there delivered Apollo."[11]

Mourad gives one account of the myth from the *Hymn to Delos* by Callimachus (who died around 240 BCE)

> So you spoke, and she let go the long pang of her wandering with a sigh and sat down by the stream Inopos, abounding then in waters sprung from the earth in the season when the Nile comes at its greatest, cascading down the Ethiopian plateau. She untied her belt, leaning backwards, her shoulders against the trunk of a palm tree, utterly exhausted, her skin glistening with sweat, and said, in a whisper almost, "Why, boy, why so hard on your mother? Here, darling, is your island, sailing on the sea. Be born, boy, be born and come, gently, from the womb." (*Hymn to Delos* 205–1421)

Mourad adds that the legend was widely known, and alluded to in Homer's *Odyssey*, the *Hymn to Apollo*, Euripedes' *Hecuba*, Thucydides' *Peloponnesian War*, Cicero's *Laws* and Pliny's *Natural History*. He suggests that appropriation and adaptation of ancient myths was common practice, and that this was first taken up in *Pseudo-Matthew* and from there came to be in *surah Maryam*. Mourad's argument is that Christians adapted the legend of Leto, replacing Leto and Apollo with Mary and Jesus; the Qur'an takes up this revised legend and recounts it for its own purposes.[12]

When he discusses the flight of Mary and Jesus, Mourad argues that when contrasted with the biblical and extrabiblical versions, the Qur'an's account of the flight to Egypt is much vaguer in terms of geographical location.[13] The Arabic word is *rabwa*, which means *peaceful hillside*. Although a few Muslim exegetes identified this as being in Egypt, most suggested Syria, with the most popular precise locations being Ramallah or Damascus. Mourad is clear that in this case the Muslim exegetes are not following Christian sources, all of which located the destination of the flight as Egypt. Instead, he argues that they comfortably contradict Christian views, presenting alternatives primarily for regional purposes,

---

11. Mourad, "Mary in the Qur'an," 168.
12. Mourad, "Mary in the Qur'an," 168.
13. Mourad, "Mary in the Qur'an," 169–71.

or perhaps for promoting polemic against Christians. Christians have a theological and ideological commitment to locating Joseph and Mary's destination as Egypt. The clearest evidence of this commitment is the fulfillment text in Matthew 2:15, which quotes Hosea 11:1 (*out of Egypt I called my son*), and makes Jesus into the perfect Israel and the true Moses. But Muslims do not share this concern and therefore do not share the geographical location of the events.

The Church of the Nativity in Bethlehem demonstrates a striking conflation of the Christian and Muslim accounts. The Church is built over a cave that is claimed to be the place where Jesus was born. There is a shrine for the place of Jesus' birth and a second shrine for the place where Jesus was wrapped in swaddling clothes. But there is also a third, a small hole that is claimed to be the place where the date palm of the Muslim story used to grow. This amalgamation of Christian and Muslim accounts provides a fascinating way into discussion between people of both faiths, focused on the historicity of these events and the way in which they are commemorated. Reynolds discusses the Kathisma church on the outskirts of Jerusalem, where the birth of Jesus was commemorated along with the miracle of the palm tree and spring given to Mary during her flight to Egypt. He points out the rivalry with the Church of the Nativity without making any judgment as to the historicity of either claim.[14]

Mary Maintains Her Virginity / Conceives by the Spirit of God (Imran 3:47; Maryam 19:20; al-Anbiya' 21:91; at-Tahrim 66:12)

The Qur'an records four incidents of Mary affirming her virginity. Two of these come in the accounts of Mary's life already discussed above. As noted there, the theological concern is to demonstrate the ease with which God can create out of nothing. The statement in *al-Anbiya'* comes in a list in which God explains how he has been working in the world through his Prophets. The previous statement concerns Zechariah and the birth of John the Baptist. Attention then turns to Mary: *And she who guarded her private part—We breathed into her some of Our spirit, and made her and her son a sign to the worlds* (al-Anbiya' 21:91). There then follows a rebuke to Christians and Jews, who have separated into two communities rather than remaining united as one as they ought to have.

---

14. Reynolds, *Qur'an and the Bible*, 477–78.

The fourth reference is in *surah at-Tahrim*. The preceding verses introduce two disbelieving wives: the wives of Noah and the wife of Lot, both of whom were married to a righteous servant of God, but both of whom were disobedient and so condemned to the fires of hell (*at-Tahrim* 66:10). These two faithless unrighteous women are then contrasted with two righteous, faithful women:

And God has struck a parable for those who believe: the wife of Pharaoh, when she said, *My Lord build a house in the Garden for me in Your presence, and rescue me from Pharaoh and his deed(s), and rescue me from the people who are evildoers*; and Mary, daughter of Imran, who guarded her private part: *We breathed into it some of Our spirit, and she affirmed the words of her Lord and his Books, and became one of the obedient* (*at-Tahrim* 66:11–12).

Discussing this special status of Mary, Reynolds notes the discussion within Islam as to what it means that Mary is above all other women.[15] For some it is because she gave birth without sexual intercourse; for others it means she is the best woman of her generation. There are three *hadith* of Muhammad in which he names Mary and his wife Khadija as the best of women. In a further four, he names four women: Mary, Khadija, the wife of Pharaoh (see *at-Tahrim* 66:11) and his daughter Fatima. Finally, there is a *hadith* in which Muhammad says his wife Aisha is the best of women, except for the Virgin Mary. Reynolds also cites the writings of the Syriac Christian father Jacob of Serugh, who extols Moses who *chose an adopted mother and made her his mother and in the same way Christ chose as his mother a daughter of the poor* (*Homélies contre les Juifs*, 57, homily 1.11.179–84).[16] This suggests that the juxtaposition of Moses' surrogate mother with Mary, the mother of Jesus, had Christian precedent.

Miracle of Jesus Speaking as an Infant / in the Cradle (Imran 3:46; al-Ma'idah 5:110; Maryam 19:24–34)

The Qur'an attributes to Jesus the miracle of speech as an infant in three places. The first (*Imran* 3:46) is part of the annunciation to Mary by Gabriel, who tells her that her son will speak from the cradle. The second (*al-Ma'idah* 5:110) comes in a reminder to Jesus of the miracles that he has been given by God. The third (*Maryam* 19:24–34) comes during the

---

15. Reynolds, *Qur'an and Its Biblical Subtext*, 139.
16. Reynolds, *Qur'an and the Bible*, 842.

time in the desert, when Jesus speaks to Mary to reassure her. As seen above, while this miracle has no parallel in the canonical Gospels, there are similar accounts in the pseudepigraphal literature, such as the episode in *Pseudo-Matthew* 20 recorded above.

Mary as "Sister of Aaron"

In this section, I will discuss the issues raised by the Qur'an's description of Mary as *sister of Aaron*. The problem was touched upon in the chapter on Moses, but is worth revisiting here. In essence, the issue is that *Mary* and *Miriam* are two versions of the same name, the former the Greek version and the latter the Hebrew/Arabic version. The biblical Prophet Moses had an older sister Miriam and an older brother Aaron. Thus, when the Qur'an speaks of *Mary* as *sister of Aaron*, this raises the question as to whether it refers to the *Mary* (normally known as *Miriam*) who is biological sister to Aaron and Moses, or whether it is referring to *Mary* the mother of Jesus.

I will examine the explanations put forward by two scholars: Samir and Mourad. Samir notes that in the apocryphal Christian texts the parents of Mary are called Anne and Yuwakim. In the Qur'an Anne is unknown and Yuwakim is called Imran. He adds that according to 1 Chronicles 5:29 the children of Amran are Aaron, Moses and Miriam (Mary). Moreover, in Exodus 15:20, Miriam is called *sister of Aaron*. In the Qur'an, Mary is also called *sister of Aaron* (*Maryam* 19:28) and *daughter of Imran* (*at-Tahrim* 66:12). However, Samir also adds that church fathers such as Gregory of Nyssa, well known to Syriac Christians, often compared the two Marys of the Old and New Testaments, and that the motif was also a popular one in preaching. This could explain the Qur'an's reference. Muslims commentators are aware of the difficulty, and suggest the two Imrans were different people.[17]

Mourad proposes that the key references are *Imran* 3:35–36; *Maryam* 19:29; *at-Tahrim* 66:12.[18] At first glance, these three passages appear to state that the Qur'an identifies Mary as daughter of Amram and sister of Aaron, leading many to argue that Muhammad confused Mary, mother of Jesus, with Miriam, sister of Aaron and Moses. Mourad notes also that some Muslim medieval commentators apply the Gospel lineage

---

17. Samir, "Theological Christian Influence," 142–43.
18. Mourad, "Mary in the Qur'an," 163–66.

of Joseph to Mary. The *Protoevangelium of James* identifies Mary's father as Joachim. Mourad explains that this report has no historical value but nevertheless it became the accepted way Christians identified her, and so the statement that "Mary is daughter of Amram" cannot be a correct way of identifying her. Unless, that is, *daughter* does not mean a direct child; in the Christian canonical sources, *son* does not always denote a direct child. Thus, for example, in Matthew 1:1 Jesus is described as *the son of David, the son of Abraham*. In the same way, in Matthew 1:20 Joseph is described as a *son of David*. Thus, in these texts *son* denotes ancestral descent, and it is perfectly plausible that the Qur'an is doing the same thing. This is supported by reference to the *sons of Israel* in *al-Baqarah* 2:246; *Imran* 3:49; and *al-Ma'idah* 5:72, and to the *sons of Adam* in *al-A'raf* 7:35; *al-Isra* 17:70 and *Ya Sin* 36:60.

Mourad explains that the expression *sister of Aaron* is used in the context of the temple priests questioning Mary about her moral transgression (that is her pregnancy). Their point is that by appealing to her ancestor Aaron, whose descendants are the only ones qualified to serve in the temple, they are magnifying the significance of her transgression. To put it another way, Mary, a descendant of Aaron, should keep the sanctuary pure, not defile it by having sex outside of marriage. Mourad concludes that medieval Muslim exegetes resorted to one of two explanations for the *sister of Aaron* phrase. Either it is the allegorical reference as outlined above, or else it refers to an otherwise unknown biological relative.

In conclusion, we can therefore state that we do not have to assume the Qur'an is confused as to the identity of Mary, but rather that it is making an allegorical statement of her spiritual lineage, or else it is making reference to a relative who is not attested in any other sources. On balance, the former explanation is the more convincing as the Qur'an shows little interest in the personal names or histories of the protagonists it discusses.

Mary in the New Testament

This section focuses primarily on mentions of Mary in the four Gospels, especially those that have parallels with the Qur'an's references to Mary. After a brief discussion of the historicity of the Gospel accounts, the bulk of the discussion focuses on the birth narratives in Matthew and Luke, before concluding with an examination of Mary's appearances in John's Gospel.

Do the Gospels Recount History?

Scholars debate whether the accounts of Jesus' birth in the New Testament are historical. Keener defends their historicity, citing four points. First, he states that just because Matthew's account has midrashic elements, that does not preclude an historical basis. Second, although Matthew has embroidered the stories of Jesus' birth, he has done so sparingly, especially in contrast with Jewish accounts that embroidered biblical births (such as 1 Enoch 106:2–3) or the apocryphal gospels. Third, the scriptural texts that Matthew cites are unusual. He ignores the more obvious messianic passages, and selects ones his contemporaries did not regard as messianic. Fourth, the vocabulary of the infancy narratives is as Matthean as the rest of the Gospel. He concludes that although historicity cannot be presumed, neither can it be disproved. The overlaps with Luke indicate an historical core that lies behind what each Gospel records.[19] France concurs that there is no reason to doubt the historicity of the record; even if there is no independent historical verification of the events, they fit well with our general knowledge of the period.[20]

The Annunciation and Birth Narratives

In his discussion of the virgin birth, Keener argues that most alleged parallels with Roman, Greek or postbiblical Jewish sources are too distant to be of any value. Rather, he suggests that although there is no Old Testament precedent for a virgin birth, there are supernatural births (Genesis 21:2; 25:21; 30:6; Judges 13:3) and prenatal annunciations (Genesis 16:11; Judges 13:3–14). Keener also points out that there was no contemporary messianic speculation centered on Isaiah 7, which allows him to argue that rather than derive a doctrine from the text, the first followers of Jesus found evidence of God's plan in Isaiah 7. This is why the text is quoted in Matthew 1:22–23. Keener correctly observes that the Hebrew term *'almah* in Isaiah 7:14 does not always mean *virgin* (the Hebrew word for virgin is *betulah*), and so most Jewish interpreters rejected the messianic interpretation of the text. The Greek word *parthenos* did conventionally mean *virgin*, and this is the basis of Matthew's case. But it is not a simplistic correspondence of words. Rather, Keener explains, Isaiah's child

---

19. Keener, *Matthew*, 81–83.
20. France, *Matthew*, 43.

was a sign to Ahaz. Named *Swift is the plunder, speedy is the loot*, this child performed a similar function to *Emmanuel* (Isaiah 8:1–4), acting as a sign, reminding the people of God's presence and the ultimate triumph for Judah of the Davidic Messiah, who would be born in Israel (Isaiah 9:1–7). Matthew's main point is clear: scripture reveals the divine plan, and God is active in the world bringing his plan to fulfillment.[21] France adds that both Matthew and Luke attribute Mary's pregnancy to the Holy Spirit (Matthew 1:18, 21; Luke 1:35) and both refer explicitly to Mary as a virgin (Matthew 1:23, 25; Luke 1:34).[22]

Nolland discusses Luke's account, and agrees that virginal conception has no precedent within Judaism. But he is equally clear that attempts to find a parallel in Greek thought are unsatisfactory, because the Greek legends of divine parentage all involve sexual relations, which Luke is at pains to deny. There is precedent within Jewish tradition for the Holy Spirit having a creative role in human origins (*The spirit of God has made me, and the breath of the Almighty gives me life*, Job 33:4; see also Psalm 104:30; Ecclesiastes 11:5). Moreover, in Jewish thought being a son of God is not a matter of physical origin; rather, the focus is on adoption or election into a special relationship with God (Exodus 4:22; 2 Samuel 8:14; Psalm 2:7; 89–26-27; Jeremiah 21:10; Hosea 11:1; Sirach 36:11; *4 Ezra* 6:58). There are also references to the nation (Isaiah 43:6–7; 63:16; 64:8) that use sonship language. Nolland argues that Luke's language of sonship stands within this tradition.[23]

Nolland also examines the annunciation of Jesus' birth to Mary.[24] He points out the parallels with the annunciation of John the Baptist's birth to Zechariah, but suggests that while the latter follows the model of Old Testament birth annunciations (Genesis 16:7–14; 17–18; Judges 13:2–23), Mary's experience is more of a call narrative (as in Judges 6:11–24; Exodus 3; Jeremiah 1:4–10). He explains that in Luke 1:35 "God is not Father as Mary is mother. Rather, by the creative power of his Spirit, God miraculously enables a true parthenogenesis, and creates a child who will stand in special relationship to himself as messianic Son."[25] Furthermore, Nolland expands, the language of Jesus as son indicates designation as

21. Keener, *Matthew*, 83–88.7
22. France, *Matthew*, 48.
23. Nolland, *Luke 1:1—9:20*, 44–48.
24. Nolland, *Luke 1:1—9:20*, 57–59.
25. Nolland, *Luke 1:1—9:20*, 58.

Messiah and recognition of the exalted status and special relationship he has with God. Finally, Nolland recognizes that the miracle of Jesus' virgin birth remains a mystery, emphasizing the fact that it is God who sends the Messiah. Green remarks that Mary is introduced as an obscure figure; with nothing to indicate she is particularly worthy of divine favor. This makes the encounter with Gabriel all the more significant, as it indicates God has favored one with no claim to worthy status, raising her up and giving her a central place in salvation history. Yet the initiative remains God's. Thus, although Mary questions how this will all take place (Luke 1:34), the purpose of the question is to emphasize the divine deed, as Gabriel answers, giving a sign and a word of reassurance (Luke 1:35–37). Mary's faith is clear as she "unreservedly embraces the purpose of God, without regard to its cost to her personally."[26]

Mary's song (Luke 1:46–55) is a major piece of theology. Marshall is surely correct that it is not a spontaneous composition, but rather a carefully constructed speech that expresses the significance of the moment in appropriate language.[27] Green argues that Mary's song draws together threads from the surrounding narrative, as well as exhibiting the parallelism common to Hebrew poetry. Green stresses that Mary's song is primarily about God, who is the main active agent. Yet he does not act alone, seeking out other actors who share in God's work. There are echoes of other great biblical songs, including those of Moses (Exodus 15:1–18), Miriam (Exodus 15:19–21), Deborah (Judges 5:1–31), Asaph (1 Chronicles 16:8–36), Judith (Judith 16:1–17) and especially Hannah (1 Samuel 1:2–10). This means that Mary is celebrating God's action throughout history, while also looking to the future. Green finds two key themes in Mary's song: first, a picture of God as the divine warrior who brings deliverance; second, God as merciful in fulfilling the promises of his covenant, lifting up the lowly, feeding the hungry, remembering his promises and more. These two themes, Green concludes, reoccur throughout Luke-Acts.[28]

When he examines the account of Jesus' birth, Nolland argues that the description of Mary's pregnancy coming to term echoes the experience of Rebekah when she gave birth to Esau and Jacob (Genesis 25:24). Luke's description of Jesus' birth is "spare in the extreme," focusing instead

---

26. Nolland, *Luke 1:1—9:20*, 86–92, quote from 92.
27. Marshall, *Luke*, 46.
28. Green, *Luke*, 98–102.

on the origin (Luke 1:35), identity (2:11) and destiny (1:32–33) of the child. Nolland recognizes that Luke 2:7 is somewhat cryptic, but argues it describes Mary and Joseph sharing space within a one-room Palestinian home. There are others beside Mary and Joseph in the home, and so when Jesus is born, there is no space for him. But space is found for him "by making use of a manger on an adjacent wall of the animal stall that formed part of such a peasant home."[29] Green concurs that most likely Mary and Joseph were staying with family or friends, in a small house where family and animals all slept in a single enclosed space. Everywhere is so full that the only space for Jesus is an animal feeding trough.[30]

Nolland also proposes that the angels' hymn of praise to Jesus, honoring him as Savior and bringer of peace (Luke 2:14), echoes language used of Emperor Augustus. The shepherds travel to Bethlehem to see Jesus for themselves, but having seen the sign fulfilled, their focus is on sharing the angelic message they have received, so that all know the special status of the child.[31] Green suggests that as well as co-opting imperial language, Luke is also drawing on Old Testament themes, citing Isaiah 9:1–7 as one source text, referencing embrace of the Gentiles, darkness and light, eschatological joy, deliverance from the oppressor, a child born for "us," peace, the throne of David and the kingdom.[32]

Turning to Joseph's decision to marry Mary, Keener makes five points.[33] First, first-century culture valued the wisdom of age, and so Joseph and Mary's youth makes their piety all the more striking. Keener argues that convention dictated people married young, and so the lack of mention of age indicates this was a young couple. Joseph was probably between eighteen and twenty, and Mary might have been as young as fourteen. Second, Mary and Joseph model sexual restraint. A godly man did not sleep with his fiancée before marriage. Thus, in *Joseph and Aseneth*, the Old Testament patriarch Joseph says, *It does not befit a man who worships God to sleep with his wife before the wedding* (21:1/20:8). But Mary and Joseph refrain from sexual relations until after Jesus is born (Matthew 1:25). The sexual restraint of the Old Testament Joseph may be relevant background. Keener adds that since Mary and Joseph were

29. Nolland, *Luke 1:1—9:20*, 111.
30. Green, *Luke*, 129.
31. Nolland, *Luke1:1—9:20*, 112.
32. Green, *Luke*, 134.
33. Keener, *Matthew*, 88–95.

poor, they presumably shared a bed but "controlled their passions for the honor of God's Messiah."[34] Their restraint may also be to ensure Scripture is fulfilled, so that the virgin both conceived and bore a son (Matthew 1:22–23; Isaiah 7:14). Their failure to produce the bloody sheet after their wedding night, which would confirm Mary's virginity, would instead confirm their shame, while also preserving God's call on their lives.

Keener's third point is that although Matthew allows divorce in some circumstances, he actually views infidelity as always being unjust. Hence Joseph is called righteous, as Matthew invites his audience to learn from Joseph's example of fidelity and discipline, as Joseph prefers God's honor to his own. At this point in the narrative, Joseph presumes Mary's guilt. Keener argues that Joseph lived in a society that presumed a man must divorce his wife is she is guilty of infidelity. Moreover, if Joseph did not send Mary away, then the presumption would be that he is the father. Mary does not claim she has been raped, and therefore the only possibility Joseph can see is that she has had sexual relations with another man.

Fourth, Keener argues Joseph tempers the principle of justice with compassion. He is righteous in choosing to divorce Mary, but he wants to do so privately, so as to minimize her shame. Jewish courts at this time did not have the power of capital punishment, but the potential for social ostracism is great. Moreover, Keener proposes, if Joseph had made his actions public, he could have impounded her dowry, and perhaps even recouped the bride price he had paid. Joseph chooses to forego these economic benefits for the sake of reducing Mary's shame.

Fifth, Joseph values obedience to God above his own honor. When God reveals the truth to Joseph in a dream, he immediately believes and responds in faith, trusting God despite the personal and social cost of his actions. Keener concludes that "Joseph's obedience to God cost him the right to value his own reputation."[35] There is a story within the Babylonian Talmud, tractate *Gittin*, of a Jewish couple who *were carried off by heathens who married them to one another. The woman said: I beg of you not to touch me as I have no Kethubah* [marriage contract] *from you. So he did not touch her till his dying day. When he died, she said: Mourn for this man who has kept his passions in check more than Joseph, because Joseph was exposed to temptation only a short time, but this man every day.* Joseph

---

34. Keener, *Matthew*, 90.
35. Keener, *Matthew*, 95.

was not in one bed with the woman but this man was; in Joseph's case she was not his wife, but here she was (Gittin 57a).³⁶

France concurs that betrothal was a binding marriage contract, only terminated by death or divorce. He argues the description of Joseph as *righteous* (Matthew 1:19) indicates someone who is careful to keep the law, which in the case of suspected infidelity by a betrothed would require divorce. Therefore, God has to guide Joseph to a different conclusion, which is why he has no sexual relations with her once they are married.³⁷

When he discusses the flight to Egypt, Keener argues that the story is one that would have resonated with contemporary audiences. There were other stories of divine children overcoming superhuman opposition, but the closest parallel comes in the story of Moses. Pharaoh, like Herod, kills male Israelite children (Exodus 1:16—2:5).³⁸ France also identifies parallels with Moses, arguing that Matthew is here laying the foundations of his typology of Jesus as the new Moses who leads the people of God in a new exodus.³⁹

Keener observes that elements of Josephus' stories of Moses have parallels with Matthew's account: a scribe predicts to Pharaoh that a deliverer for Israel will be born, but Moses' father is warned in a dream and protects him.⁴⁰ Josephus (*Antiquities* 2.205–17, 234–36) describes Moses' birth in hagiographic terms. He begins by explaining how Pharaoh was warned by one of his key advisors that *there would be a child born to the Israelites, who, if he were reared, would bring the Egyptian dominion low, and would raise the Israelites; that he would excel all men in virtue, and obtain a glory that would be remembered through all ages* (*Antiquities* 2.205). Pharaoh naturally takes steps to avoid this threat to his power, ordering every male Israelite baby to be thrown into the Nile. One noble Israelite, Amram, recognizing that his wife was pregnant and concerned for the future of his people, began to pray, asking God to have mercy on him. God came to him in a dream, encouraging him that he would be cared for and as his piety would be rewarded. He would have a son and *he shall deliver the Hebrew nation from the distress they were under from the*

---

36. Translation from Simon, *Gittin*.
37. France, *Matthew*, 50–59.
38. Keener, *Matthew*, 106–7.
39. France, *Matthew*, 63.
40. Keener, *Matthew*, 107.

Egyptians. His memory shall be famous while the world lasts; and this not only among the Hebrews but foreigners also (Antiquities 2.216).

The story develops much as it does in the book of Exodus, albeit with more detail. Pharaoh's daughter, having found Moses in the basket in the river, takes him to her father, describing the baby Moses as *a child who is of a divine form* (Antiquities 2.232). Pharaoh consents to his daughter's wishes, and takes the child in his arms. Pharaoh even gives baby Moses his diadem to play with; but Moses takes it off, kicking it around and treading on it. The scribe who foretold Egypt's doom witnesses this, and realizing this is the baby whose birth he has foretold, tries to kill him. But Pharaoh's daughter snatches the baby away, protecting him. Josephus concludes that God's own providence had protected Moses (*Antiquities* 2.232–37). This raises some interesting points for reflection as to how Christians should understand the accounts of Jesus' own birth.

The biblical annunciation and birth narratives are crucial for the formation of Christian doctrine. The Muslim accounts are similar, yet also very different. Muslim and Christian understandings of Jesus' identity and mission are shaped by our varying accounts of his origins. Careful and respectful conversation is needed to elucidate all the subtle differences and explore their implications.

Does Jesus' Family Believe in Him?

There is an incident recorded in all three Synoptic Gospels where Mary and some of her children come to Jesus. The implication is that they want to prevent him from continuing with his ministry. Mark's version is as follows:

> Then his mother and his brothers came; and standing outside, they sent to him and called him. A crowd was sitting around him; and they said to him, "Your mother and your brothers and sisters are outside, asking for you." And he replied, "Who are my mother and my brothers?" And looking at those who sat around him, he said, "Here are my mother and my brothers! Whoever does the will of God is my brother and sister and mother." (Mark 3:31–35)

Guelich argues that, at least at this point in his life, Jesus' family misunderstand and even discredit his ministry. Jesus responds by redefining family on the basis of faith, not biology. That does not preclude his biological relatives from entering the family of faith, but it does require them to make an active choice to do so.[41] Nolland discusses the parallel text in Luke (8:19–21), noting that although it is briefer than Mark's account, Luke is equally clear that Jesus' family members are outside because they have no sympathy with Jesus' actions at this moment. Nolland argues that in Luke's Gospel Mary is a positive figure, and so one of Luke's concerns is to avoid painting a negative picture of her.[42] The text does not explicitly record it, but presumably Mary, who treasured all she saw and heard of the child Jesus in her heart (Luke 2:51), eventually came to have full faith in her son as the Messiah.

The question of belief and unbelief in Jesus is a crucial one for Christian-Muslim dialogue, especially since in the Qur'an Jesus states that his followers have misunderstood (or willfully distorted) his teachings. The Qur'an does not make specific statements about the faith of Jesus' own family, but nevertheless this point is one that should be explored in dialogue.

Mary in John's Gospel

John's Gospel does not have a birth narrative for Jesus. But Mary is still present, perhaps most notably at Jesus' crucifixion:

> Meanwhile, standing near the cross of Jesus were his mother, and his mother's sister, Mary the wife of Clopas, and Mary Magdalene. When Jesus saw his mother and the disciple whom he loved standing beside her, he said to his mother, "Woman, here is your son." Then he said to the disciple, "Here is your mother." And from that hour the disciple took her into his own home. (John 19:25–27)

Jesus addresses his mother somewhat indirectly, as *woman*. This is the same term he uses at the wedding at Cana (John 2:4). Church tradition has identified *the disciple whom he [Jesus] loved* as John, the author of the Gospel, but this is by no means certain. Michaels discusses the issue at length, noting inconclusive arguments that this John was in fact one of Jesus' own biological younger brothers, but preferring the possibility that he might simply be one of Jesus' closest followers. Michaels also rejects any symbolic interpretations of the text, arguing that it is simply pastoral practice, Jesus ensuring his mother will be provided for after his

---

41. Guelich, *Mark 1—8:26*, 180–86.
42. Nolland, *Luke 1:1—9:20*, 394–95.

own death.[43] Beasley-Murray agrees that the focus is on ensuring Mary is cared for. He finds fulfillment of the promise of the wedding at Cana. In Cana Mary looked to Jesus for provision for the wedding guests; now here, at the moment of his death, Jesus provides for his mother's future needs as well.[44]

These incidents do not have direct Qur'anic parallels, but they underscore the importance of Mary as a figure within Christian devotion, a subject to which I now turn.

Mary in Christians and Muslim devotion

While it is undoubtedly true that Christians and Muslims both hold Mary in high regard, precisely what that means varies not only from person to person, but also between the two faiths. What follows is not an exhaustive treatment of the subject, but rather a few pointers for discussion.

In his discussion of early Christian doctrines, Kelly traces the development of Christian devotion to Mary from the close of the first century to the middle of the fifth. He argues that during the first three centuries of the Christian Era devotion to Mary was overshadowed by devotion to the cult of the martyrs. While her role in the working out of God's plan for redemption was recognized from an early stage, there is relatively little evidence of prayers being addressed to her, or of her help and protection being sought.

Several Christian texts develop devotion to Mary. Kelly notes that in the *Ascension of Isaiah* 2:8–14 there is the first affirmation that Mary was a virgin not only in conceiving Jesus, but also in giving birth to him. Another account explains, *[The Spirit] opened the womb of the Virgin and she received conception and brought forth; and the Virgin became a Mother of many mercies; and she travailed and brought forth a Son, without incurring pain* (Odes of Solomon 19:6–7).[45]

The *Protoevangelium of James*, discussed above, was written primarily to glorify Mary. Crucially, although some Christians taught and propagated these understandings, others disputed them. The church father Tertullian, for example, argued that Exodus 13:2 was a prophecy of Mary's womb opening, and Origen argued she needed the purification

---

43. Michaels, *John*, 956–59.
44. Beasley-Murray, *John*, 349–50.
45. Translation from Harris, *Odes and Psalms of Solomon*.

prescribed by the law. But while this debate was a live one, the main focus of the early church was in replacement theology; namely, that Mary was the antithesis of Eve. Thus, Justin Martyr taught that while both Eve and Mary were virgins, Eve had transgressed God's command, and so brought disobedience and death into the world. Mary, on the other hand, had obeyed God, bringing obedience and life.

Kelly explains that interest in Mary increased in the centuries after the Council of Nicaea. Mary came to be described by the title *Theotokos*, *God-bearer*, and as *aeiparthenos* or *ever-virgin*. This latter title was disputed, as the New Testament indicates Jesus had siblings. Interest in the parallel between Eve and Mary continued; some argued Mary should be the "mother of all living" (Genesis 3:20). But Eastern teachers in particular also recognized Mary's human frailty, questioning for example whether her behavior at the wedding at Cana (John 2) was as it should have been. In the West, the idea that Mary was *ever-virgin* became a more established teaching, and the argument developed that Jesus' siblings were in fact his cousins. Augustine drew together and refined the teachings about Mary, defending her permanent virginity. He argued that since the risen Christ could enter through closed doors, there was no reason why he could not emerge from her womb without violating it. He also argued that she was the recipient of God's special grace that meant she remained sinless, enabling Jesus to be born untouched by the stain of sin.

Kelly also comments that there is some evidence of a cult of devotion to Mary also emerged around this time, and that people were beginning to pray to her. The remark made by Nestorius that he does not object to people calling Mary the Blessed Virgin *Theotokos*, provided they do not treat her as a goddess, can be taken as indicating some people were doing precisely that. Kelly cites evidence of a fourth-century (or perhaps later) papyrus fragment which reads, *Mother of God, [listen to] my petitions; do not disregard us in adversity, but rescue us from danger*. He proposes this may reflect a trend within popular piety of the time.

The christological debates of the mid-fifth century, including the Councils of Ephesus and Chalcedon, included discussion about Mary, not in the context of honoring her, but rather as part of the process of clarifying and defining the union of the divine and human in the incarnation. The generally agreed conclusion was that Mary must be *Theotokos*, which meant festivals in her honor and inclusion of her name within liturgy and celebrations. Mary thus came to be called blessed, as her speech in Luke 1 predicts.[46]

Devotion to Mary has developed over the centuries in certain expressions of Christianity. Most Roman Catholics, for example, would say the *Hail Mary* as a normal part of their devotional prayers:

> Hail Mary full of Grace, the Lord is with thee.
> Blessed are thou among women and
> blessed is the fruit of thy womb Jesus.
> Holy Mary Mother of God,
> pray for us sinners now and at the hour of our death
> Amen.

Some, both within the Roman Catholic Church and the Anglo-Catholic part of the Anglican Church, would include the *Angelus* and *Regina Coeli* during services. The Angelus, which comes from the Latin for angel, is a devotional prayer that centers on repetition of the *Hail Mary*. In the text below, "V." indicates the leader and "R." the congregational response.

> V. The Angel of the Lord declared unto Mary.
> R. And she conceived of the Holy Spirit.
> Hail Mary, full of grace . . .
>
> V. Behold the handmaid of the Lord.
> R. Be it done unto me according to thy word.
> Hail Mary, full of grace . . .
>
> V. And the Word was made Flesh.
> R. And dwelt among us.
> Hail Mary, full of grace . . .
>
> V. Pray for us, O holy Mother of God.
> R. That we may be made worthy of the promises of Christ.

During the Easter season (that is, from Easter Sunday to Pentecost), the *Angelus* is replaced by the *Regina Coeli* (*Queen of Heaven*), which commemorates the resurrection of Jesus.

> Queen of Heaven, rejoice. Alleluia.
> For He, whom thou wast worthy to bear. Alleluia.
> Has risen as He said. Alleluia.

---

46. Kelly, *Early Christian Doctrines*, 491–99.

Pray for us to God. Alleluia.
V. Rejoice and be glad, O Virgin Mary. Alleluia.
R. Because the Lord is truly risen, Alleluia.
Let us pray
O God, Who by the Resurrection of Thy Son, our Lord Jesus Christ, hast been pleased to give joy to the whole world, grant we beseech Thee, that through the intercession of the Blessed Virgin Mary, His Mother, we may attain the joys of eternal life. Through the same Christ, our Lord. Amen.

Perhaps the most commonly used Marian text is the *Magnificat*, which is part of the Evening Prayer service of both the Anglican and Catholic Churches. The name comes from the Latin text of the first line of the prayer, *Magnificat anima mea Dominum*, which is reproduced in English in full below:

> My soul magnifies the Lord, and my spirit rejoices in God my Savior,
> for he has looked with favor on the lowliness of his servant.
>   Surely, from now on all generations will call me blessed;
> for the Mighty One has done great things for me,
>   and holy is his name.
> His mercy is for those who fear him
>   from generation to generation.
> He has shown strength with his arm;
>   he has scattered the proud in the thoughts of their hearts.
> He has brought down the powerful from their thrones,
>   and lifted up the lowly;
> he has filled the hungry with good things,
>   and sent the rich away empty.
> He has helped his servant Israel,
>   in remembrance of his mercy,
> according to the promise he made to our ancestors,
>   to Abraham and to his descendants forever. (Luke 1:46–55)

Of course, not all Christians would say these prayers, and not all those who do say them understand themselves as praying to Mary. Indeed, the words of the *Hail Mary* are a request that she prays for the petitioner. Christians whose faith is of a more Reformed Protestant character would be at pains to avoid any hint of devotional prayer to Mary. They would study New Testament texts about her, regard her with great respect, but would certainly not say the *Angelus* or *Regina Coeli*, and when saying the *Magnificat* would understand it primarily as repetition of scripture rather than as a distinctly Marian prayer.

Mary is held in high esteem within Islam. Abu Hurayrah reports this saying of the Prophet:

> Every person born is attacked by Satan and is thus prone to desire, except for Mary the daughter of Imran. When Hannah gave birth to her, she said: "Lord, I put her and her offspring in your protection from the stoned Satan." A veil was placed around her, and Satan attacked it.

Mary is held up as one of the best of women. Abi b. Abi Talib reports Muhammad saying she is one of the two best women (the other being Khadijah daughter of Khuwayld), while Anas bin Malik has the Prophet list four women, adding Asiyah, wife of Pharaoh, and Fatimah, daughter of Muhammad.[47]

Much is made of her piety in relation to Jesus' conception. Thus, for example, Wahb b. Munabbih records that Gabriel blew into an opening in her clothes *so that the breath reached her womb*, enabling her to conceive Jesus. Mary and Joseph, who is described as a relative, travelled together to the place of prayer at Mount Zion, which was amongst the greatest of the places of prayer at that time. They both served there; over time Joseph became aware Mary was pregnant and became distressed by this. He challenges her, and she explains that God can cause crops to grow without seed, trees without rain and children without a penis (that is, without sexual intercourse). Joseph realizes that he is witnessing an act of God and ceases his questioning.[48]

There is, unsurprisingly, no comparable tradition in Islam of devotional prayer that involves Mary. I have noted above some teachings that indicate the great respect afforded to Mary, and the way she is considered to be an example of sound service to God. But she is only an example to learn from, nothing more. As seen above, the Qur'an has stories of Mary's childhood and upbringing in the temple, which are in postbiblical but not in biblical tradition. Jesus speaks to his mother to reassure her as soon as he is born (*Maryam* 19). Note also the polemic in *Maryam* 19:34–40, which is designed to show that the earlier praise of Jesus does not mean his claim to divinity is true. Thus, the Qur'an takes Christian Christology and reshapes it for its own purpose, that is, to deny those christological claims.

---

47. Wheeler, *Prophets in the Qur'an*, 298.
48. Wheeler, *Prophets in the Qu'ran*, 299–300.

Christians and Muslims will all have their own different understandings of Mary; there is a variety of devotional practice and understanding within each faith tradition. The purpose of this discussion is not to claim any sort of universal application but rather to open up discussion about one of the most spiritually revered women of all time.

Jesus

IN ODDBJØRN LEIRVIK'S HISTORICAL survey of *Images of Jesus Christ in Islam*, he begins by pointing out that since Islam was developed subsequent to Christianity within the same geographical area, it "challenges Christianity by competing in its own field."[1] Leirvik notes that all too often discussion of Jesus in Islam descends into polemics or apologetics, rather than remaining at the level of dialogue. This chapter will endeavor to remain dialogical. Leirvik makes four observations that are helpful for maintaining this stance. First, he suggests that Christology must include dialogue with faiths other than Christianity, because Christ cannot be constrained within the walls of the church. Second, he argues that the Christian image of Christ as suffering servant is incompatible with Islam's vision of the believer's victory over sin and evil, and so Islam will develop its own vision of Christ. Therefore, even if the same terminology is used, it will be given a very different meaning. Third, what the Qur'an says about Christ is interrelated to what it says about Jews, Christians and the Jewish-Christian scriptures, although I will not discuss these latter topics in detail here. Fourth, for Muslims it is Muhammad, not Christ, who is the Seal of the Prophets, and the miracle of the Qur'an itself is the greatest of all miracles.[2] Christians will of course disagree with this understanding, but the purpose of the exercise is not to agree, but to understand differences.

The chapter is divided into four main parts. First is a short discussion of what the Qur'an says about Jesus, and second, what the Qur'an denies about Jesus, focused especially on refutation of the crucifixion. The third section contrasts two Christian responses to Islam's understanding of

---

1. Leirvik, *Images of Jesus Christ in Islam*, 2.
2. Leirvik, *Images of Jesus Christ in Islam*, 2–4.

Jesus, before the fourth discusses the transfiguration as a New Testament text to use to explore different Christian and Muslim understandings of Jesus at greater length. Practicalities have precluded a detailed discussion of everything the New Testament says about Jesus, as that would take at least one book in and of itself.

What the Qur'an says about Jesus

The most fundamental point the Qur'an makes about Jesus is that he is a human being. Reynolds notes that in Luke 24, after the resurrection, Jesus eats to show that he is human (Luke 24:41).[3] In the Qur'an both Jesus and his mother eat food, also with the intent of showing they are human (*al-Ma'idah* 5:75; Reynolds suggests *al-Anbiya'* 21:8; *al-Furqan* 25:7; *al-Mu'minun* 23:51 as cross references[4]). Although the point is similar, it is also radically different, for Luke wants his readers to understand this means Jesus is both human and divine, while the Qur'an wants to make only the former assertion.

Jesus as Prophet and Messenger

Kaltner and Mirza explain that Jesus is a "prophet and messenger" in the Qur'an, mentioned by name twenty-five times.[5] Of these, nine occurrences are just his name, and the other sixteen also use a title such as *son of Mary* or *Messiah*. Kaltner and Mirza suggest the frequent use of *son of Mary* in the Qur'an is to underscore the humanity of Jesus; the phrase only comes once in the New Testament, in Mark 6:3. The Qur'an does not tell the story of what Jesus did, and as such there is little overlap with the accounts in the Gospels. Rather, the concern in the Qur'an is to emphasize who Jesus was. The main overlap is in the birth narratives, as both Bible and Qur'an affirm that Jesus was born of a virgin named Mary. This is discussed in the previous chapter, and will not be repeated here.

Kaltner and Mirza suggest that *an-Nisa'* 4:171 encapsulates the Qur'an's view of Jesus, a human messenger and Prophet sent by God:

---

3. Reynolds, *Qur'an and Its Biblical Subtext*, 95.
4. Reynolds, *Qur'an and Its Biblical Subtext*, 209.
5. Kaltner and Mirza, *Bible and the Qur'an*, 76.

> People of the Book! Be not go beyond the limits of your religion, and do not say about God (anything) but the truth. The Messiah, Jesus, son of Mary, was only a messenger of God, and His word, which He cast into Mary, and a spirit from Him. So believe in God and His messengers, but do not say, "Three". Stop! (It will be) better for you. God is only one God. Glory to Him! (Far be it) that He should have a son! To Him (belongs) whatever is in the heavens and whatever is on the earth. God is sufficient as a guardian.

Reynolds concurs that this verse emphasizes Jesus as a human being, but focuses on the statement, *do not say, "Three"* (which is sometimes mistranslated as, *do not say "[God is] a trinity"*). For Reynolds, the "critique of Christians here is not predicated on abstract rationality, but rather on the jealousy of the Qur'an's God, who insists he alone be worshipped." There are arguably parallels with Exodus 34:12–14, amongst other Old Testament passages.[6] Nasr proposes that the Qur'an's critique of Christians is that they "*exaggerate* in their religion, by ascribing divine status to their prophet, Jesus."[7]

The Qur'an adds that Jesus is the one who received and passed on a written book called the *injil*, the Gospel:

> And in their footsteps We followed up with Jesus, son of Mary, confirming what was with him of the Torah, and We gave him the Gospel, containing guidance and light, and confirming what was with him of the Torah, and as guidance and admonition to the ones who guard (themselves). (*al-Ma'idah* 5:46)

The Qur'an does describe Jesus as God's word (*Imran* 3:45), but although this is the same terminology as used in John 1:1–18, the meaning is very different. For John, describing Jesus as the Word of God is a way of making him divine, coequal and coeternal with God. For the Qur'an, the designation of Jesus as the Word of God marks him as a Prophet given a divine message to share with his people. Similarly, while the Qur'an describes Jesus as being the spirit of God, the focus is on Jesus' conception, not a claim to divinity. Thus, in *at-Tahrim* 66:12 God breathes his spirit into Mary to impregnate her, and God comforts Jesus with is Spirit (*al-Baqarah* 2:87, 253; *al-Ma'idah* 5:110).[8]

---

6. Reynolds, *Qur'an and the Bible*, 186.
7. Nasr, *Study Qur'an*, 267.
8. Kaltner and Mirza, *Bible and the Qur'an*, 76–77.

Jesus is also exhorted in the Qur'an to practice almsgiving and prayer, two of the pillars of Islam. Here, as with other biblical Prophets, Jesus is a true believer who is fully submitted to the divine will. According to the Qur'an, Jesus' first miracle is speaking as an infant; his subsequent miracles are making real live birds out of clay, healing the blind, the leprous and raising the dead. The miracles are described as follows:

> And (He will make him) a messenger to the Sons of Israel. "Surely I have brought you a sign from your Lord: I shall create for you the form of a bird from clay. Then I will breathe into it and it will become a bird by permission of God. And I shall heal the blind and the leper, and give the dead life by permission of God. And I shall inform you of what you may hear, and what you may store up in your houses. Surely in that is a sign indeed for you, if you are believers." (*Imran* 3:49)

Notice that the miracles are done with God's permission, rather than on Jesus' own initiative. This is an important distinction, emphasizing the fact that Jesus is merely a human being uniquely equipped by God for a particular purpose. It is also striking that the Qur'an cites miracles from both the canonical and noncanonical gospels. There are numerous stories in the four canonical Gospels of Jesus giving sight to the blind, cleansing lepers and raising the dead. The story of the clay bird is found in the noncanonical *Gospel of Thomas*, which recounts this incident:

> When this boy Jesus was five years old he was playing at the crossing of a stream, and he gathered together into pools the running water, and instantly made it clean, and gave his command with a single word. Having made soft clay he molded from it twelve sparrows. And it was the sabbath when he did these things. And there were also many other children playing with him. When a certain Jew saw what Jesus was doing while playing on the sabbath, he at once went and told his father Joseph, "See, your child is at the stream, and he took clay and molded twelve birds and has profaned the sabbath." And when Joseph came to the place and looked, he cried out to him saying, "Why do you do on the sabbath things which it is not lawful to do?" But Jesus clapped his hands and cried out to the sparrows and said to them, "Be gone!" And the sparrows took flight and went away chirping. The Jews were amazed when they saw this, and went away and told their leaders what they had seen Jesus do. (*Gospel of Thomas* 2:1–5)

The account in the *Gospel of Thomas* contains elements to which the Qur'an does not allude, most significant of which is the context on the debate about work on the Sabbath. For the Qur'an, the clay birds are simply a further sign that God has given Jesus. But for the *Gospel of Thomas*, they show how Jesus redefines (and possibly abrogates) the Sabbath command, albeit in a fashion that is different from the challenges brought in the canonical Gospels. In the canonical Gospels, Jesus teaches that healing miracles can be performed on the Sabbath, because healing and transforming lives is of greater importance than observing the command to rest from work (see, for example, Luke 13:10–17 or John 5). The account of the birds in the *Gospel of Thomas* is of a different order; the animation of the birds reads more as a way of conveniently disposing of the evidence of transgression of the command to rest and/or a sign of indifference to the command to rest. As noted in the discussion of creation, the Qur'an has no interest in the Sabbath rest command, and so that context is not included. But as Reynolds points out, one point the *Gospel of Thomas* makes with this story is that Jesus creates living beings from clay just as God creates human beings from clay. The inclusion of this story within the Qur'an means that the Qur'an also equates Jesus' creative activity with divine creative activity.[9]

The Qur'an does not mention Jesus' teaching as found in the New Testament. Thus, discussion of the kingdom of God/kingdom of heaven (Matthew 13, 22; Luke 13, 15), social justice (Matthew 23), forgiveness (Matthew 18:1–35; Mark 2; Luke 19:1–10) and concern for the poor and marginalized (Luke 10:25–37) are all missing, and also there is less teaching about the end times (Matthew 25; Mark 13; Luke 17). Nor does Jesus speak in parables in the Qur'an.[10]

An important caveat to the fact that Jesus does not speak in parables in the Qur'an is the fact that God does. There are a number of parables in the Qur'an. *Al-Kahf* 18:32–44 is one such example, which Reynolds equates with the parable of the rich fool, Luke 12:16–21.[11]

I will discuss one other example of a Qur'anic parable here:

> Do you not see how God has struck a parable? A good word is like a good tree. Its root is firm and its branch (reaches) to the sky, giving its fruit every season by the permission of its Lord.

---

9. Reynolds, *Qur'an and the Bible*, 121–22.
10. Kaltner and Mirza, *Bible and the Qur'an*, 79.
11. Reynolds, *Qur'an and the Bible*, 460.

God strikes parables for the people so that they may take heed. But the parable of the bad word is like a bad tree, uprooted from the earth, without any support for it. God makes firm those who believe by the firm word in this present life and in the Hereafter. But God leads astray the evildoers. God does whatever He pleases. (*Ibrahim* 14:24–27)

The *Enlightening Commentary* explains:

> A good tree and a tidy noble one has got several ensuing outcomes like: growing, bearing fruits abundantly, casting shadows and sustaining itself, and bearing fruits under all kinds of circumstances.
>
> A monotheistic person is never stagnant and the signs of his faith constantly reveal themselves in his speech and his acts. His faith is continuous and not seasonal, and he always calls others to the faith, persuading them to act according to what is allowed.
>
> The tree of faith always bears fruits and a believer is under all circumstances remembering Allah (s.w.t.) and is seeking to perform his duties, whether be it in welfare or in hardship, in happiness or in disaster, in poverty or in wealth, and in time of the threat of the oppressors he will resist until the end.[12]

There are at least four possible biblical parallels to this parable. In his translation of the Qur'an, Droge suggests Psalm 1:1–6 provide a parallel. This psalm reads:

> Happy are those who do not follow the advice of the wicked, or take the path that sinners tread, or sit in the seat of scoffers; but their delight is in the law of the Lord, and on his law they meditate day and night. They are like trees planted by streams of water, which yield its fruit in its season, and their leaves do not wither. In all that they do, they prosper.
>
> The wicked are not so, but are like chaff that the wind drives away. Therefore, the wicked will not stand in the judgment, nor sinners in the congregation of the righteous; for the Lord watches over the way of the righteous, but the way of the wicked will perish.

The main parallel idea is of the good tree that is firmly rooted in God's word in contrast with the bad tree that has no roots and so no

---

12 https://www.al-islam.org/enlightening-commentary-light-holy-quran-vol-8/section-4-disbelievers-shall-be-disappointed-truth.

stability. This is similar to the parable that Jesus tells of the wise and foolish builders; the former builds his house on a rock and the latter on sand. When the storms come, the house built on the rock stands firm, while the house built on sand collapses. Jesus says his words are the rock on which we are to build our lives (Matthew 7:24–27). Elsewhere, Jesus talks about trees and their fruit; good trees produce only good fruit and bad trees only bad fruit, which is a warning about true and false prophets (Matthew 7:15–20; Luke 6:43–45). Reynolds suggests Jeremiah 17:5–8 as another parallel.[13]

Finally, Jesus also tells a parable about the sowing of seeds that contains similar ideas. The seeds fall on four types of soil, each corresponding with a different response to Jesus' own preaching. The seeds that fall on the path and are eaten by birds are those in whom the word takes no root, for Satan immediately snatches it away. The seeds that fall on rocky ground and are soon scorched by the sun because they have no roots are those who fall away from faith as soon as trouble or persecution comes. The seeds that fall among thorns and are choked by the thorns are those who are lured away by the cares of the world or the attraction of wealth. Those seeds that fall on good soil, yielding thirty, sixty or even a hundred times what is sown, are those who hear the word, accept it and bear fruit (Mark 4:1–20; Matthew 13:1–24; Luke 8:4–15). This parable is more sophisticated than the one in the Qur'an, with four alternative responses rather than two. But the main point is similar; there are those who bear fruit by responding positively to God's word, and those who are fruitless by being faithless. Guelich argues it is a statement about "the outcome of God's eschatological activity in history" in bringing a harvest of those who believe.[14] France concurs, arguing the purpose of the parable is to point both to the happy ending of the harvest and also the reality that the harvest is not as big as it could have been. Those who hear the parable are invited to reflect as to why this might be.[15]

---

13. Reynolds, *Qur'an and the Bible*, 399–400.
14. Guelich, *Mark 1—8:26*, 197.
15. France, *Matthew*, 504.

Jesus and the End Times

Reynolds argues that the Qur'an makes two main points about Jesus' role in the end times.[16] First, he will be raised alive to heaven, and second, he will return and punish Christians for their unbelief. One verse of the Qur'an that implies that Jesus will return to earth at the end times, although this is by no means certain. The text reads:

> (Remember) when God said, "Jesus! Surely I am going to take you and raise you to Myself, and purify you from those who disbelieve. And I am going to place those who follow you above those who disbelieve until the Day of Resurrection. Then to Me is your return, and I shall judge between you concerning your differences. (*Imran* 3:55)

The final sentence is taken as indicating Jesus has some role in returning to the earth, and is part of God's judgment of humanity (*your* and *you* in this sentence are plural). The Qur'an does not say anything else about Jesus' role in the end times, but there is significant speculation in the later traditions. Thus, Ibn Kathir explains:

> Jesus will descend on the white minaret in Damascus just as the dawn prayer is happening. This is the easternmost minaret in Damascus which is built of white rock. It was built in the place of the one destroyed by Christians. Jesus will descend, kill all the pigs, break the crosses, and no one will accept anything but Islam. He will remain for 40 years and then he will die and be buried with the Prophet Muhammad and his two companions Abu Bakr and Umar b. al-Khattab.[17]

Cook explains that in Islamic teaching Jesus' arrival ushers in the messianic age. Jesus will kill the antichrist and convert Christians to Islam. There are also traditions of the Mahdi, who appears either at this point or in wars with the Byzantines that precede Jesus' return. Cook argues that Muslims were concerned about ascribing all apocalyptic functions to Jesus because of concerns about ceding ground to Christian devotion. Thus, Jesus is often subordinate to the Mahdi, even in strands of Muslim apocalyptic thought which draw inspiration from biblical texts such as Isaiah 11:6-9.[18]

16. Reynolds, *Qur'an and the Bible*, 124–25.
17. Wheeler, *Prophets in the Qu'ran*, 317.
18. Cook, *Contemporary Muslim Apocalyptic Literature*, 9.

The Qur'an's View of Jesus

The summary found in this section is based primarily on Khalidi.[19] Khalidi begins his discussion of the Qur'an's view of Jesus with a preliminary discussion of the Qur'an's understanding of Prophets in general. He proposes that the Qur'an parades a large number of Prophets in an admonitory narrative style quite unlike that of the Bible. This narrative style, in its rhythm and economy, is most often closer to poetry than it is to prose, and may well have had parallels with the oracular style of pre-Islamic diviners. There is no essential difference in diction between the narrative and nonnarrative portions of the text. Throughout, the language is couched in a grammatical tense that might be called the eternal present. Past, present and future are laid out in a continuum. There is thus a degree of similarity between all the Prophets, who have similar experiences as they speak divine truth largely to people who are not ready to hear it.

The interrelations among all the Qur'anic Prophets are visible at the level of both narrative styles and actual experience of prophethood. This is made more salient by the fact that the stories of various Prophets are not found together but are scattered throughout the Qur'anic text. Prophetic narrative reinforces itself in a number of ways. Words spoken by a Prophet or to him by God tend to find echoes, sometimes verbatim repetition, among other Prophets. The same may be said for acts performed or experiences encountered. One may thus speak of a typology of Qur'anic Prophets, a model of prophecy recognizable by the manner in which a particular Prophet sets about his mission of warning a proud or sarcastic or ignorant community, the (often violent) rejection of his message and ultimate vindication by God in the form of retribution. This typology is reinforced by the Qur'an itself, which proclaims that no distinction is, or should be, made among Prophets and that true belief must include belief in all Prophets (*an-Nisa'* 4:150). It is in some such general typological framework of prophecy that the Jesus of the Qur'an should be placed, and often is not.

There is something about Jesus in the Qur'an that is quite different from the figure portrayed in the Gospels. This difference lies not so much in narrative tone (although the tone is wholly other), for the same may be said of the tone in which all the stories of Prophets are presented in the Qur'an. Rather, the difference is that Jesus is a controversial Prophet. He is the only Prophet in the Qur'an who is deliberately made to distance

---

19. Khalidi, *Muslim Jesus*, 9–17.

himself from the doctrines that his community is said to hold of him. The term the Qur'an employs in this regard is *cleansing* (*Imran* 3:55): Jesus will be cleansed from the perverted beliefs of his followers, and furthermore he himself plays an active role in the cleansing process. In answer to God, Jesus explicitly denies any responsibility for advocating tritheism. God meanwhile denies the crucifixion. With Jesus, as with no other prophetic figure, the problem is not only to retell his story accurately; there are major doctrinal difficulties with the Christian version of his life and teachings to which the Qur'an repeatedly returns. In sum, the Qur'anic Jesus, unlike any other Prophet, is embroiled in polemic, as the Qur'an questions the Christian account of Jesus' crucifixion and vigorously denounces the Trinity as tritheism.

Khaladi suggests there are four types of references to Jesus in the Qur'an. First, birth and infancy stories (*Maryam* 19:16–36); second, miracles (*Imran* 3:49; *al-Ma'idah* 5:110); third, conversations between Jesus and God or between Jesus and the Israelites (*al-Ma'idah* 5:72–81); and fourth, divine pronouncements on his humanity, servanthood and place in the prophetic line, which stipulate that "fanatical" opinions about him should be abandoned (*an-Nisa'* 4:157–58; *al-Ma'idah* 5:111–20). The focus in the Qur'an is on Jesus' birth more than his death; hence the frequent reference to him as *son of Mary*. His death is nevertheless miraculous: he is lifted up to God, where according to later Islamic tradition he remains alive and waiting to fulfill his appointed role at the end of time, a role merely hinted at in the Qur'an (*az-Zukhruf* 43:61).

His speech and divine pronouncements concerning him seem to echo the prophetic career of Muhammad himself, or else seem designed to show that he is merely a servant of God, that is, a human being, who does not disdain that status. There is no Sermon on the Mount, no parables, no teachings on the law and the Spirit and of course no passion. Instead he has his faithful disciples who believe in him, he is humble and pious toward his mother, and he bears a message of God's unity, which confirms earlier prophetic messages.

Jesus and the Christian communities are approached in a variety of moods: conciliatory, reassuring and diplomatic, as well as menacing. The gates of God's mercy are left perpetually ajar. Christians are repeatedly invited to examine their scriptures for evidence of the coming of Muhammad, and Jesus is then given the distinction of explicitly announcing this coming, establishing a special affinity between the two Prophets (*as-Saff* 61:6). The Qur'an pronounces Christians the closest of all religious communities to the Muslims, for among them are found priests and monks humbly devoting themselves to God, their eyes overflowing with tears as they listen to the Qur'an and come, presumably, to recognize its truth (*al-Ma'idah* 5:82–85). Reynolds cites stories within Islamic tradition based on this passage, all of which involve the Negus, the Christian Ethiopian king to whom Muhammad purportedly sent some of his followers. The Negus, and his priests and monks, on hearing the message of the Qur'an, weep and declare how similar it is to their own Christian faith, and then receive Islam as the true faith.[20]

There is thus no single picture of Jesus in the Qur'an. Khalidi argues that a close reading of the Qur'an that pays special attention to its structure and diction would convey the impression of a text revealed in an environment of argument and counterargument, of a text struggling to establish its authority amid the sneers and sarcasm of unbelievers or the babble of quarrelsome religious communities. In the Qur'an, the followers of Jesus are an egregious example of man's tendency to distort or exaggerate the single message that God revealed to the Prophets. The Qur'anic Jesus is in fact an argument addressed to his more wayward followers, intended to convince the sincere and frighten the unrepentant. As such, he has little in common with the Jesus of the Gospels, canonical or apocryphal. Rather, the Qur'anic image bears its own special and corrective message, pruning, rectifying and rearranging an earlier revelation regarded as notorious for its divisive and contentious sects.

What the Qur'an Denies about Jesus

The Qur'an is equally concerned with negative definition of Jesus; that is to say, there are several passages that clearly set out who Jesus is not. This discussion below focuses on two main points, first, the denial of the doctrines of the Trinity and the incarnation, and second, the denial of the crucifixion of Jesus.

Denial of the Trinity and the Incarnation

An-Nisa' 4:171 is clear that Jesus is not part of *three*. Kaltner and Mirza argue that this is a specific repudiation of both the Trinity and the incarnation. They explain that the doctrines of both of the Trinity and the

---

20. Reynolds, *Qur'an and the Bible*, 211.

incarnation are, for Muslims, the sin of *shirk*, "associating something from creation with the uncreated deity in a way that compromises the divine unity."[21] This is also seen in *al-Ma'idah* 5:17, 72–76. Reynolds regards the former verse as the Qur'an's *reductio ad absurdum* of Christian doctrine, and the latter as denying that God is Christ.[22]

Later in *al-Ma'idah* there is a passage that is difficult for Christians for two reasons: first, because it presents an understanding of the Trinity that is not what orthodox Christianity teaches, and second, because in it Jesus denies both the Trinity and the incarnation. The crucial passage is:

> (Remember) when God said, "Jesus, son of Mary! Did you say to these people, 'Take me and my mother as two gods instead of God (alone)?'" He said, "Glory to You! It is not for me to say what I have no right (to say). If I had said it, You would have known it. You know what is within me, but I do not know what is within You. Surely You—You are the Knower of the unseen. I only said to them what You commanded me: 'Serve God, my Lord and your Lord!' And I was witness over them as long as I was among them. But when You took me, You became the Watcher over them. You are a Witness over everything." (*al-Ma'idah* 5:116–17)

The passage appears to assert that Christians claim Mary is part of the Trinity. Kaltner and Mirza recognize that this is not orthodox Christian theology, but also note that over time there have been Christian groups that have venerated Mary so highly that outsiders might have thought she had been given divine status. This may, they propose, underlie the rebuttal of *al-Ma'idah* 5:116–17. Kaltner and Mirza add that Jesus' refusal to accept divine status is less an attack on Christianity and more a defense of the unity of God. Similarly, in *Maryam* 19:30–31 Jesus explains his lowly status primarily to ensure God is exalted.[23] Reynolds notes that some scholars argue these verses indicate that Muhammad was influenced by heretical Christians who believed in Mary's divinity.[24] Reynolds is not persuaded by this argument, arguing the verses may not reflect exactly what Christians believed. But Reynolds does also argue that the Qur'an teaches the Christian understanding of Trinity to be Father, Mother, Son (or God, Mary and Jesus), because the Qur'an nowhere

---

21. Kaltner and Mirza, *Bible and the Qur'an*, 78.
22. Reynolds, *Qur'an and the Bible*, 194, 208.
23. Kaltner and Mirza, *Bible and the Qur'an*, 78–79.
24. See for example McGrath, *Heresy*, 225–29.

makes connections between the Holy Spirit and Christian teaching on the Trinity.[25]

There are significant differences on the death of Jesus. Jesus appears to allude to his own death in *al-Ma'idah* 5:117, but the key passage is *a-Nisa'* 4:157–58. The wider context of this passage means that *they* refers to the Jews who are Jesus' contemporaries; these Jews are described in the previous verses as going against God's will in a number of ways. They thought they were in charge, but it was in fact God who remained in control the whole time (see also *Imran* 3:54–55).

Kaltner and Mirza note that a key phrase in *an-Nisa'* 4:157–58 can be read in two ways.[26] The Arabic phrase *shubbiha lahum* can be translated either as *it was made to appear so to them* or else *he was made to appear so to them*. The former translation suggests that Jesus appeared to die but in fact did not die. But if the latter translation is adopted, then the verse can be read as teaching that it was in fact not Jesus who died. This understanding has given rise to the interpretation that someone else was substituted for Jesus, and this substitute died in his place. Either option is grammatically possible, and I will discuss the issue in greater detail below.

Finally, Jesus appears to predict the coming of Muhammad.

> And remember when Jesus, son of Mary, said, "Sons of Israel! Surely I am the messenger of God to you, confirming what was before me of the Torah, and bringing good news of a messenger who will come after me, whose name will be Ahmad." (*as-Saff* 61:6)

Kaltner and Mirza explain that although the messenger named in that *ayat* is Ahmad, the three root letters are the same as for Muhammad, and the two names are considered to be variants of each other.[27] Reynolds finds a parallel with *al-Baqarah* 2:129, where Abraham prays for a Prophet to be raised up, and *al-A'raf* 7:157, which argues the Qur'an's Prophet is found in the books of the Jews and the Christians.[28] Kaltner and Mirza also note that Muslims make a similar claim about two verses in John's Gospel.[29] Jesus promises, *I will ask the Father, and he will give you another Advocate to be with you forever* (John 14:16); he subsequently

---

25. Reynolds, *Qur'an and the Bible*, 218.
26. Kaltner and Mirza, *Bible and the Qur'an*, 80.
27. Kaltner and Mirza, *Bible and the Qur'an*, 80.
28. Reynolds, *Qur'an and the Bible*, 826.
29. Kaltner and Mirza, *Bible and the Qur'an*, 81.

adds, *When the Advocate comes, whom I will send you from the Father, the Spirit of Truth who comes from the Father, he will testify on my behalf* (John 15:26). Christians normally understand this *Advocate* to be a reference to the gift of the Holy Spirit, developing their understanding from other references in John's Gospel. Thus, 14:26 speaks of the *Advocate, the Holy Spirit* guiding believers into all truth, and in 16:7 Jesus says it is good that he leaves his disciples so that the *Advocate* can come to them in his stead.

Michaels explains that there is no agreement amongst scholars as to how to best translate the Greek word *parakletos*, with *Comforter, Counsellor, Helper* and *Advocate* all being used.[30] The use of the word *another* in John 14:16 makes it clear that Jesus himself also fulfills this role (so 1 John 2:1, *we have an advocate with the Father, Jesus Christ the righteous*). The function of this *Advocate* is to remind the disciples of what they have been taught, without the constraints of time or place that Jesus faced. Michaels is clear that the role of the *Advocate* has no conceptual background in Jewish thought, proposing the paradigm of successive prophetic and redemptive figures, for example, Moses and Joshua or Elijah and Elisha. This must be caveated with the observation that Jesus' role remains primary, while the *Advocate's* role is derivative of what has been pioneered.

Some Muslims argue that the verses are in fact a reference to Muhammad. There are two distinct arguments as to why the mention of the *Advocate* is in fact a reference to Muhammad: first, the origin and etymology of the Greek word *parakletos*, and second, the context in which the *Advocate* is mentioned. In the first argument, Muslim apologists claim that the *parakletos* is the corrupted form of a very similar word *periklitos*, which means *admired one* or *glorified one*, which is the identical meaning of the name Ahmad in Arabic, which as noted above is the other name of Muhammad. There is no manuscript or textual evidence for the corruption of the text, which for the Christian might be conclusive proof that it has no basis in fact. But a Muslim apologist would simply counter that all the extant manuscripts are corrupt, leading to an impasse in the debate.

The contextual argument is primarily that the Holy Spirit was already present and active when Jesus was ministering, and so the reference to Jesus leaving in order for the *Advocate* to come is better understood as someone arriving who had not been previously present. For the Muslim,

---

30. Michaels, *John*, 783, 791–92.

it makes sense to argue that this person in Muhammad But for the Christian, the experience of Pentecost, of a new revelation of the Spirit, is the counterargument. Whether either argument convinces the other is, of course, a moot point.

Does the Qur'an Deny or Assert Jesus' Crucifixion and Death?

I now discuss the Qur'anic view of Jesus' crucifixion in greater detail, first setting out the arguments of Suleiman Mourad before second examining the views of Todd Lawson. Mourad discusses this question at some length. He notes that "although Muslim scholars have overwhelmingly rejected the crucifixion of Jesus, they are divided regarding the reality of his death."[31]

Mourad suggests the Qur'an's denial is directed not at the reality of Jesus' crucifixion, but against the theological implications of the crucifixion.[32] He points out that even radical teachers such as Sayyid Qutb could not come to any firm conclusions about what the Qur'an actually teaches about the death of Jesus. This is a complex problem with no clear solution. The key verses are:

> (Remember) when God said, "Jesus! Surely I am going to take you and raise you to Myself, and purify you from those who disbelieve. And I am going to place those who follow you above those who disbelieve until the Day of Resurrection. Then to Me is your return, and I shall judge between you concerning your differences." (*Imran* 3:55)

> And for their saying, "Surely we killed the Messiah, Jesus, son of Mary, the messenger of God"—yet they did not kill him, nor did they crucify him, but it (only) seemed like (that) to them. Surely those who differ about him are indeed in doubt about him. They have no knowledge about him, only the following of conjecture. Certainly they did not kill him. No! God raised him up to Himself. God is mighty, wise. (*an-Nisa'* 4:157–58)

> I [Jesus] only said to them what you commanded me: "Serve God, my Lord and your Lord!" And I was witness over them as long as I was among them. But when You took me, You became

---

31. Mourad, "Does the Qur'an Deny or Assert?," 349.
32. Mourad, "Does the Qur'an Deny or Assert?"

the Watcher over them. You are a Witness over everything. (*al-Ma'idah* 5:117)

In *Imran* 3:55, Mourad explains, the interpretative difficulty lies with the combination of the phrases *mutawaffika* and *make you ascend to Me*. Some suggest that *mutawaffika* means *overcome by sleep*. If this is correct, then the Qur'an means that God caused Jesus to be overcome by sleep and then raised him to himself. A second view is that both phrases refer *to removing Jesus from this world to the next without death*. A third view holds that *mutawaffika* refers to Jesus' future death, and the verse is not a strictly chronological sequence. Hence God first raises Jesus to Paradise, then brings him to earth in the future, and then he will die. A fourth understanding is that both expressions refer to Jesus' physical death and resurrection from death by God, both events having occurred in the past. Mourad suggests that those who hold the first three views do so because they believe God would not (or could not) let Jesus be killed by his enemies; they turn to *an-Nisa'* 4:157–58 for support, although whether the Jewish group referred to made those claims in the time of Jesus or the time of Muhammad is unclear.

Further support for this view comes from a prophetic *hadith* to the effect that Jesus will return at the End of Days to kill the antichrist, after which he will die and be buried by Muslims. If this *hadith* is true, then there can have been no past death, for no human being can die twice, because God creates humans, causes them to die and then resurrects them (*Maryam* 19:33). Mourad questions the logic of this claim. He explains that this *hadith* is anti-Christian polemic, spoken by Muhammad when a Christian delegation came from Nagran and argued with him over the crucifixion of Jesus. Muhammad's refutation is based on his belief in Jesus' future return. Mourad points out that the circumstances of this *hadith* are different from that presumed in *an-Nisa'* 4:157–58, the only place in the Qur'an when the issue of Jesus' crucifixion is raised. The Qur'anic text refers to a Jewish group who claim to have killed Jesus. The group in the *hadith* are Christians who, as Mourad points out, would not have claimed to have killed Jesus. Thus the two groups are different.

Mourad adds that those who hold the fourth view also maintain that God rescues Jesus from crucifixion. They interpret *mutawaffika* to mean *cause to die*, but argue this was not on the cross. Jesus did die, was raised and then ascended to heaven. They disagree amongst themselves as to whether this resurrection was just his soul, or his body and soul.

Mourad concludes that while there is complete agreement amongst Muslim exegetes that Jesus was not crucified, there is no unity as to who died in his place. Some argue God made someone look like Jesus, and that person was crucified, although again there is no agreement as to who that person was. A less popular view is that one of Jesus' disciples volunteered to take his place, and was made to look like Jesus.

But some Muslim exegetes raise problems with this view. Mourad cites the philosopher al-Razi (died 1210 CE) as an example. He rejected the idea that God made someone else look like Jesus, pointing out that if that was the case, then it would mean the certainty of everything was in doubt, "for how can we be certain of anything if its reality can be different from its apparent manifestation?"

In his discussion of *an-Nisa'* 4:157–58, Mourad focuses on the phrase *shubbiha lahum*, which he suggests means something to the effect that *something was made to appear to them that essentially was not true*. This is more than simple visual confusion; Mourad suggests it means something that, if accepted as literally true, would lead to confusion or error. Thus, he proposes, the phrase *shubbiha lahum* in *an-Nisa'* 4:157 makes sense only if it refers either to the act of killing or to Jesus. Thus, rather than referring to someone being made to look like Jesus and that substitute being crucified, *an-Nisa'* 4:157 either denies that the killing took place or it denies that Jesus died as a consequence of his crucifixion.

Mourad continues his survey of the rest of the verse, suggesting that it reinforces the interpretative possibilities he has proposed, favoring the second alternative. Thus, he argues, the Qur'an questions the certainty of Jesus' death, not the fact of crucifixion taking place. Mourad understands *an-Nisa'* 4:157–58 to argue that Jesus has not been killed for he was resurrected from death and is alive with God. That is to say, for someone to be killed they must remain dead; therefore, those who claim Jesus was killed by crucifixion are mistaken. Mourad proposes the following translation of *an-Nisa'* 4:157–58.

> For their saying: "It is we who killed the Messiah Jesus son of Mary, the messenger of God." Nay, they did not kill him by crucifying him. They thought they did, and those who affirm that are uncertain; they have no knowledge about it except by speculation. In certainty they did not kill him because God raised him from death up to Him.

Mourad also finds support for his argument in *Imran* 3:169, which teaches that those who are killed in the path of God are not dead but alive with their Lord. Mourad concludes that the Qur'an is cautioning against deciding on the basis of perception of reality; the revealed truth is different and can inspire faith. As an aside, Mourad notes that the phrase *shubbiha la hum* cannot be used to support Docetic theology. This is because Docetism argues that Jesus merely seemed to be human, while the Qur'an is clear that Jesus is human.

Mourad notes that *Maryam* 19:33 is not the subject of discussion by Muslim exegetes, as it is merely a statement of the sequence of birth-death-resurrection in which God acts on Jesus. This is the entirely normal sequence for a Prophet (or indeed any person) and so not especially worthy of comment. Mourad concludes:

> The Qur'an reflects the insistence of the early Muhammad movement that the crucifixion of Jesus does not represent a defeat of God. In other words, this movement could not accept, as a matter of basic belief, that Jesus's career ended on the cross, with God unable to intervene. For what would that mean about God's commitment to protecting them? Thus they argue that God was the ultimate victor because He could do something those who crucified Jesus could not: He could annul Jesus's death by resurrecting him.[33]

The idea of Jesus not dying on the cross was, Mourad proposes, a later development, borne from a theological conviction that God protects his Prophets. Moreover, once *an-Nisa'* 4:157–58 was embedded in anti-Christian polemic, then the only way Muslim exegetes could interpret these verses was to deny Christian belief in the crucifixion of Jesus. If you free the verses from that context, then other readings become possible.

In his discussion of *The Crucifixion and the Qur'an*, Todd Lawson argues that exegetes tend to overlook the history of interpretation that holds the Qur'an actually denies the historicity of Jesus' crucifixion in *an-Nisa'* 4:157.[34] He explains that it "is important to recognize that the earliest textual evidence for such an interpretation is not Muslim at all; rather it is from the pen of none other than the last great Church Father, John of Damascus (d. 749)."[35] But, he adds, what is not clear is whether (a) John

---

33. Mourad, "Does the Qur'an Deny or Assert?," 356.
34. Lawson, *Crucifixion and the Qur'an*.
35. Lawson, *Crucifixion and the Qur'an*, 7.

knew the denial to be the Muslim interpretation of the verse or (b) John made that interpretation himself, in order to present Islam as a heresy to his audience. We must remember he was writing in Greek, for a Christian audience, and it is not certain whether Muslims read his writings.

Lawson points out the exegetical moves that Christians make which portray their vested interest. The argument is that if this text denies the crucifixion of Jesus, then the text is clearly wrong, because there is clear historical evidence that Jesus was crucified. And if the text is clearly wrong on this point of fact, then the text cannot be in any way holy, and thus cannot be anything from God—and so Muhammad cannot be a messenger of God. Whatever interpretation we end up with, John of Damascus's interpretation will not stand. Lawson argues that "the Qur'an itself only asserts that the Jews did not crucify Jesus. This is obviously different from saying that Jesus was not crucified."[36] Lawson explains that John of Damascus, and many Qur'an exegetes, deny the crucifixion, but the Qur'an itself does not do so. The most frequent interpretation is that God saved Jesus from death by crucifixion in a miraculous manner and that someone else was substituted for Jesus on the cross. This is a form of Docetism, a Christian heresy. This interpretation is sometimes demonized, for example, by Ibn Kathir, as intrusive to Islam and a form of *Isra'iliyyat* (erroneous Jewish legend).

Lawson proposes that the problem that Muslim exegetes faced was not Jesus' death on the cross, but the incompatibility of that death with their view of Prophets. We must reconcile the Qur'an's view of death with its understanding of what happened to Jesus (see *Imran* 3:169). He focuses on problem phrase in *an-Nisa* 4:157, *shubbiha lahum*, and lists some possible translations.

Yusuf Ali	*but so it was made to appear to them*
Pickthall	*but it appeared so unto them*
Abdul Haleem	*though it was made to appear like that to them*
Dakhtiar	*but a likeness was shown to them*
Sale	*but he was represented by one in his likeness*
Bell	*but he was counterfeited for them*
Arberry	*only a likeness of that was shown to them*
Jones	*but it was made to seem so to them*

The point Lawson wants to make is that the Qur'an itself neither confirms nor denies the fact of the crucifixion. It certainly does say that

---

36. Lawson, *Crucifixion and the Qur'an*, 12.

the Jews did not kill Jesus. But that is not the same as saying the crucifixion did not happen. While it is the case that much later *tafsir* (exegesis) of the Qur'an denies that Jesus was crucified, this position is nowhere stated in the Qur'an itself. While John of Damascus wanted to show Islam to be heresy from a Christian perspective, the Muslim exegetes who followed him probably wanted to show how distinct Islam was from Christianity, and so also put forward a perspective that denied the death of Jesus—to show the superiority of Islam over against Christianity. There are three broad interpretations of *an-Nisa'* 4:157–58. First, no one was crucified. Second, Jesus was crucified, but this happened only because God decided it would, not because of any Jewish plots. Third, someone other than Jesus was crucified. This third view is the most common in the Muslim world today.[37]

Turning to the Qur'anic context, Lawson notes that Jesus' crucifixion is only mentioned once, in *an-Nisa'* 4:157, and inferred in 4:158. The context of the discussion is the "general edification of its audience" in relation to unbelief.[38] The Jews are singled out for idol worship (*an-Nisa'* 4:153), breaking the covenant, killing Prophets, having hard hearts (*an-Nisa'* 4:155), general unbelief and slander of Mary (*an-Nisa'* 4:156), saying they killed Jesus, the messenger of God (*an-Nisa'* 4:157), general wrongdoing (*an-Nisa'* 4:160), taking usury and devouring people's wealth under false pretenses (*an-Nisa'* 4:161). There follows a promise of immense reward for those who avoid such behavior (*an-Nisa'* 4:162). Thus, the crucifixion verse is *not* in the context of a discussion of Christian doctrine. Rather, the assertion is "parenthetic support of the condemnation of *kufr*."[39] This means that *an-Nisa'* 4:157 is understood as condemning the Jews for their boast that they could contravene the will of God by killing his Prophet and messenger, Jesus, the son of Mary.

Lawson adds that the death of Jesus is directly mentioned in *Maryam* 19:33; *Imran* 3:55 and *al-Ma'idah* 5:117 and indirectly mentioned in *al-Ma'idah* 5:17. In *Maryam* 19:33, the infant Jesus speaks from the cradle, saying, *Peace (be) upon me the day I was born, and the day I die, and the day I am raised up alive.* This *ayat* is normally taken as referring to Jesus' death in the Last Days, when he returns to earth, kills the antichrist, lives for a while and then dies naturally. He will then be buried

---

37. Lawson, *Crucifixion and the Qur'an*, 12–23.
38. Lawson, *Crucifixion and the Qur'an*, 26.
39. Lawson, *Crucifixion and the Qur'an*, 27.

next to Muhammad, and they will rise together on the Day of Resurrection. A different word is used in *Imran* 3:55 and *al-Ma'idah* 5:117, generally taken as indicating physical death. In both instances, the instigator of the action is God. Thus, Lawson concludes that "Jesus, according to the Qur'an, can die a normal 'biological' death."[40]

Lawson then shifts his discussion to the phrase *shubbiha lahum*. He explains that the most common verbal usage within the Qur'an is "to be similar or nearly identical to the point of confusion of true identity." Examples include that cows are like us (*al-Baqarah* 2:70) and that their hearts are all alike (*al-Baqarah* 2:118). It is also used as a particle, *and it is given to them in resemblance* (*al-Baqarah* 2:25).[41] The precise phrase *shubbiha lahum* is a *hapax legomenon* within the Qur'an, occurring only in this verse, and it is therefore difficult to be certain what it means. Lawson's main point is to emphasize the fact that the Qur'an "neither supports nor rejects the substitution of another human being for Jesus in this context, being serenely indifferent to the entire question."[42] Lawson also discusses the Qur'an's conception of death, arguing that the Qur'an is clear that death is inevitable for all human beings, but that the timing and manner of a person's death is entirely in God's hands. The implication for exegesis of *an-Nisa'* 4:157–58 is that the point being made is that the Jews did not arrange for Jesus' crucifixion because the death of everyone—even a Prophet—is entirely in God's, not human, hands.[43] In his conclusion Lawson argues that the origin of the substitution legend was not concern over the historicity of Jesus' crucifixion, but rather disagreement with Christian theories of salvation. Moreover, differences between the Christian and Muslim conceptions of Prophets—especially the Muslim belief that Prophets cannot be defeated by death—were also relevant.[44]

For Christians who want to engage with Muslims in conversation about Jesus, it is crucial to be able to distinguish between what the Qur'an argues and how the text has been interpreted throughout the centuries. As the arguments of Mourad and Lawson make clear, these are two very different things. Yet they are intimately interlinked, and it is not easy to separate them in conversation. Anyone wishing to do so must advance

---

40. Lawson, *Crucifixion and the Qur'an*, 30.
41. Lawson, *Crucifixion and the Qur'an*, 32.
42. Lawson, *Crucifixion and the Qur'an*, 36.
43. Lawson, *Crucifixion and the Qur'an*, 39–42.
44. Lawson, *Crucifixion and the Qur'an*, 144–45.

Christian Responses to the Qur'an's Views about Jesus

This section brings two views into dialogue: Wessels and Glaser. The former argues for similarities; the latter stresses the differences between the Christian and Muslim views of Jesus.

Anton Wessels: The Torah, the Gospel and the Qur'an

In his discussion of the three holy books of Abrahamic monotheism, Wessels is at pains to draw out the similarities he finds. To give one example, he argues that for Christians Jesus is the embodiment and fulfillment of the Torah, a position he proposes is also taken by the Qur'an, which states Jesus confirms the Torah (*Imran* 3:50; *al-Ma'idah* 5:46; *as-Saff* 61:6).[45]

Elsewhere, Wessels discusses Herod the Great, who attempts to kill the child Jesus but fails, and the adult Jesus who comes into conflict with Herod Antipas and Pilate, who fail to understand him and condemn him to death. He compares this experience with Muhammad's experience of the unjust leaders of Mecca, who resisted him and his message.[46] Another contrast Wessels draws is between the night of exodus for the people of Israel from Egypt; Jesus' own exodus from Egypt, and also from Jerusalem, in particular to the mount of transfiguration, where his glory is revealed; and Muhammad's *hijra* from Mecca, as well as his night journey to Jerusalem.[47]

Wessels's work in finding connections and commonalities between Islam and Christianity is to be commended. The chapter began with the observation that discussion about Jesus can quickly turn polemical. Exploring commonalities is the best way of preventing polemic dominating discussion. But even so, we must also make space to explore differences.

---

45. Wessels, *Torah, the Gospel and the Qur'an*, 45.
46. Wessels, *Torah, the Gospel and the Qur'an*, 69–71.
47. Wessels, *Torah, the Gospel and the Qur'an*, 90–95.

Ida Glaser and Hannah Kay: Thinking Biblically about Islam

The main focus of Glaser and Kay's discussion of Jesus is the transfiguration, which they argue draws out clear contrasts with the Qur'anic understanding of Jesus. As they begin to discuss the transfiguration, they suggest Muslim readers would not find Luke 8 surprising because the Qur'an also records that Jesus did miracles (see *Imran* 3:49; *al-Ma'idah* 5:110). They cite *Imran* 3:59 and *an-Nisa'* 4:171 as giving the Qur'an's understanding of who Jesus is. Jesus is a Prophet like other Prophets, even though titles such as Messiah, Word and Spirit are unique to him; only he is born of a virgin, which somehow makes him like Adam; and only he has miracles attributed to him. Luke 9, however, challenges an Islamic understanding of Jesus. First, Luke 9:1–6 suggest Jesus acts on his own authority, whereas the Qur'an would argue all authority must be God's. Second, while *an-Nisa'* 5:112–15 may refer to the feeding of the five thousand, which is recorded in Luke 9:10–17, in the Qur'an the food comes from heaven, not from Jesus' own hands. (The other possibility is that *an-Nisa'* 5:112–15 refers to the Last Supper.) Third, Glaser and Kay suggest that when Jesus asks *Who do the crowds say I am?* the answers that the disciples give are very Islamic ones. The Qur'an is comfortable with the concept that Jesus is the Messiah, but not with the idea of his dying on a cross; Glaser and Kay suggest most Muslims would agree with Peter in Matthew 16:22. However, a call for disciples to die for their faith is something that Muslims would agree with.[48]

For Glaser and Kay, the transfiguration is a clear picture of who Jesus is; it demonstrates that God has come to be with his people. They note the ancient Christian tradition that the Trinity is present at the transfiguration, pointing to the voice of the Father, the glory of the Son and the Holy Spirit as the bright cloud. But, they explain, from an Islamic perspective, the transfiguration is impossible because God is simply too transcendent to appear on earth in human form. Glaser and Kay cite some of the Qur'an's strong denials that God could ever have a son, including *al-Ikhlas* 112:1–4; *Maryam* 19:35, 88–92 and *an-Nisa'* 4:171. They point out the two different Arabic words that can be translated *son*. *Walad* is always used of a biological child, and is used in all of these verses. The other term, *ibn*, can be metaphorical as well as literal (see *al-Baqarah* 2:215). The only time *ibn* is used in the context of denying Jesus is the Son of God is *at-Taubah* 9:30.

---

48. Glaser and Kay, *Thinking Biblically about Islam*, 164–65.

Glaser and Kay also explain that the Qur'an's main concern is to deny that God had sexual relations with Mary, a notion that is equally repugnant to the New Testament, and indeed to all Christians. God did not physically beget Jesus. Glaser and Kay argue that when the New Testament refers to Jesus as the Son of God, it is a way of referring to him as the Messiah, a Davidic king, as seen in the promises God makes to David in 2 Samuel 7:12–16, and expanded upon in some psalms (2:7; 89:26–27). They further explain that in the New Testament the other "son" of God is Israel, as seen in Hosea 11:1, quoted also in Matthew 2:15, and in Exodus 4:22–23.[49]

Conclusions and Pointers for Discussion

This chapter has outlined some of the contours of difference between Muslim and Christian understandings of Jesus. Glaser and Kay's suggestion that the transfiguration provides the best focal point for examination of these differences is taken up in this final section, which explores Christian exegesis of the transfiguration as a way into conversation about who Muslims and Christians think Jesus is.

Thomas Martin suggests that in Luke's Gospel Jesus' glory is primarily his humility. He argues there is a "purposeful tension of ambiguity" between the concept of glory, understood in terms of triumphalism, and humility, understood as the converse. Luke does emphasize Jesus' royal exaltation as Lord of all creation, but he does so by stressing both glory and humility. This acts as a "counter-sign of all normal expectations for kings, princes, presidents, nations, multi-national corporations, pop-stars and splendidly robed bishops, well-dressed pastors, or famous church buildings."[50]

This point about Jesus' glory shown in his humility can be developed in a number of places in the Gospel accounts, such as the fact that Jesus is not accepted as a Prophet by his own (Luke 4:23–30) and the fact that Jesus deliberately chooses someone who would betray him to be in his most intimate circle (Luke 6:16). Elsewhere, Jesus teaches we should love our enemies (Luke 6:27–36); the Son of Man is accused of being a glutton and a drunkard (Luke 7:34) and the glory of Jesus is shown in his humility when he is anointed by a sinful woman (Luke 7:36–50; see also John 12:1–11). Jesus goes to the margins, meeting foreigners, such as the

---

49. Glaser and Kay, *Thinking Biblically about Islam*, 169–73.
50. Martin, "What Makes Glory Glorious?," 5.

centurion (Luke 7:1–10), women, for example, raising the widow's son (Luke 7:11–17) and societal outcasts, such as Zacchaeus (Luke 19:1–10). Moreover, the triumphal entry is a further demonstration of glory through humility (John 12:12–19; see also Matthew 21:1–11). In John's Gospel, the cross as the revelation of God's glory to the world (John 12:20–36; 17:1–5; 19:28–37). Finally, in the transfiguration it is actually the humble Jesus, not the exalted Jesus, whom we are called to listen to (Luke 9:34).

Martin expands on the point that even in the transfiguration Jesus' glory is actually in his humility, stating that

> Jesus' true glory is not articulated brightness to be captured in the verbal photograph of 9:29. His true glory is instead hidden in the dark mysterious cloud out of which emanates the voice of God. And Jesus when he emerges from the cloud is alone and very normal.[51]

Jesus' experience as he comes down the mountain further emphasizes the point that humility is the glory of God's Son (Luke 9:37–62). Thomas argues that Jesus' "humiliated glory" is demonstrated in the fact that Jesus continues his ministry amidst a lack of comprehension of his role or identity (Luke 9:41), as he embraces humility (Luke 9:44). Jesus shows us that greatness is not in having authority, but in being a slave to all (Luke 9:48). It does not seek revenge or coercion (Luke 9:55). Humiliated glory is homeless (Luke 9:58), lacking human security (Luke 9:60). Glory "eschews triumphalism and, instead, embraces humility, not as a tool to achieve triumph, but as glory's very essence."[52]

In his discussion of the transfiguration, Nolland explores links with the experience of Moses on Mount Sinai (Exodus 24, 34–35). Jesus is here in the place of God, taking on the form of glory he has in the heavenly realm. Nolland recognizes that mountains are places of encounter with God. Jesus meets with Moses and Elijah on the mount of transfiguration because they are the two figures associated with meeting God on Sinai (Exodus 24; 1 Kings 19). Moses' role was, in the formation of the people of God and Elijah, both the restorer of God's people and also the figure who was "the immediate precursor to God's final intervention in this world, as set out in Malachi 4:4–5."[53]

---

51. Martin, "What Makes Glory Glorious?," 22.
52. Martin, "What Makes Glory Glorious?," 24.
53. Nolland, *Luke 9:21—18:34*, 503.

Keener develops four themes in his exploration of Matthew's account of the transfiguration (Matthew 16:28—17:13). First, Jesus is the glorious Lord before whom all other heroes of the faith must bow (16:28—17:3). Keener finds some Jewish parallels, citing examples involving angels (Daniel 10:6; *2 Enoch* 19:1; *3 Enoch* 18:25; 22:4–9), the righteous after death (*3 Ezra* 7:97), specific mention of Noah (*1 Enoch* 106:2, 10), Abel (*Testament of Abraham* 12A), Enoch (*1 Enoch* 71:11; *2 Enoch* 22:10) and even God himself (Daniel 7:9–10; *1 Enoch* 14:18–20; 46:1; 71:10). But the closest parallels are with Moses, whose face shines with God's glory after he has seen it (Exodus 34:29–35). Moreover, in the Babylonian Talmud, *the countenance of Moses was like that of the sun* (Baba Bathra 75a).[54]

Second, God the Father expects his people to listen to Jesus as they would listen to the God's law (Matthew 17:4–5). Keener argues Peter's suggestion to build tabernacles is merely an attempt to provide temporary shelter and so prolong the encounter. But there is nevertheless a resonance with the tabernacle in the wilderness, where God's law was promulgated. Third, Keener argues that although Jesus is powerful, he does not flaunt that power, but rather cares for his people (Matthew 17:6–8). The disciples fall on their faces, and Jesus touches them, providing words of reassurance. Fourth, Jesus, God's chosen Messiah, must walk in God's way of martyrdom, as have the Prophets before him. Jesus' death is the logical fulfillment of his life in obedience to his Father.[55]

There is a wealth of scholarly discussion of the meaning of Jesus' transfiguration, but the three brief accounts above are sufficient to introduce some mainstream Christian views. Christian understandings of Jesus are very different from Muslim ones. For the Christian, Jesus' glory is shown primarily in his weakness, in his death on the cross. But for a Muslim, Jesus is the obedient Prophet who is in some senses a precursor to Muhammad. It is unlikely that Christians and Muslims will come to a common mind about Jesus, but these passages provide a good way into discussing those differences in a spirit of friendship and mutual appreciation.

---

54. Translation from Simon and Slotki *Baba Bathra*, vol. 1.
55. Keener, *Matthew*, 436–40.

Postscript

The charity that I work for, the St. Philip's Centre, organizes all its activities around four core values: encounter, understand, trust and co-operate. We do not necessarily regard these values as operating in a linear fashion, but at times it is a convenient shorthand to describe interfaith encounters in these terms. The purpose of this book has been to enable Christians and Muslims to encounter each other's understandings of key figures in both their traditions. Whether Christians would describe all the characters discussed in this book as Prophets is a moot point, but examining this designation is part of the experience of encountering and understanding different worldviews and perspectives. I have written this book in the hope that, by reading it, Muslims and Christians are able to understand each other better, and so come to trust each other more. Often dialogue and interfaith encounter focuses primarily on encouraging arm's-length tolerance or grudging respect for perspectives that seem alien or incomprehensible. If people of faith remain at this level of distance from each other, misunderstandings will abound and positive community relations will be next to impossible. We must develop relationships of trust with those we fundamentally disagree with if we are to coexist peacefully in the same neighborhoods. It is only when we have learnt to trust each other that we can begin to cooperate together for the good of all.

Bibliography

Alexander, T. Desmond. *Exodus*. Apollos Old Testament Commentary 2. London: Apollos, 2017.
Allen, Leslie C. *Ezekiel 1–19*. Word Biblical Commentary 28. Dallas: Word, 1994.
———. *Ezekiel 20–48*. Word Biblical Commentary 29. Dallas: Word, 1990.
Anderson, A. A. *2 Samuel*. Word Biblical Commentary 11. Dallas: Word, 1989.
Ansari, Humayun. *"The Infidel Within": Muslims in Britain since 1800*. London: Hurst, 2004.
Bakhos, Carol. *The Family of Abraham: Jewish, Christian and Muslim Interpretations*. Cambridge, MA: Harvard University Press, 2014.
Bal, Mieke. *Loving Yusuf: Conceptual Travels from Present to Past*. Chicago: University of Chicago Press, 2008.
Barnett, Paul. *The Second Epistle to the Corinthians*. New International Commentary on the New Testament. Grand Rapids: Eerdmans, 1997.
Bauckham, Richard J. *James*. New Testament Readings. London: Routledge, 1999.
———. *Jude, 2 Peter*. Word Biblical Commentary 50. Nashville: T. Nelson, 1983.
Beasley-Murray, George R. *John*. 2nd ed. Word Biblical Commentary 36. Nashville: T. Nelson, 1999.
Block, Daniel I. *The Book of Ezekiel Chapters 1–24*. New International Commentary on the Old Testament. Grand Rapids: Eerdmans, 1997.
Bray, Gerald. *God Has Spoken: A History of Christian Theology*. Nottingham: Apollos, 2014.
Butler, Trent C. *Joshua 13–24*. 2nd ed. Word Biblical Commentary 7b. Grand Rapids: Zondervan, 2014.
Bruce, F. F. *The Book of the Acts*. New International Commentary on the New Testament. Grand Rapids: Eerdmans, 1988.
Chapman, Colin. *Cross and Crescent: Responding to the Challenge of Islam*. Downers Grove, IL: InterVarsity, 1988.
Charlesworth, James H. *The Old Testament Pseudepigrapha*. 2 vols. New York: Anchor, 1985.
Childs, Brevard S. *Exodus*. Old Testament Library. Louisville: Westminster John Knox, 1974.
———. *Isaiah*. Old Testament Library. Louisville: Westminster John Knox, 2001.
Conti, Marco. *1–2 Kings, 1–2 Chronicles, Ezra, Nehemiah, Esther*. Ancient Christian Commentary on Scripture. Downers Grove, IL: InterVarsity, 2008.

Cook, David. *Contemporary Muslim Apocalyptic Literature*. Syracuse, NY: Syracuse University Press, 2005.

Cuypers, Michel. *The Composition of the Qur'an: Rhetorical Analysis*. Translated by Jerry Ryan. London: Bloomsbury, 2015.

Dahood, Mitchell. *Psalms 51–100*. Anchor Bible Commentary. New York: Doubleday, 1968.

Davids, Peter H. *Letters of 2 Peter and Jude*. Pillar New Testament Commentary. Grand Rapids: Eerdmans, 2006.

DeSilva, David A. *Perseverance in Gratitude: A Socio-Rhetorical Commentary on the Epistle "to the Hebrews"*. Grand Rapids: Eerdmans, 2000.

DeVires, Simon J. *1 Kings*. Word Biblical Commentary 12. Waco: Word, 1985.

Droge, Arthur J., translator. *The Qur'an*. Sheffield: Equinox, 2013.

DuGuid, Iain M. *Ezekiel*. NIV Application Commentary. Grand Rapids: Zondervan, 1999.

Eaton, John. *The Psalms: A Historical and Spiritual Commentary with an Introduction and New Translation*. London: Continuum, 2003.

Elliott, J. K. *The Apocryphal New Testament*. Oxford: Oxford University Press, 1993.

Fee. Gordon. *The First Epistle to the Corinthians*. New International Commentary on the New Testament. Grand Rapids: Eerdmans, 1987.

Firestone, Reuven. "Merit, Mimesis, and Martyrdom: Aspects of Shi'ite Meta-Historical Exegesis on Abraham's Sacrifice in Light of Jewish, Christian, and Sunni Muslim Tradition." *Journal of the American Academy of Religion* 66 (1998) 93116.

France, R. T. *The Gospel of Matthew*. New International Commentary on the New Testament. Grand Rapids: Eerdmans, 2007.

———. *Matthew: Evangelist and Teacher*. Carlisle: Paternoster, 1989.

Franke, John R. *Joshua, Judges, Ruth, 1–2 Samuel*. Ancient Christian Commentary on Scripture. Downers Grove, IL: InterVarsity, 2005.

Freedman, H. *Shabbath Volume 2: Hebrew-English Edition of the Babylonian Talmud*. London: Soncino, 1972.

Galadari, Abdulla. *Qur'anic Hermeneutics: Between Science, History, and the Bible*. London: Bloomsbury, 2018.

Garrett, Duane, and Paul R. House. *Songs of Songs and Lamentations*. Word Biblical Commentary 23B. Nashville: T. Nelson, 2004.

Gathercole, Simon. *The Pre-Existent Son: Recovering the Christologies of Matthew, Mark, and Luke*. Grand Rapids: Eerdmans, 2006.

Glaser, Ida. *The Bible and Other Faiths: What Does the Lord Require of Us?* Leicester: InterVarsity, 2005.

Glaser, Ida with Hannah Kay. *Thinking Biblically about Islam: Genesis, Transfiguration, Transformation*. Carlisle: Langham Global Library, 2016.

Grogan, Geoffrey W. *Psalms: The Two Horizons Old Testament Commentary*. Grand Rapids: Eerdmans, 2008.

Grossfeld, Bernard. *The Two Targums of Esther: Translated, with Apparatus and Notes*. Edinburgh: T. & T. Clark, 1991.

Green, Joel. *The Gospel of Luke*. New International Commentary on the New Testament. Grand Rapids: Eerdmans, 1997.

Guelich, Robert. A. *Mark 1—8:26*. Word Biblical Commentary 34a. Nashville: T. Nelson, 1989.

Guezzou, Mokrane. *Tanwir al-Miqbas min Tafsir Ibn 'Abbas*. Royal Aal al-Bayt Institute for Islamic Thought, 2007. Accessed at https://www.altafsir.com/Books/IbnAbbas.pdf.

Hagner, Donald. *Matthew 1–13*. Word Biblical Commentary 33a. Dallas: Word, 1993.

———. *Matthew 14–28*. Word Biblical Commentary 33b. Nashville: T. Nelson, 1995.

Haleem, Muhammad Abdel. *Understanding the Qur'an: Themes and Style*. London: Tauris, 2012.

Hamilton, Victor P. *The Book of Genesis 1–17*. New International Commentary on the Old Testament. Grand Rapids: Eerdmans, 1990.

———. *The Book of Genesis 18–50*. New International Commentary on the Old Testament. Grand Rapids: Eerdmans, 1995.

Harris, J Rendell. *The Odes and Psalms of Solomon, Published from the Syriac Version*. Cambridge: Cambridge University Press, 1911.

Harris, Murray J. *The Second Epistle to the Corinthians*. New International Greek Testament Commentary. Grand Rapids: Eerdmans, 2005.

Ho, Craig Y. S. "The Stories of the Family Troubles of Judah and David: A Study of Their Literary Links." *Vetus Testamentum* 49 (1999) 514–31.

Japhet, Sara. *I & II Chronicles*. Old Testament Library. London: SCM, 1993.

Jenson, Robert W. *Ezekiel*. London: SCM, 2009.

Johnson, Luke Timothy. *Letters to Paul's Delegates: 1 Timothy, 2 Timothy, Titus*. Harrisburg, PA: Trinity, 1996.

Kaltner, John, and Younus Y. Mirza. *The Bible and the Qur'an: Biblical Figures in the Islamic Tradition*. London: T. & T. Clark, 2018.

Keener, Craig. *A Commentary on the Gospel of Matthew*. Grand Rapids: Eerdmans, 1999.

———. *The Gospel of John*. Vol. 1. Peabody, MA: Hendrickson, 2003.

Kelly, J. N. D. *Early Christian Doctrines*. London: Continuum, 1977.

Khalidi, Tarif. *The Muslim Jesus: Sayings and Stories in Islamic Literature*. London: Harvard University Press, 2001.

Kim, Dohyung. "The Structure of Genesis 38: A Thematic Reading." *Vetus Testamentum* 62 (2012) 550–60.

Klein, Ralph W. *1 Samuel*. Word Biblical Commentary 10. Nashville: T. Nelson, 1983.

Knight, George W. *Commentary of the Pastoral Epistles*. New International Greek Testament Commentary. Grand Rapids: Eerdmans, 1992.

Koptak, Paul E. *Proverbs*. NIV Application Commentary. Grand Rapids: Zondervan, 2003.

Kruse, Colin G. *Paul's Letter to the Romans*. Pillar New Testament Commentary. Grand Rapids: Eerdmans, 2012.

Kugel, James L. *In Potiphar's House: The Interpretive Life of Biblical Texts*. Cambridge, MA: Harvard University Press, 1994.

Lane, William L. *The Gospel of Mark*. New International Commentary on the New Testament. Grand Rapids: Eerdmans, 1974.

———. *Hebrews 9–13*. Word Biblical Commentary 47b. Waco, TX: Word, 1991.

Lawson, Todd. *The Crucifixion and the Qur'an: A Study in the History of Muslim Thought*. London: Oneworld, 2009.

Leaman, Oliver. *The Qur'an: A Philosophical Guide*. London: Bloomsbury, 2016.

Leemhuis, F. "Ibrahim's Sacrifice of His Son in the Early Post-Koranic Tradition." In *The Sacrifice of Isaac: The Aqudah (Genesis 22) and Its Interpretations*, edited by Ed Noort and Eibert Tigchelaar, 125–39. Leiden: Brill, 2002.

Leirvik, Oddbjørn. *Images of Jesus Christ in Islam*. 2nd ed. London: Continuum, 2010.

Leuchter, Mark. "Genesis 38 in Social and Historical Perspective." *Journal of Biblical Literature* 132 (2013) 209–27.

Lienhard, Joseph. *Exodus, Leviticus, Numbers, Deuteronomy*. Ancient Christian Commentary on Scripture. Downers Grove, IL: InterVarsity, 2001.

Lodahl, Michael. *Claiming Abraham: Reading the Bible and the Qur'an Side by Side*. Grand Rapids: Brazos, 2010.

Longenecker, Bruce W. *Galatians*. Word Biblical Commentary 41. Nashville: Nelson, 1990.

———. *The Triumph of Abraham's God: The Transformation of Identity in Galatians*. Edinburgh: T. & T. Clark, 1998.

Longman, Tremper. *The Book of Ecclesiastes*. New International Commentary on the Old Testament. Grand Rapids: Eerdmans, 1998.

———. *Song of Songs*. New International Commentary on the Old Testament. Grand Rapids: Eerdmans, 2001.

Louth, Andrew. *Genesis 1–11*. Ancient Christian Commentary on Scripture. Downers Grove, IL: InterVarsity, 2001.

Marshall, I Howard. *The Gospel of Luke*. New International Greek Testament Commentary. Carlisle: Paternoster, 1978.

Martin, Ralph P. *2 Corinthians*. Word Biblical Commentary 40. Nashville: Nelson, 1986.

Martin, Thomas W. "What Makes Glory Glorious? Reading Luke's Account of the Transfiguration Over Against Triumphalism." *Journal for the Study of the New Testament* 29 (2006) 3–26.

McConville, J. G. *Deuteronomy*. Apollos Old Testament Commentary. London: Apollos, 2002.

McGrath, Alister. *Heresy: A History of Defending Truth*. London: SPCK, 2009.

McGuire, Meredith. *Lived Religion: Faith and Practice in Everyday Life*. Oxford: Oxford University Press, 2008.

McKnight, Scott. *The Letter of James*. New International Commentary on the New Testament. Grand Rapids: Eerdmans, 2011.

Metzger, Bruce M. *The Canon of the New Testament: Its Origin, Development and Significance*. Oxford: Oxford University Press, 1997.

Michaels, J. Ramsey. *The Gospel of John*. New International Commentary on the New Testament. Grand Rapids: Eerdmans, 2010.

———. *1 Peter*. Word Biblical Commentary 49. Nashville: T. Nelson, 1988.

Millar, J. Gary. *Now Choose Life: Theology and Ethics in Deuteronomy*. Leicester: Apollos, 1998.

Moo, Douglas. *The Epistle to the Romans*. New International Commentary on the New Testament. Grand Rapids: Eerdmans, 1996.

Motyer, J. Alec. *The Prophecy of Isaiah: An Introduction and Commentary*. Downers Grove, IL: InterVarsity, 1999.

Mounce, William D. *The Pastoral Epistles*. Word Biblical Commentary 46. Nashville: Nelson, 2000.

Mourad, Suleiman A. "Mary in the Qur'an: A Reexamination of Her Presentation." In *The Qur'an in Its Historical Context,* edited by Gabriel Said Reynolds, 163–74. London: Routledge, 2008.

Mourad, Suleiman A. "Does the Qur'an Deny or Assert Jesus's Crucifixion and Death?" In *New Perspectives on the Qur'an. The Qur'an in Its Historical Context 2,* edited by Gabriel Said Reynolds, 349–57. London: Routledge, 2011.

Murphy, Roland E. *Ecclesiastes.* Word Biblical Commentary 23a. Nashville: T. Nelson, 1992.

———. *Proverbs.* Word Biblical Commentary 22. Nashville: T. Nelson, 1998.

Nashim, Seder *Nazir, Sotah: Hebrew-English Edition of the Babylonian Talmud.* London: Soncino, No Date.

Nasr, Seyyed Hossein. *The Study Qur'an: A New Translation and Commentary.* London: HarperOne, 2015.

Nolland, John. *The Gospel of Matthew.* New International Greek Testament Commentary. Grand Rapids: Eerdmans, 2005.

———. *Luke 1:1—9:20.* Word Biblical Commentary 35a. Nashville: T. Nelson, 1989.

———. *Luke 9:21—18:34.* Word Biblical Commentary 35b. Nashville: T. Nelson, 1993.

———. *Luke 18:35—24:53.* Word Biblical Commentary 35c. Nashville: T. Nelson, 1993.

Oswalt, John N. *The Book of Isaiah 40–66.* International Commentary on the Old Testament. Grand Rapids: Eerdmans, 1998.

Pitkänen, Pekka M. A. *Joshua.* Apollos Old Testament Commentary. London: Apollos, 2010.

Pratt, Richard L. *1 and 2 Chronicles.* Mentor Commentary. Fearn: Christian Focus, 1998.

Reinink, Gerrit J. "The Lamb on the Tree: Syriac Exegesis and Anti-Islamic Apologetics." In *The Sacrifice of Isaac: The Aqudah (Genesis 22) and Its Interpretations,* edited by Ed Noort and Eibert Tigchelaar, 109–24. Leiden: Brill, 2002.

Reynolds, Gabriel Said. *The Emergence of Islam: Classical Traditions in Contemporary Perspective.* Minneapolis: Fortress, 2012.

———. *The Qur'an and Its Biblical Subtext.* London: Routledge, 2010.

———. *The Qur'an and the Bible.* New Haven, CT: Yale University Press, 2018.

Samir, Samir Khalil. "The Theological Christian Influence of the Qur'an: A Reflection." In *The Qur'an In Its Historical Context,* edited by Gabriel Said Reynolds, 141–62. London: Routledge, 2008.

Schlater, Jacob, and H. Freedman. *Sanhedrin: Hebrew-English Edition of the Babylonian Talmud.* London: Soncino, 1969.

Sheridan, Mark. *Genesis 12–50.* Ancient Christian Commentary on Scripture. Downers Grove, IL: InterVarsity, 2002.

Simon, Maurice. *Berakoth: Hebrew-English Edition of the Babylonian Talmud.* London: Soncino, 1960.

———. *Gittin: Hebrew-English Edition of the Babylonian Talmud.* London: Soncino, 1977.

Simon, Maurice, and Israel W. Slotki. *Baba Bathra Volume 1: Hebrew-English Edition of the Babylonian Talmud.* London: Soncino, 1976.

Sinai, Nicolai. *The Qur'an: A Historical-Critical Introduction.* Edinburgh: Edinburgh University Press, 2017.

Slotki, Israel W. *'Erubin: Hebrew-English Edition of the Babylonian Talmud.* London: Soncino, 1983.

———. *Yebamoth: Hebrew-English Edition of the Babylonian Talmud.* London: Soncino, 1984.

Steward, Devin. "Notes on Medieval and Modern Emendations of the Qur'an" In *The Qur'an in Its Historical Context*, edited by Gabriel Said Reynods, 225–48. London: Routledge, 2008.

Tate, Marvin E. *Psalms 51–100.* Word Biblical Commentary 20. Dallas: Word, 1990.

Thiselton, Anthony C. *The First Epistle to the Corinthians.* New International Greek Testament Commentary. Grand Rapids: Eerdmans, 2000.

Tottoli, Roberto. *Biblical Prophets in the Qur'an and Muslim Literature.* London: Routledge, 2002.

Unal, Ali. *The Qur'an with Annotated Interpretation in Modern English.* The Light Inc. No date or place of publication.

Van Der Toorn, Karel. *Scribal Culture and the Making of the Hebrew Bible.* Cambridge, MA: Harvard University Press, 2007.

Weinandy, Thomas G. *Does God Suffer?* Edinburgh: T. & T. Clark, 2000.

Wenham, Gordon J. *Genesis 1–15.* Word Biblical Commentary 1. Waco: Word, 1987.

———. *Genesis 16–50.* Word Biblical Commentary 2. Dallas: Word, 1994.

Wessels, Anton. *The Torah, the Gospel and the Qur'an: Three Books, Two Cities, One Tale.* Grand Rapids: Eerdmans, 2013.

Wheeler, Brannon M. *Moses in the Qur'an and Islamic Exegesis.* London: Routledge, 2002.

———. *Prophets in the Qur'an: An Introduction to the Quran and Muslim Exegesis.* London: Continuum, 2002.

Wilson, Mark. "Noah, the Ark, and the Flood in Early Christian Literature." *Scriptura* 113 (2014) 1–12.

Wilson, Tom. *Hospitality, Service, Proclamation: Interfaith Engagement as Christian Discipleship.* London: SCM, 2019.

———. *What Kind of Friendship?: Christian Responses to Tariq Ramadan's Call for Reform within Islam.* Eugene, OR: Wipf and Stock, 2015.

Witherington, Ben. *The Acts of the Apostles: A Socio-Rhetorical Commentary.* Grand Rapids: Eerdmans, 2001.

———. *Conflict and Community in Corinth: A Socio-Rhetorical Commentary on 1 and 2 Corinthians.* Grand Rapids: Eerdmans, 1996.

———. *Grace in Galatia: A Commentary on Paul's Letter to the Galatians.* Edinburgh: T. & T. Clark, 1998.

———. *Letters and Homilies for Hellenized Christians*, vol. 2, *A Socio-Rhetorical Commentary on 1–2 Peter*. Nottingham: Apollos, 2007.

Witutum, Joseph. "Joseph among the Ishmaelites: Q12 in the Light of Syriac Sources." In *New Perspectives on the Qur'an: The Qur'an in Its Historical Context 2*, edited by Gabriel Said Reynolds, 2:425–48. London: Routledge, 2011.

Wray-Beal, Lissa M. *1 & 2 Kings.* Apollos Old Testament Commentary 9. Nottingham: Apollos, 2014.

Yarbrough, Robert W. *The Letters to Timothy and Titus.* Pillar New Testament Commentary. London: Apollos, 2018.

www.ingramcontent.com/pod-product-compliance
Lightning Source LLC
Chambersburg PA
CBHW062024220426
43662CB00010B/1464